LETTERHEAD & LOGO DESIGN 3
Creating The Corporate Image

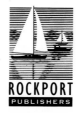

ROCKPORT PUBLISHERS, INC.
Rockport, Massachusetts

Distributed by North Light Books
Cincinnati, Ohio

First published in the United States of America by:
Rockport Publishers, Inc.
146 Granite Street
Rockport, Massachusetts 01966
Telephone: (508) 546-9590
Fax: (508) 546-7141
Telex: 5106019284 ROCKORT PUB

First published in Germany by Rockport Publishers, Inc. for:
Nippan
Nippon Shuppan Hanbai Deutschland GmbH
Krefelder Str. 85
D-40549 Dusseldorf
Telephone: (0211) 504 8089
Fax: (0211) 504 9326

Distributed to the book trade and art trade in the U.S. and Canada by:
North Light, an imprint of
F & W Publications
1507 Dana Avenue
Cincinnati, Ohio 45207
Telephone: (513) 531-2222

Other Distribution by:
Rockport Publishers, Inc.
Rockport, Massachusetts 01966

ISBN 1-56496-111-7

10 9 8 7 6 5 4 3 2 1

Art Director: *Laura Herrmann*
Designer: *Laura Herrmann*
Layout/Production: *Thom Lewis*
Production Manager: *Barbara States*
Production Assistant: *Pat O'Maley*

Printed in Singapore

CONTENTS

INTRODUCTION

Each new business begins with a letterhead and a logo . . . literally. Before anything else is accomplished, a letterhead and a logo is created. Sometimes before a business plan is created . . . a letterhead and logo is created. Often before office space is leased . . . a letterhead and logo appears! In fact, I've created entire identity systems even before the company telephone number is known . . . no kidding. Nothing is closer to the birth of an enterprise and nothing can be more important than a properly conceived, designed and executed logo and letterhead.

In addition to icons, words and numbers, business papers convey a surprisingly accurate and remarkable complete amount of additional information. In fact, that little 2 x 3½ business card is probably the most influential seven square inches in the world of print communication.

Actually, the entire nature of an organization and/or an individual is evident on the surface of the simple business card. One can detect or deduce intelligence, self assurance, innovation and leadership. In addition, characteristics such as mimicry, inauthenticity, slovenliness and miserliness are also apparent, even to the casual observer.

If you are presented with a slipshod business card, you won't be surprised when you step into a dirty lobby upon arrival for your first visit. Conversely, business papers, created by bona fide talent, can generate a powerful visual statement which can set the cultural tone for an entire organization.

Curiously, not one of the nation's leading business schools devoted even a single course to the subject of visual identities . . . in spite of the obvious success of companies who have purposefully, accidentally or otherwise tapped into the power of design.

Consider, on a personal level, the visual imagery that has been placed in your mind by enterprises such as Benetton, Apple and Nike. If you think advertising has created those feelings of yours, think again. Other advertisers have created the ads and spent the money, yet they have failed to get the job done on you.

Design is the real power behind this phenomenon of imagery. Advertising is only the conduit. Ads are the wiring, design is the electricity. You get shocked by the electricity, not by the wires.

As you thumb through the pages of this book you will see the work of some of the world's most amazing people . . . Graphic Designers. You will discover pleasant visual puns and clever metaphors as well as stunning interpretations of the traditional elements of typography, paper and color.

While all of the designs featured in this book are interesting or beautiful, some of them are brilliant. Graphic Design is ubiquitous. It's everywhere in our culture and, at it's best, it contributes to the beauty and richness of our lives.

Michael Stanard

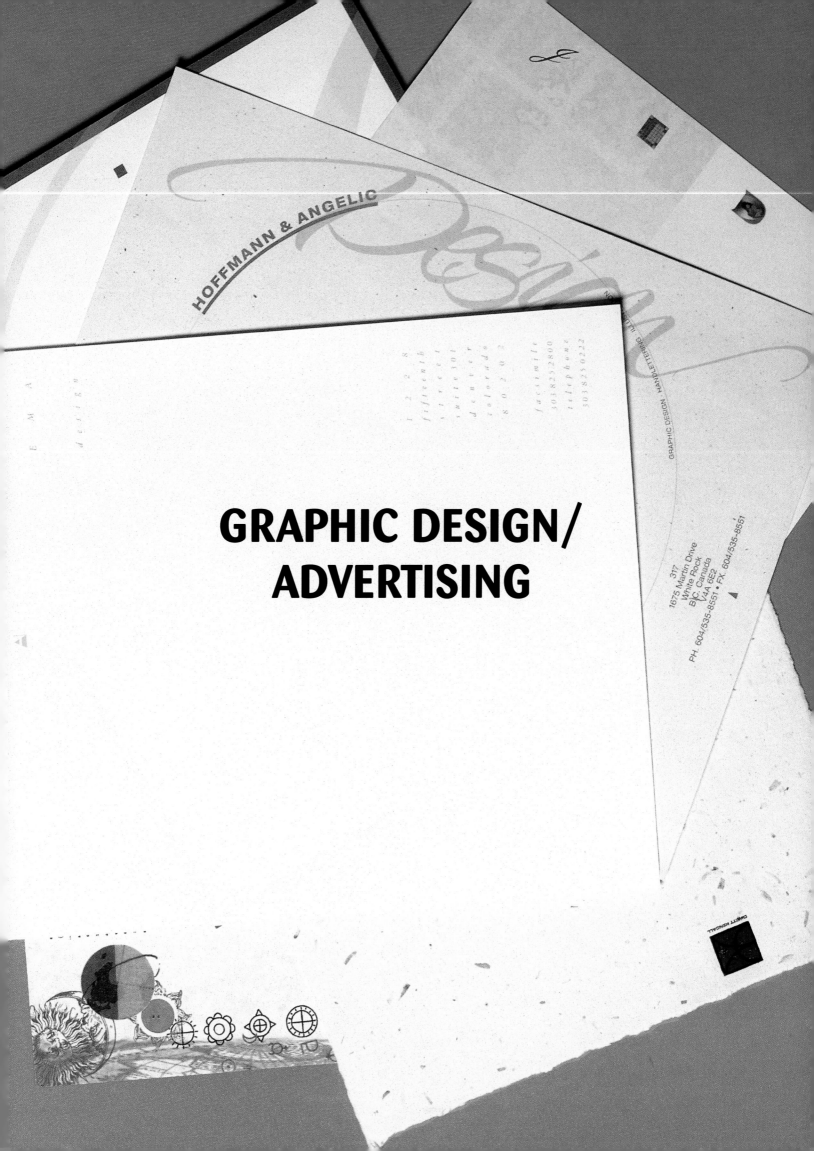

GRAPHIC DESIGN/
ADVERTISING

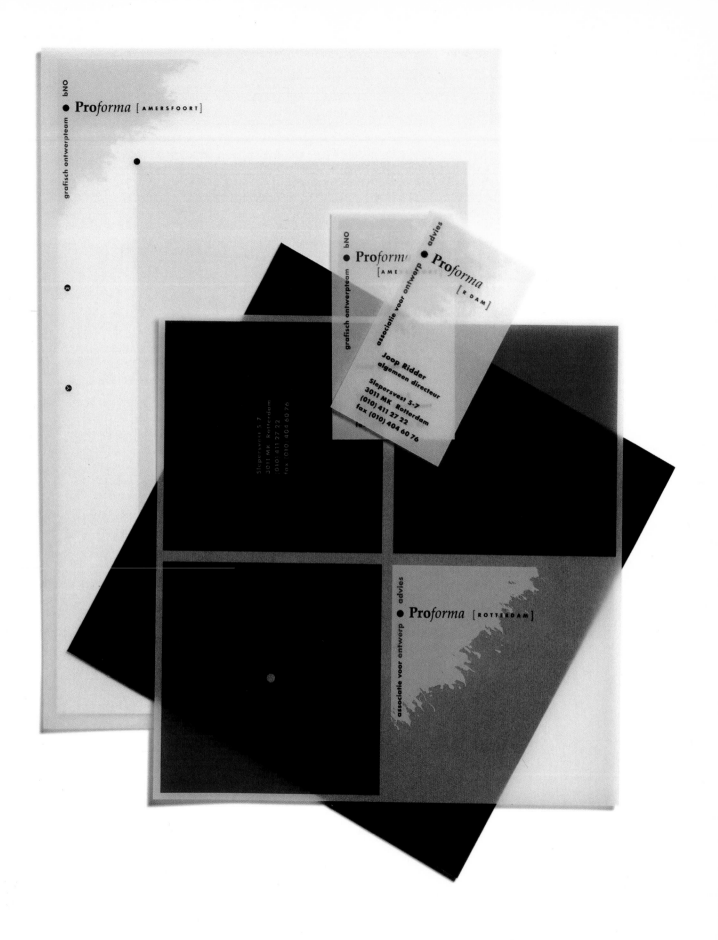

DESIGN FIRM	Proforma Rotterdam
ART DIRECTOR	Aadvan Dommelen
DESIGNER	Gert Jan Rooijakkers
CLIENT	Proforma
PAPER/PRINTING	Calque

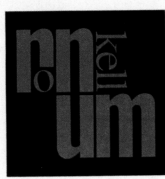

Ron Kellum Inc. 151 First Avenue PH-1 NY, NY 10003

Telephone: 212-979-2661 Fax/Modem: 212-260-3525

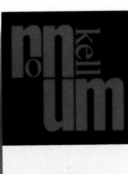

Ron Kellum

Ron Kellum Inc.
151 First Ave. PH-1 New York, NY 10003
Tel: 212-979-2661 Fax: 212-260-3525

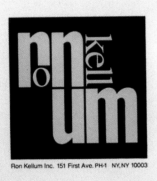

Ron Kellum Inc. 151 First Ave. PH-1   NY, NY 10003

DESIGN FIRM	Ron Kellum Inc.
ART DIRECTOR	Ron Kellum
DESIGNER	Ron Kellum
ILLUSTRATOR	Ron Kellum Inc.
PAPER/PRINTING	Strathmore Writing

DESIGN FIRM	38 North
ART DIRECTOR	Nida Zada
CLIENT	38 North
PAPER/PRINTING	4 colors

DESIGN FIRM	Musikar Design
ART DIRECTOR	Sharon R. Musikar
DESIGNER	Sharon R. Musikar
PHOTOGRAPHER	Sharon R. Musikar
CLIENT	Musikar Design
PAPER/PRINTING	Classic Crest, 2 colors

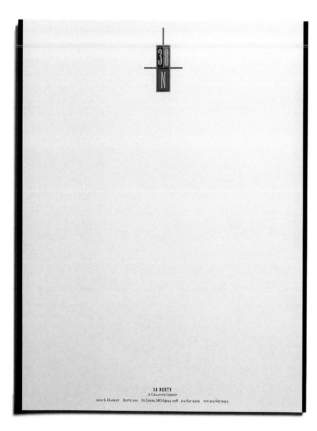

DESIGN FIRM	Bartels & Company, Inc.
ART DIRECTOR	David Bartels
DESIGNER	Brian Barclay
ILLUSTRATOR	Brian Barclay
CLIENT	Bartels & Company, Inc.

DESIGN FIRM	Cisneros Design
ART DIRECTOR	Fred Cisneros
DESIGNER	Fred Cisneros
CLIENT	Cisneros Design
PAPER/PRINTING	Classic Crest

DESIGN FIRM	Shields Design
ART DIRECTOR	Charles Shields
DESIGNER	Charles Shields
CLIENT	Shields Design
PAPER/PRINTING	Simpson Quest

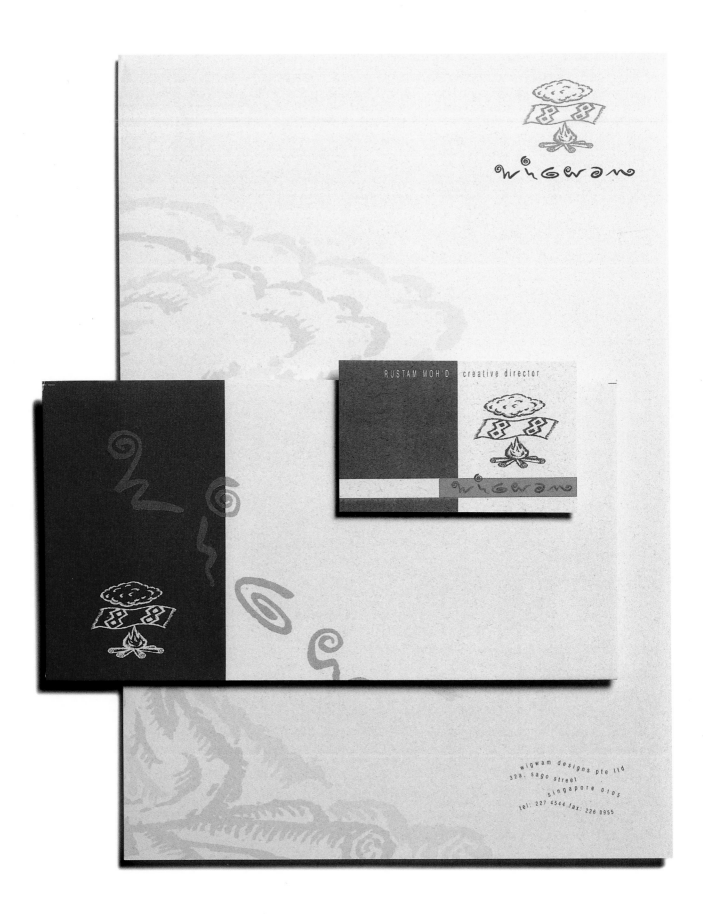

DESIGN FIRM Wigwam Designs Pte. Ltd.
ART DIRECTOR Rustam Moh'd
DESIGNER Rustam Moh'd
ILLUSTRATOR Muk Koon Hoong
CLIENT Wigwam Designs

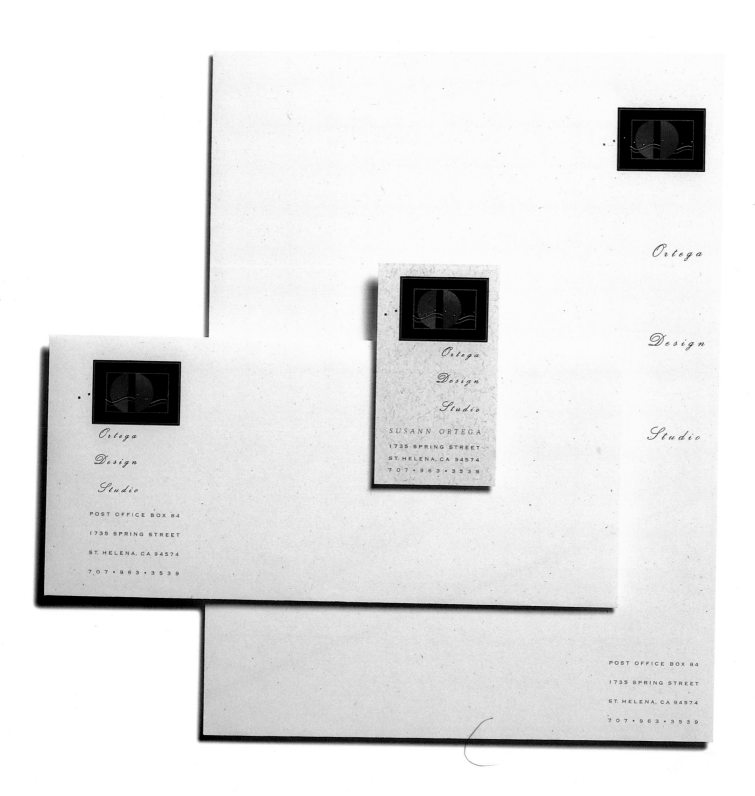

DESIGN FIRM Ortega Design
ART DIRECTOR Susann Ortega
DESIGNER Susann Ortega, Joann Ortega
ILLUSTRATOR Susann Ortega
CLIENT Ortega Design
PAPER/PRINTING Simpson Evergreen, foil stamp, embossed

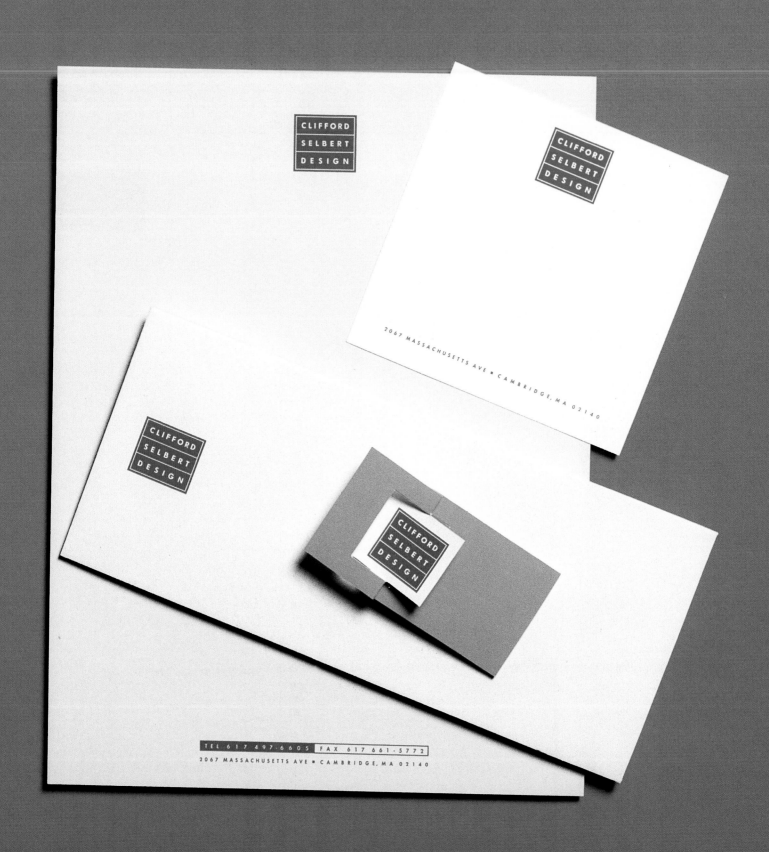

DESIGN FIRM   Clifford Selbert Design
ART DIRECTOR   Clifford Selbert, Melanie Lowe
DESIGNER   Melanie Lowe
CLIENT   Clifford Selbert Design
PAPER/PRINTING   Strathmore

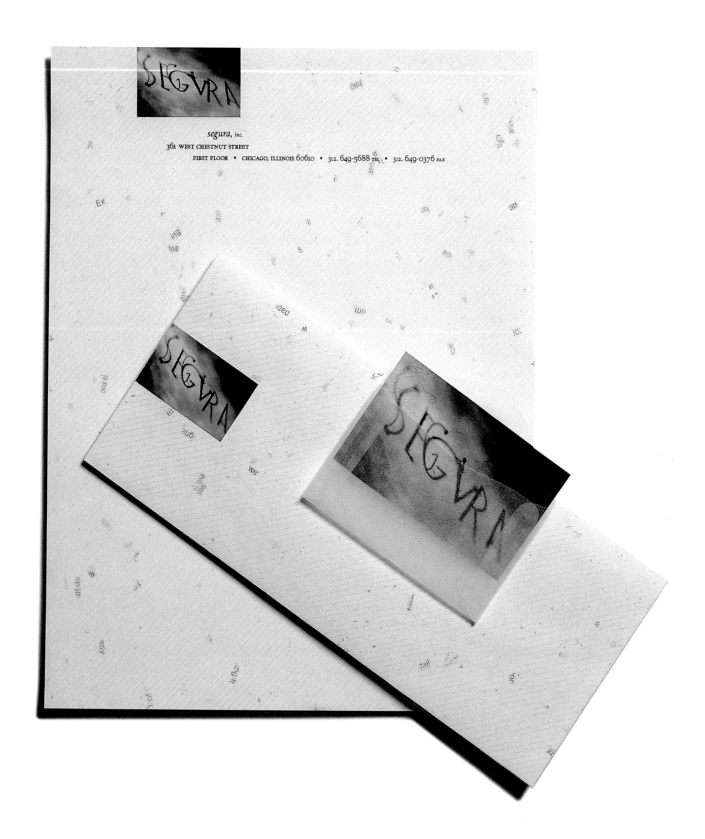

DESIGN FIRM   Segura Inc.
ART DIRECTOR   Carlos Segura
DESIGNER   Carlos Segura
ILLUSTRATOR   Greg Heck
CLIENT   Segura Inc.
PAPER/PRINTING   Wagner

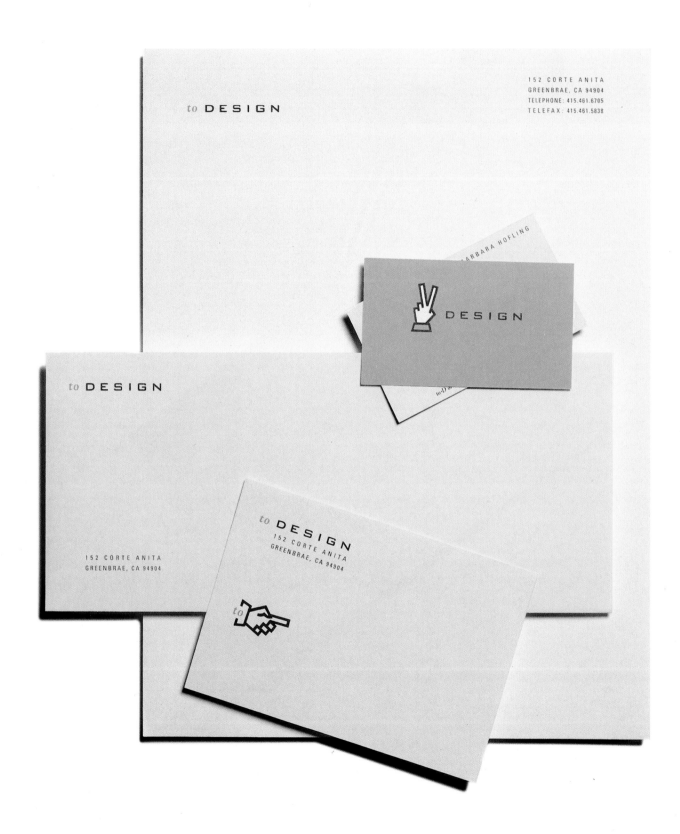

DESIGN FIRM THARP DID IT
DESIGNER Rick Tharp, Jean Mogannam
CLIENT to DESIGN/Barbara Hofling
PAPER/PRINTING Neenah Paper

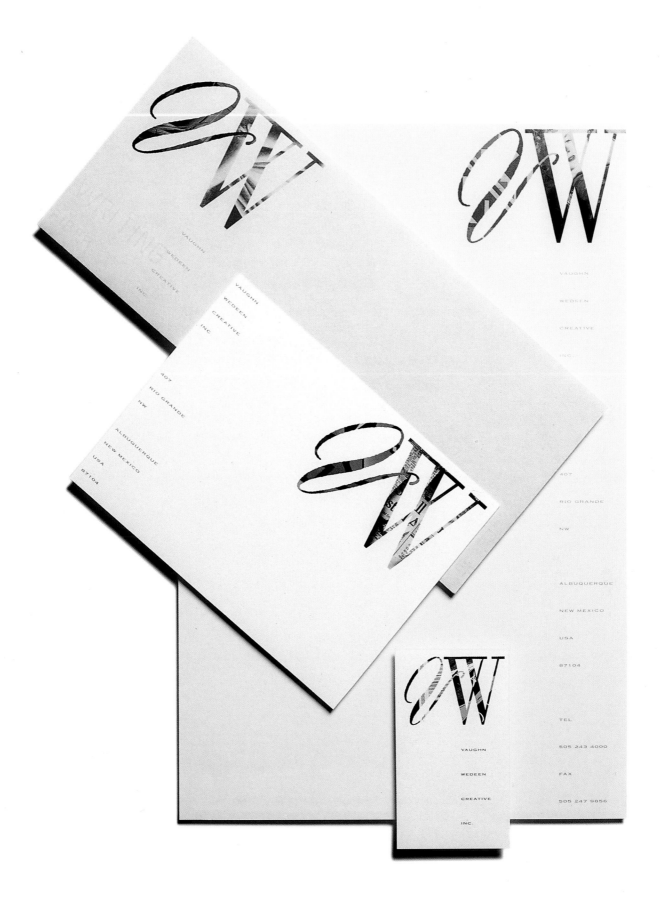

DESIGN FIRM   Vaughn Wedeen Creative
ART DIRECTOR   Rick Vaughn, Steve Wedeen
DESIGNER   Rick Vaughn, Steve Wedeen
ILLUSTRATOR   Various
CLIENT   Vaughn Wedeen Creative
PAPER/PRINTING   Strathmore Ultimate White

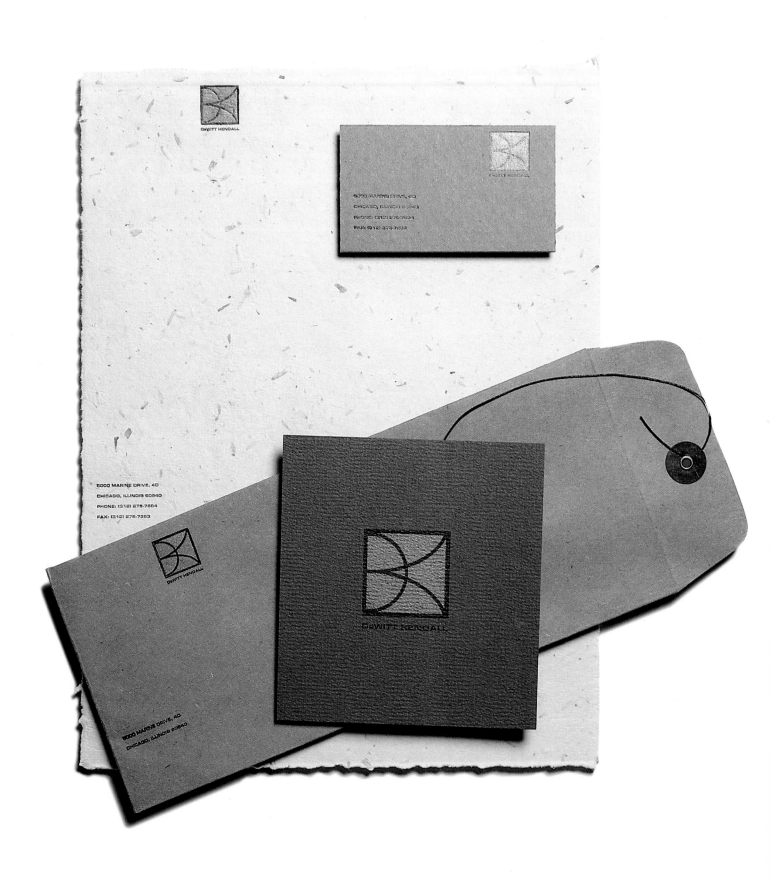

DESIGN FIRM	Dewitt Kendall – Chicago
ART DIRECTOR	Dewitt Kendall
DESIGNER	Dewitt Kendall
ILLUSTRATOR	Dewitt Kendall
CLIENT	Dewitt Kendall Chicago
PAPER/PRINTING	Kraft 3-ply industrial chipboard, handmade rice husk paper (stationery) Simpson Gainsborough, 2 hits of copper (business card)

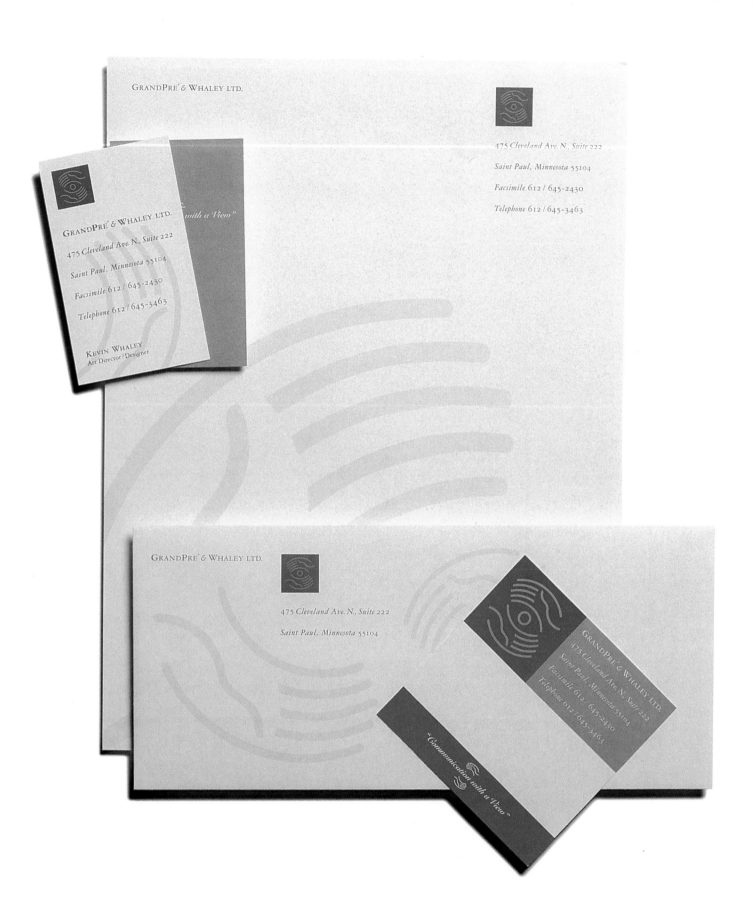

DESIGN FIRM	GrandPré and Whaley, Ltd.
ART DIRECTOR	Kevin Whaley, Mary GrandPré
DESIGNER	Kevin Whaley
CLIENT	GrandPré & Whaley, Ltd.
PAPER/PRINTING	Strathmore

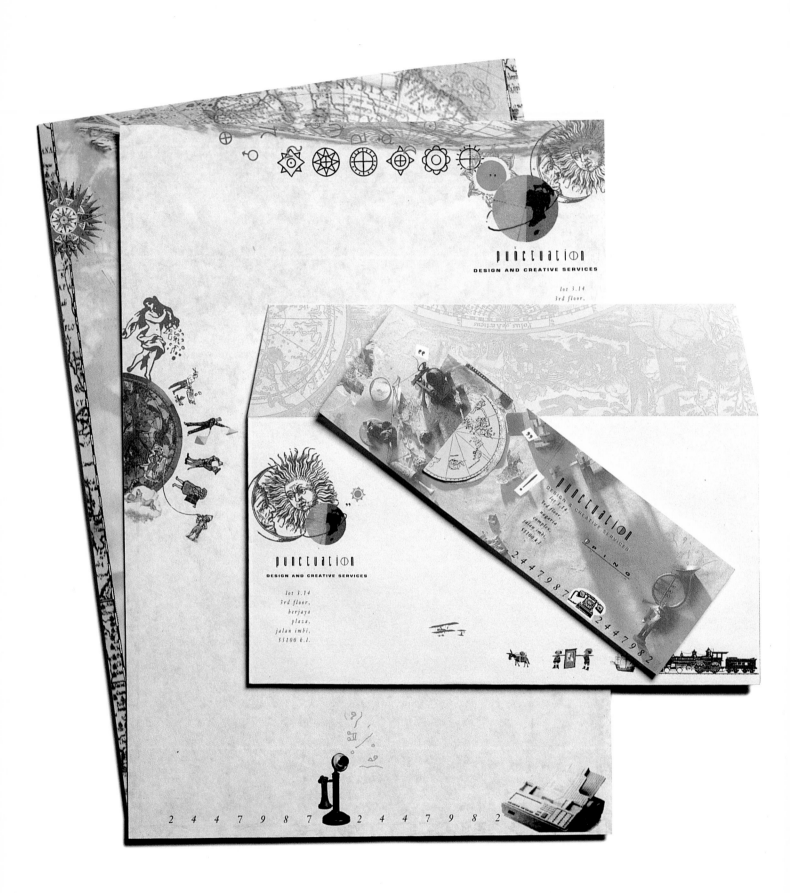

DESIGN FIRM	Punctuation
ART DIRECTOR	Ping
DESIGNER	Ping
CLIENT	Punctuation
PAPER/PRINTING	New Raglin, Stratakolour

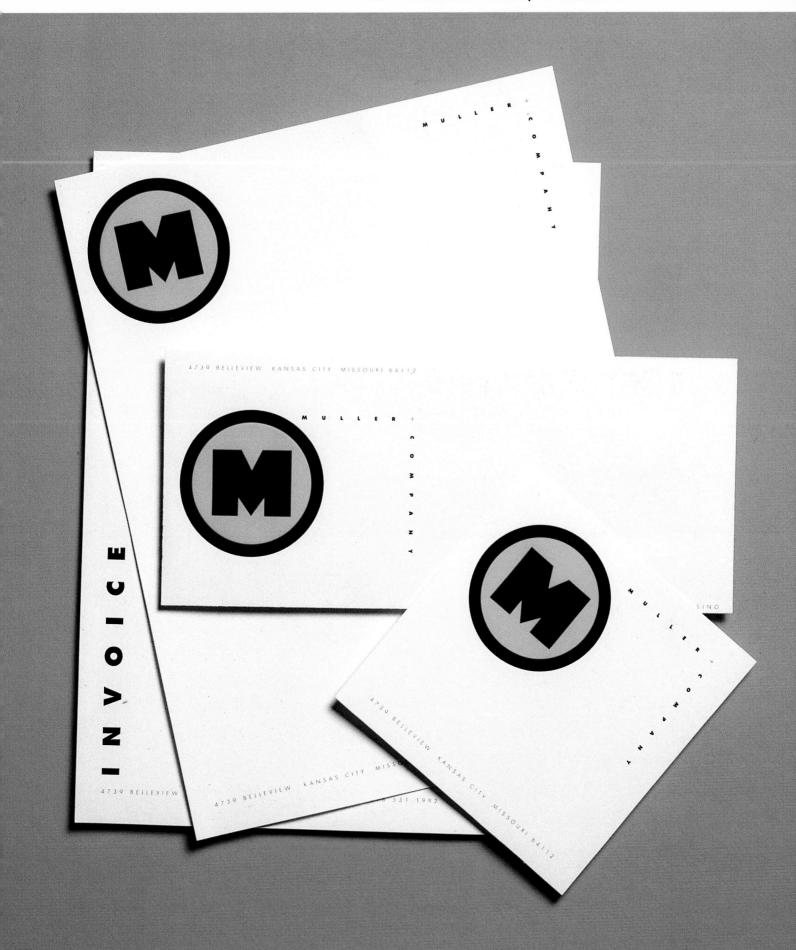

DESIGN FIRM   Muller + Company
ART DIRECTOR   John Muller
DESIGNER   John Muller
CLIENT   Muller + Company
PAPER/PRINTING   Proterra Chalk Vellum

DESIGN FIRM	Cactus Design
ART DIRECTOR	Susan Hankoff-Estrella
DESIGNER	Susan Hankoff-Estrella
ILLUSTRATOR	Theo Camut
CLIENT	Cactus Design
PAPER/PRINTING	Strathmore Renewal, Chamois

DESIGN FIRM	Jeff Shelly
ILLUSTRATOR	Jeff Shelly
CLIENT	Jeff Shelly

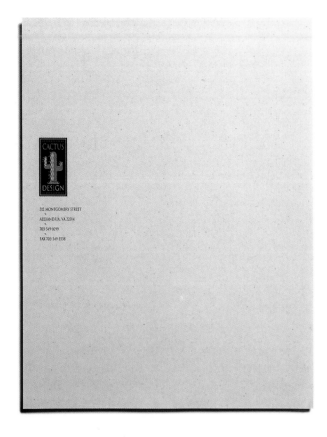

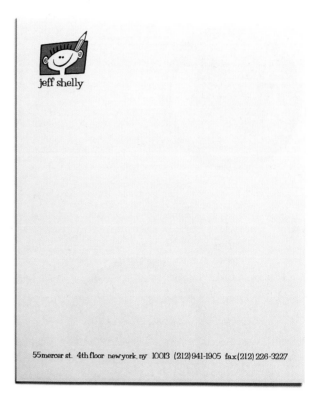

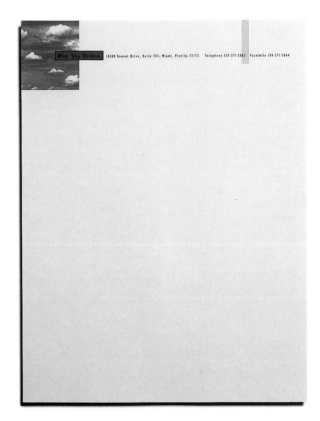

DESIGN FIRM	M. Renner Design
ART DIRECTOR	Michael Renner
DESIGNER	Michael Renner
ILLUSTRATOR	Michael Renner
CLIENT	Studio Pignatelli

DESIGN FIRM	Blue Sky Design
ART DIRECTOR	Bob Little, Joanne Little,
	Maria Dominguez
CLIENT	Blue Sky Design
PAPER/PRINTING	Crane's Crest Fluorescent White

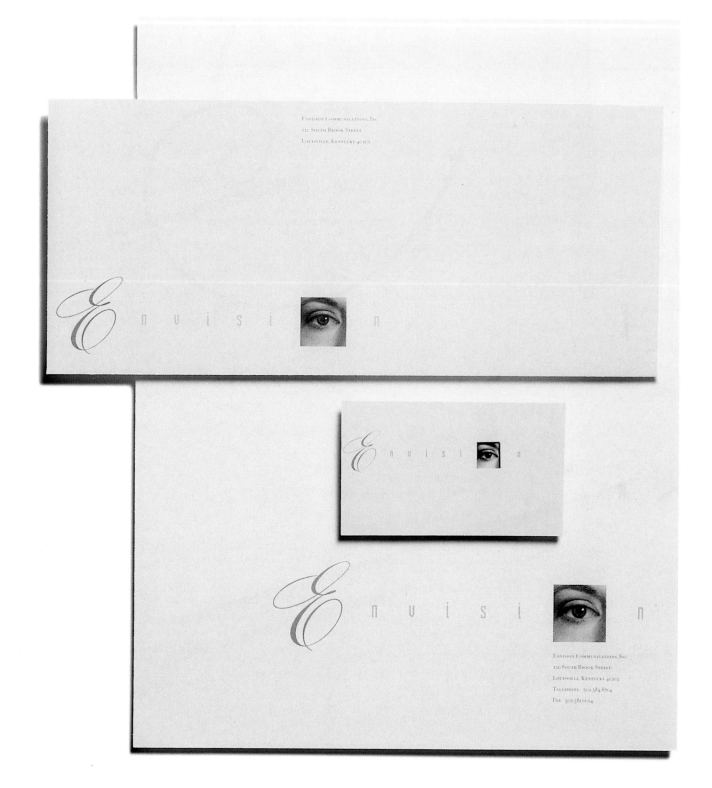

DESIGN FIRM	Envision
ART DIRECTOR	Julia Comer, Walter McCord
DESIGNER	Julia Comer, Walter McCord
ILLUSTRATOR	Julia Comer, Walter McCord
CLIENT	Envision
PAPER/PRINTING	Strathmore Alexandra Brilliant, 3 colors

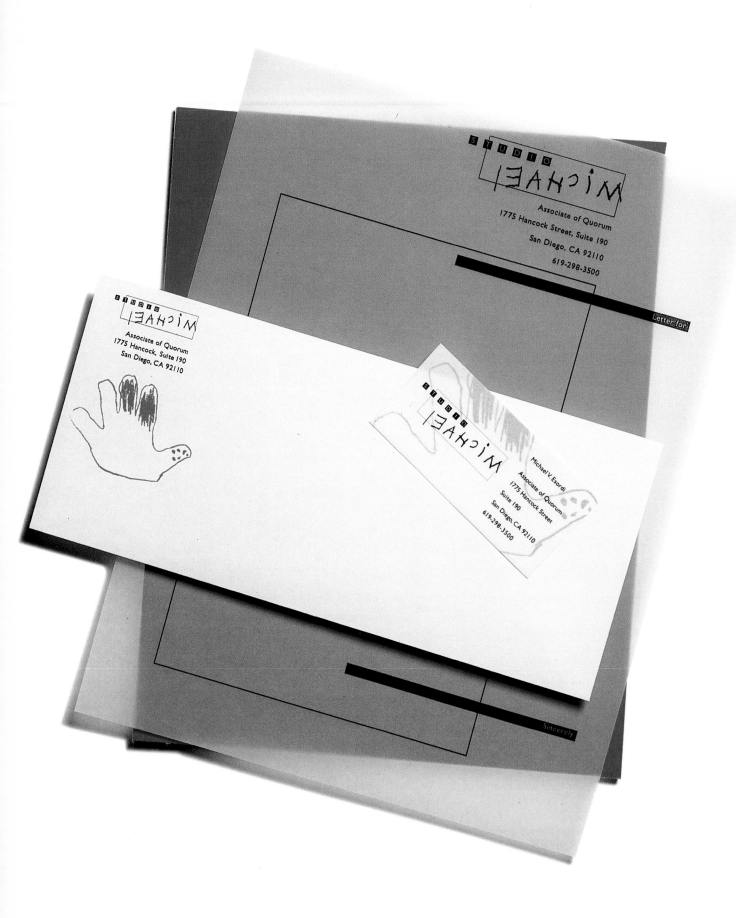

DESIGN FIRM	Studio Michael
ART DIRECTOR	Michael Esordi
DESIGNER	Michael Esordi
ILLUSTRATOR	Michael Esordi
CLIENT	Studio Michael
PAPER/PRINTING	Classic Crest, UV Vellum

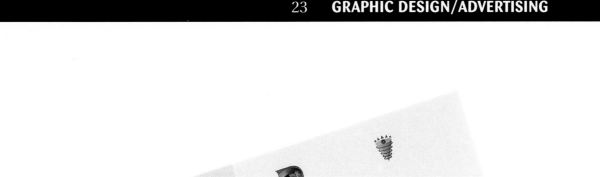

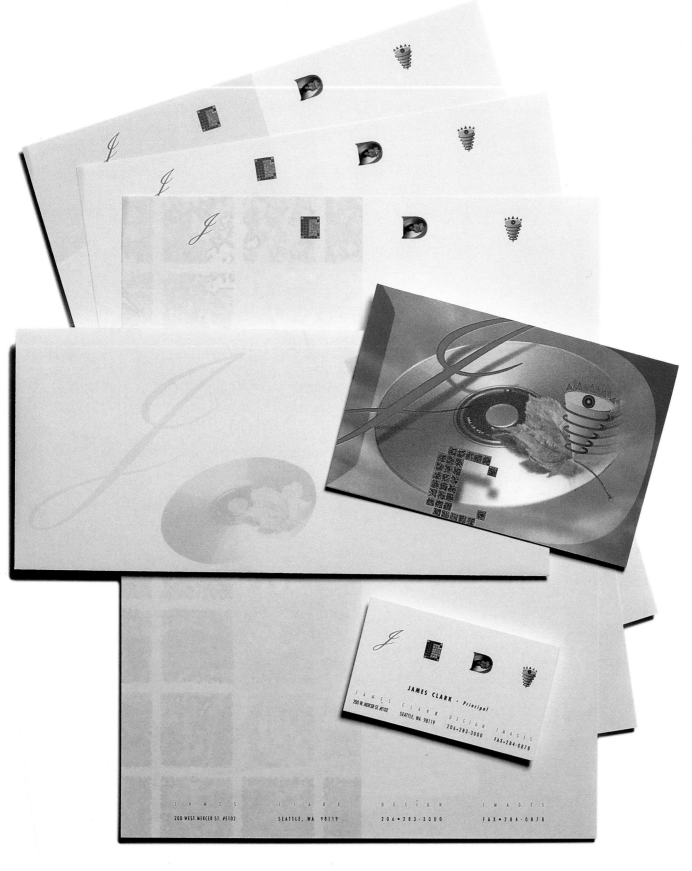

DESIGN FIRM	James Clark Design Images
ART DIRECTOR	James Clark
DESIGNER	James Clark
ILLUSTRATOR	Dyanna Kosak
CLIENT	James Clark Design Images
PAPER/PRINTING	Printing Control

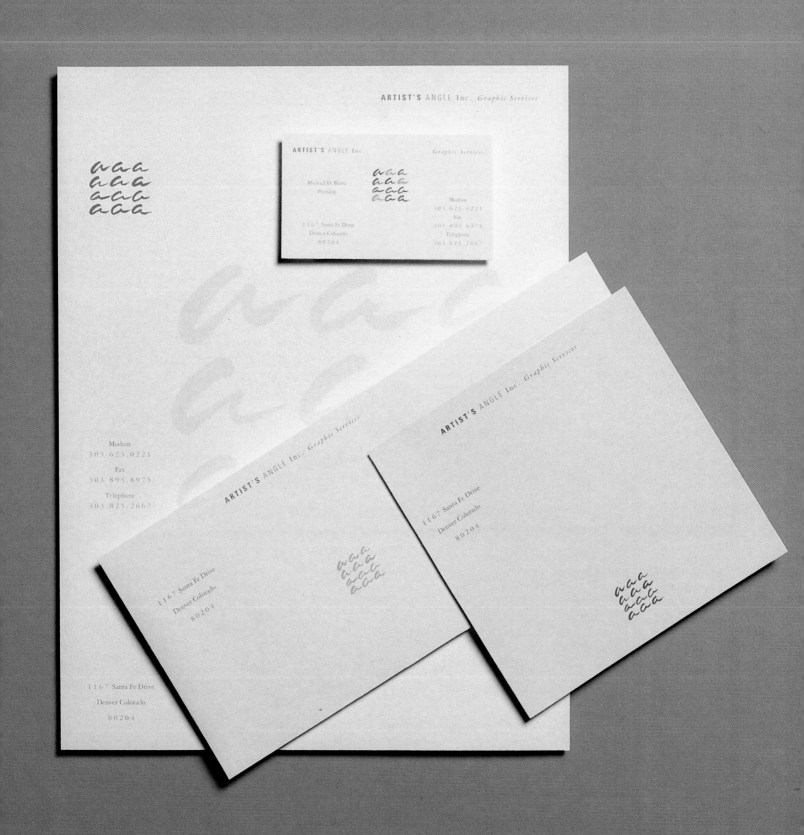

DESIGN FIRM   Ema Design
ART DIRECTOR   Thomas C. Ema
DESIGNER   Debra Johnson Humphrey
CLIENT   Artist's Angle
PAPER/PRINTING   Classic Crest

DESIGN FIRM Randy McCafferty
DESIGNER Randy McCafferty
ILLUSTRATOR Randy McCafferty
CLIENT Randy McCafferty
PAPER/PRINTING Speckletone

DESIGN FIRM Elizabeth Resnick Design
ART DIRECTOR Elizabeth Resnick
DESIGNER Elizabeth Resnick
CLIENT Elizabeth Resnick Graphic Design
PAPER/PRINTING Strathmore Writing, embossed
flourescent, offset dark green

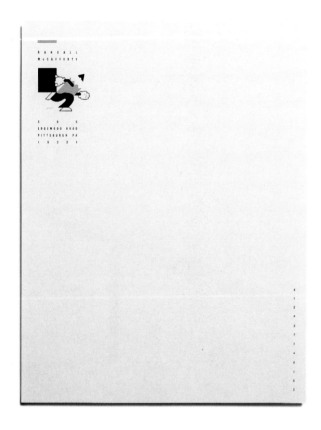

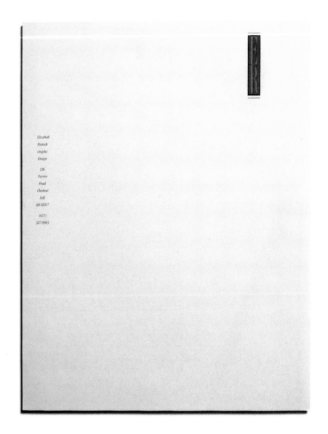

DESIGN FIRM Heart Graphic Design
ART DIRECTOR Clark Most
DESIGNER Clark Most
CLIENT Heart Graphic Design
PAPER/PRINTING Benefit Natural Flax

DESIGN FIRM Puccinelli Design
ART DIRECTOR Keith Puccinelli
DESIGNER Keith Puccinelli, Heidi Palladino
ILLUSTRATOR Keith Puccinelli
CLIENT Puccinelli Design
PAPER/PRINTING Gilbert Neo

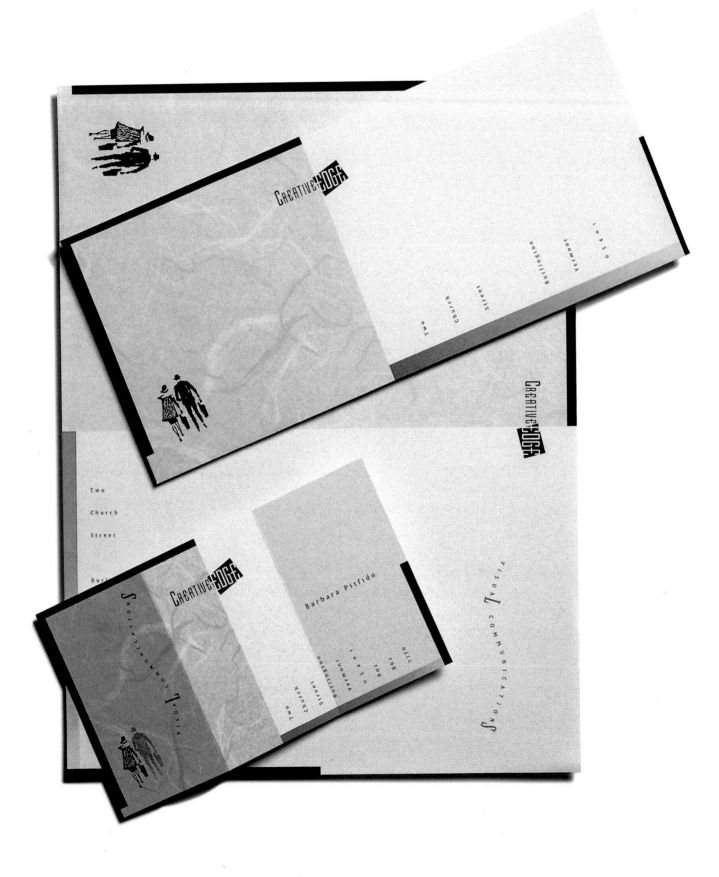

DESIGN FIRM   Creative EDGE
DESIGNER   Rick Salzman, Barbara Pitfido
CLIENT   Creative EDGE
PAPER/PRINTING   Gilbert Esse

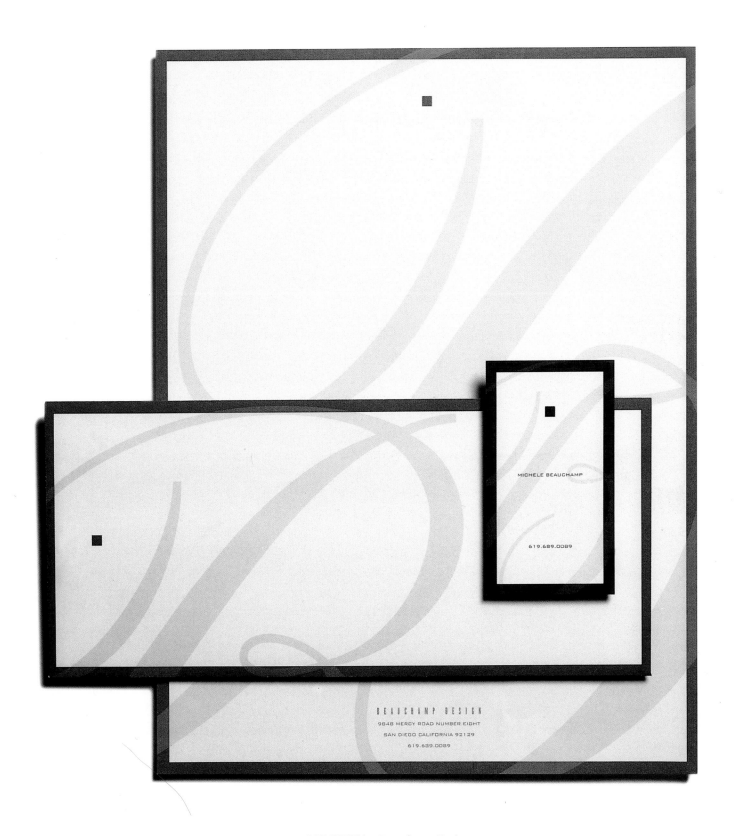

MICHELE BEAUCHAMP

619.689.0089

BEAUCHAMP DESIGN
9848 MERCY ROAD NUMBER EIGHT
SAN DIEGO CALIFORNIA 92129
619.689.0089

DESIGN FIRM   Beauchamp Design
ART DIRECTOR   Michele Beauchamp
DESIGNER   Michele Beauchamp
CLIENT   Beauchamp Design
PAPER/PRINTING   Starwhite Vicksburg

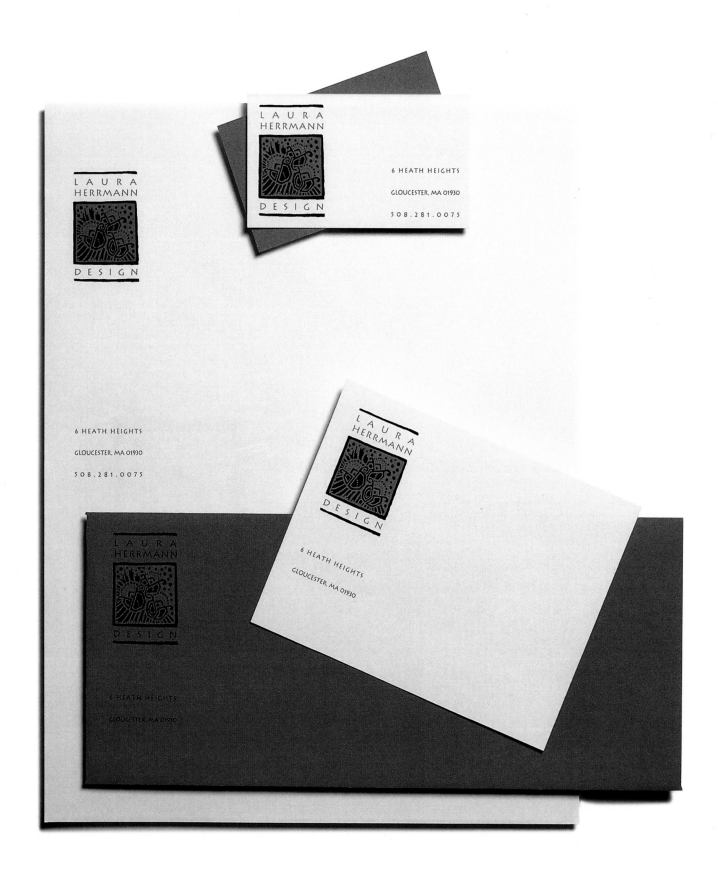

DESIGN FIRM   Laura Herrmann Design
ART DIRECTOR   Laura Herrmann
DESIGNER   Laura Herrmann
CLIENT   Laura Herrmann Design
PAPER/PRINTING   Classic Linen, Writing and Duplex

Thomas Hillman
Design

193 Middle Street
Portland, Maine 04101

PH 207 773 3727
FX 207 773 7155

I like my clients *to feel like* "a big cheese."

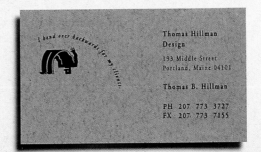

Thomas Hillman
Design
193 Middle Street
Portland, Maine 04101

Thomas B. Hillman

PH 207 773 3727
FX 207 773 7155

I bend over backwards for my clients.

Thomas Hillman
Design

193 Middle Street
Portland, Maine 04101

I'm in tune with my clients.

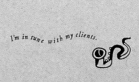

DESIGN FIRM	Thomas Hillman Design
ART DIRECTOR	Thomas Hillman
DESIGNER	Thomas Hillman
ILLUSTRATOR	Bob Aufuzdish, Eric Donelan
CLIENT	Thomas Hillman Design
PAPER/PRINTING	Neenah Environment

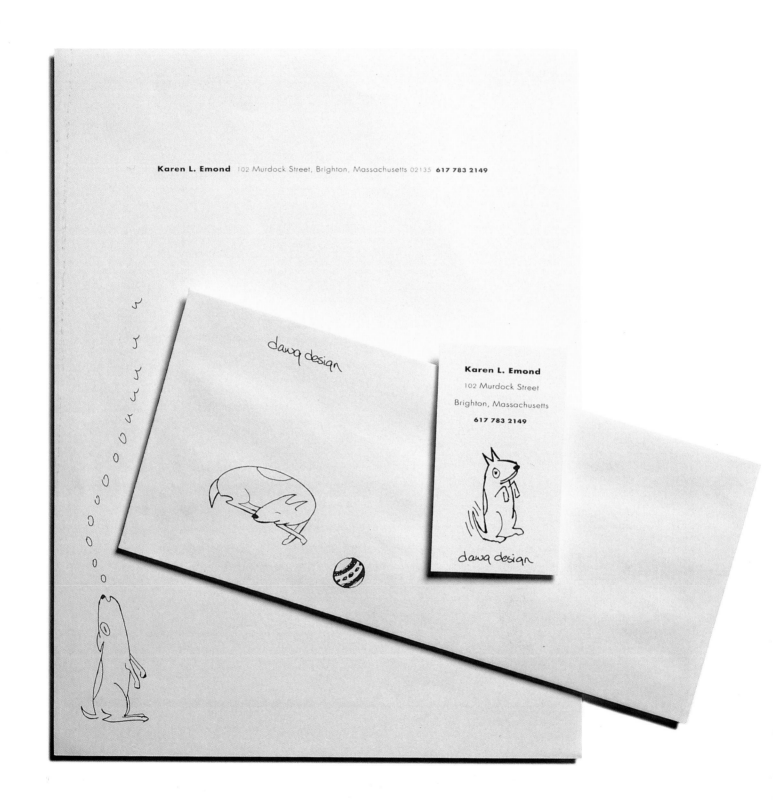

Karen L. Emond 102 Murdock Street, Brighton, Massachusetts 02135 617 783 2149

dawg design

Karen L. Emond
102 Murdock Street
Brighton, Massachusetts
617 783 2149

dawg design

DESIGN FIRM	Hawley & Armian Marketing/Design
DESIGNER	Karen Emond
CLIENT	Dawg Design
PAPER/PRINTING	Strathmore Writing

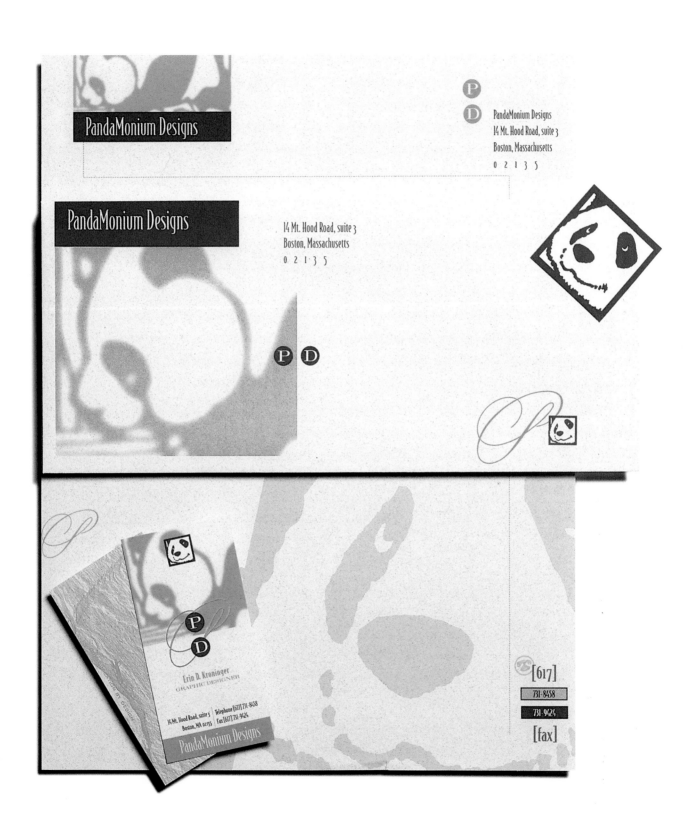

DESIGN FIRM Pandamonium Designs
DESIGNER Raymond Yu
CLIENT Pandamonium Designs
PAPER/PRINTING Howard Crush Leaf

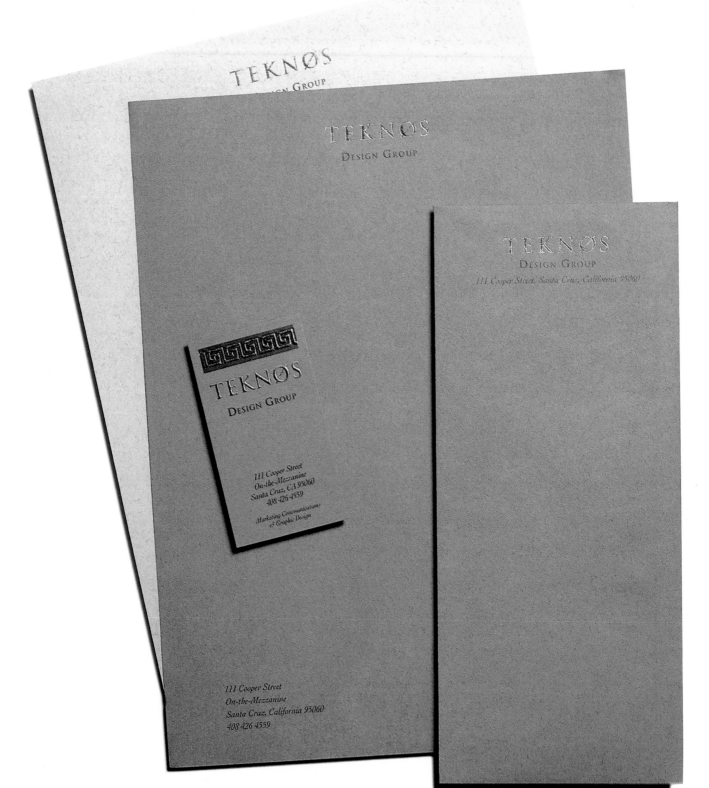

DESIGN FIRM Teknøs Design Group
DESIGNER Annaliese Fee
CLIENT Teknøs Design Group
PAPER/PRINTING Simpson Evergreen, Spruce

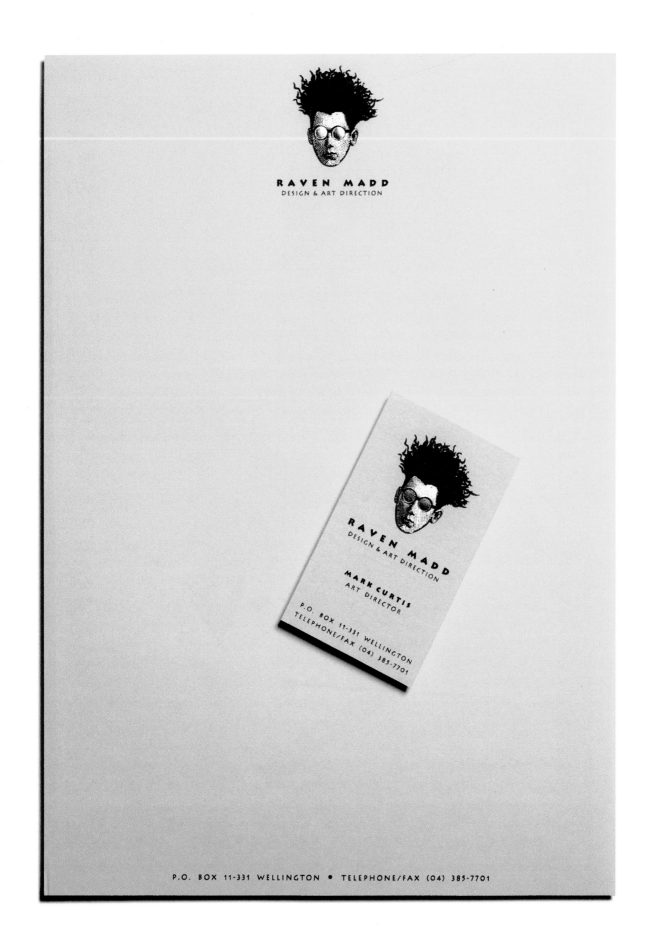

DESIGN FIRM	Raven Madd
ART DIRECTOR	Mark Curtis
DESIGNER	Mark Curtis
ILLUSTRATOR	Mark Curtis
CLIENT	Raven Madd
PAPER/PRINTING	N2 Print Ltd.

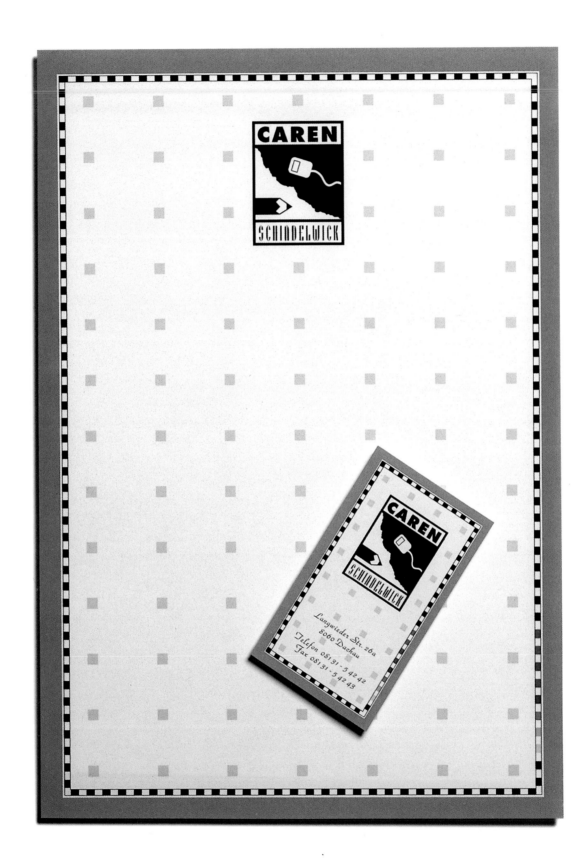

DESIGN FIRM Kom Design Munich
ART DIRECTOR Caren Schindelwick
CLIENT Caren Schindelwick
PAPER/PRINTING 4-color printing

DESIGN FIRM   Ema Design
ART DIRECTOR   Thomas C. Ema
CLIENT   Ema Design
PAPER/PRINTING   Kimberly Writing

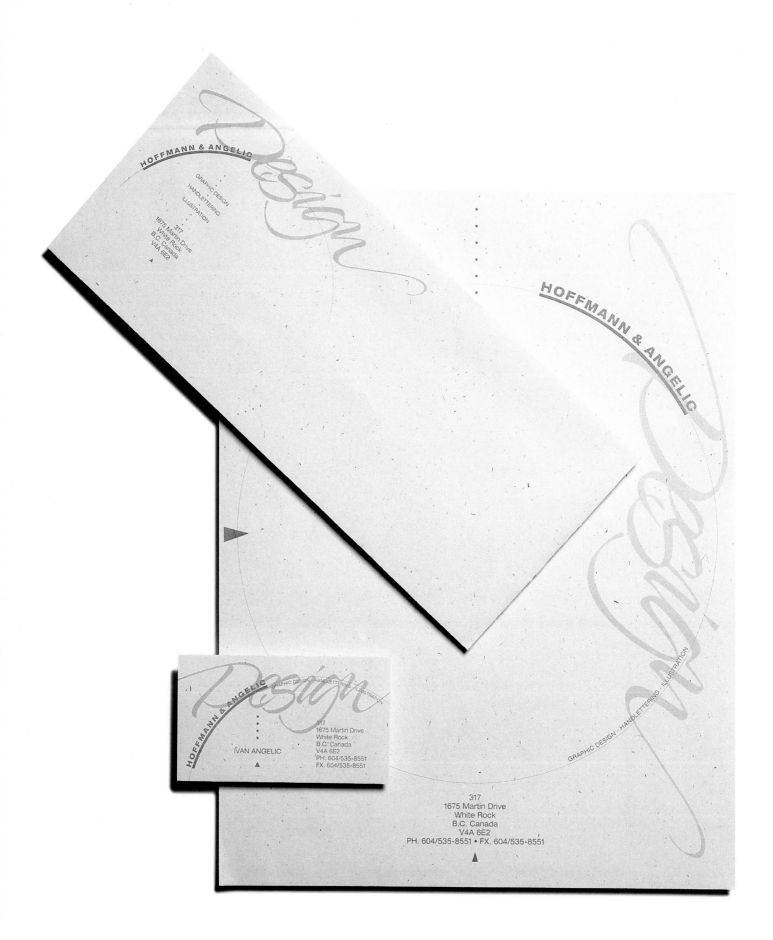

DESIGN FIRM	Hoffmann & Angelic Design
ART DIRECTOR	Ivan Angelic
DESIGNER	Andrea Hoffman
CALIGRAPHER	Ivan Angelic
CLIENT	Hoffmann & Angelic Design
PAPER/PRINTING	Genesis/Milkweed

DESIGN FIRM Sommese Design
ART DIRECTOR Kristin Sommese
DESIGNER Kristin Sommese
CLIENT Sommese Design

DESIGN FIRM Muller + Company
DESIGNER David Shultz
CLIENT Chris Muller

DESIGN FIRM Creative Services by
Pizza Hut
ART DIRECTOR Lisa Voss, Lori Cox
DESIGNER Lisa Voss
CLIENT Creative Services by
Pizza Hut

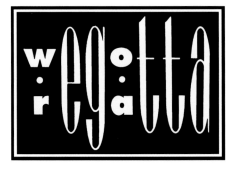

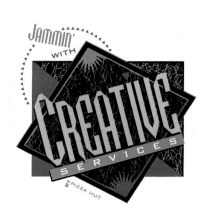

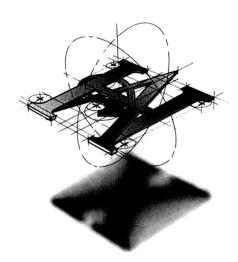

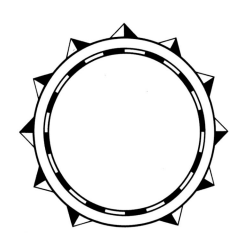

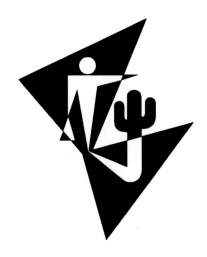

DESIGN FIRM Hornall Anderson
Design Works
ART DIRECTOR Jack Anderson
DESIGNER Jack Anderson,
David Bates, Lian Ng
ILLUSTRATOR Yutaka Sasaki
CLIENT Hornall Anderson
Design Works

DESIGN FIRM Segura Inc.
ART DIRECTOR Carlos Segura
DESIGNER Carlos Segura
ILLUSTRATOR Carlos Segura
CLIENT Sol Communications

DESIGN FIRM Tieken Design &
Creative Services
ART DIRECTOR Fred E. Tieken
DESIGNER Fred E. Tieken
CLIENT American Advertising
Federation

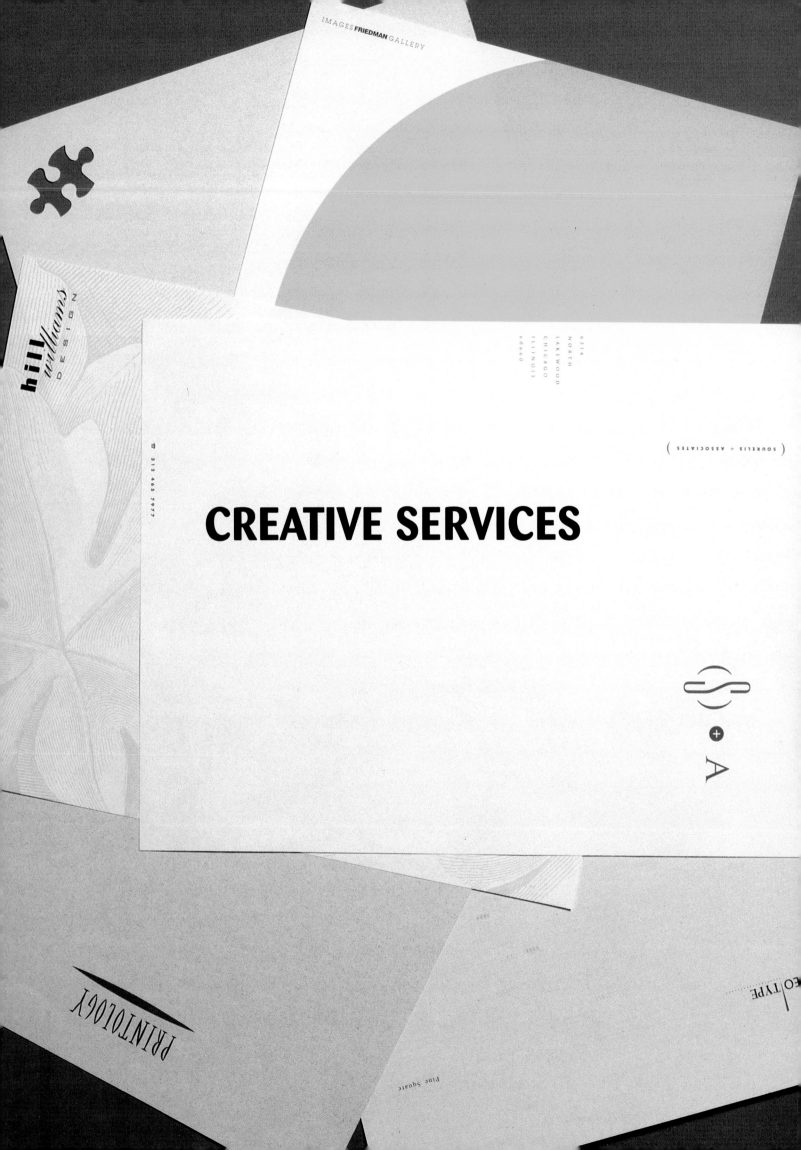

CREATIVE SERVICES

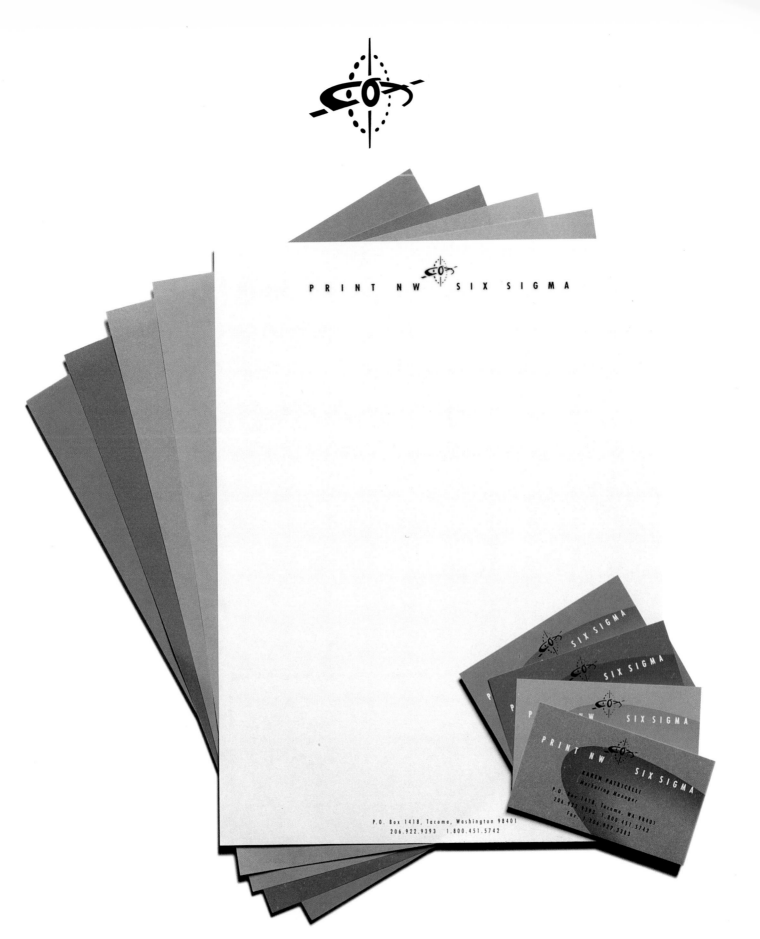

DESIGN FIRM Hornall Anderson Design Works
ART DIRECTOR Jack Anderson
DESIGNER Jack Anderson, Heidi Hatlestad, Mary Hutchinson,
Bruce Branson-Meyer
ILLUSTRATOR Scott McDougall
CLIENT Print NW/Six Sigma
PAPER/PRINTING Neenah Classic Crest Recycled

DESIGN FIRM	Dewitt Kendall – Chicago
ART DIRECTOR	Dewitt Kendall
DESIGNER	Dewitt Kendall
ILLUSTRATOR	Dewitt Kendall
CLIENT	William Wagenaar Studios
PAPER/PRINTING	Passport

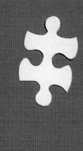

MIKE HERNACKI
Mystery Writer

2757 STATE STREET
SAN DIEGO, CA 92103

619 542 0902
FAX 297 8895

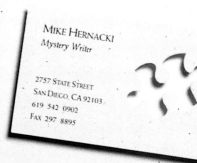

2757 STATE STREET
SAN DIEGO, CA 92103

DESIGN FIRM	Linnea Gruber Design
ART DIRECTOR	Linnea Gruber
DESIGNER	Linnea Gruber
CLIENT	Mike Hernacki
PAPER/PRINTING	Speckletone, die-cut, embossed

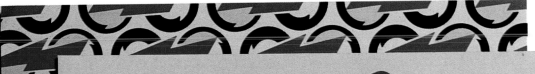

113 Arthur Avenue

Des Moines, Iowa 50313

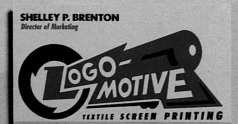

SHELLEY P. BRENTON
Director of Marketing

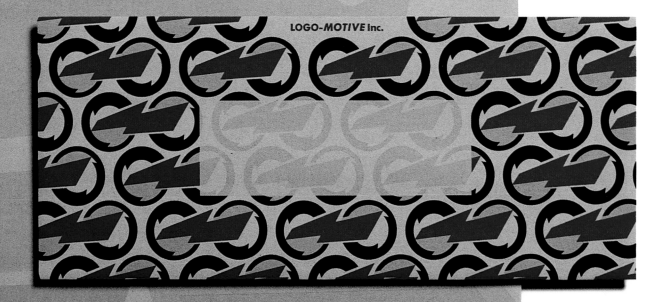

LOGO-MOTIVE Inc.

Ph. 515 · 243 · 4141   **LOGO-MOTIVE Inc.**   **FAX 515 · 243 · 7228**

DESIGN FIRM	Sayles Graphic Design
ART DIRECTOR	John Sayles
DESIGNER	John Sayles
ILLUSTRATOR	John Sayles
CLIENT	Logo-Motive
PAPER/PRINTING	James River, Retreeve Gray, 2 colors

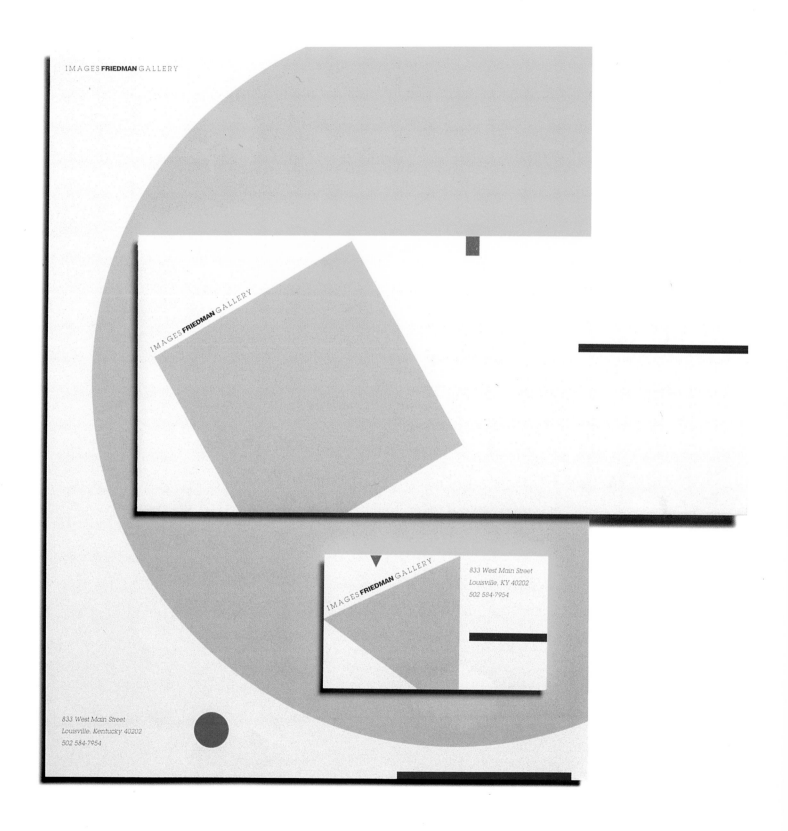

DESIGN FIRM   Images
ART DIRECTOR   Julius Friedman
DESIGNER   Julius Friedman
ILLUSTRATOR   Julius Friedman
CLIENT   Images Friedman Gallery
PAPER/PRINTING   Simpson Starwhite Vellum

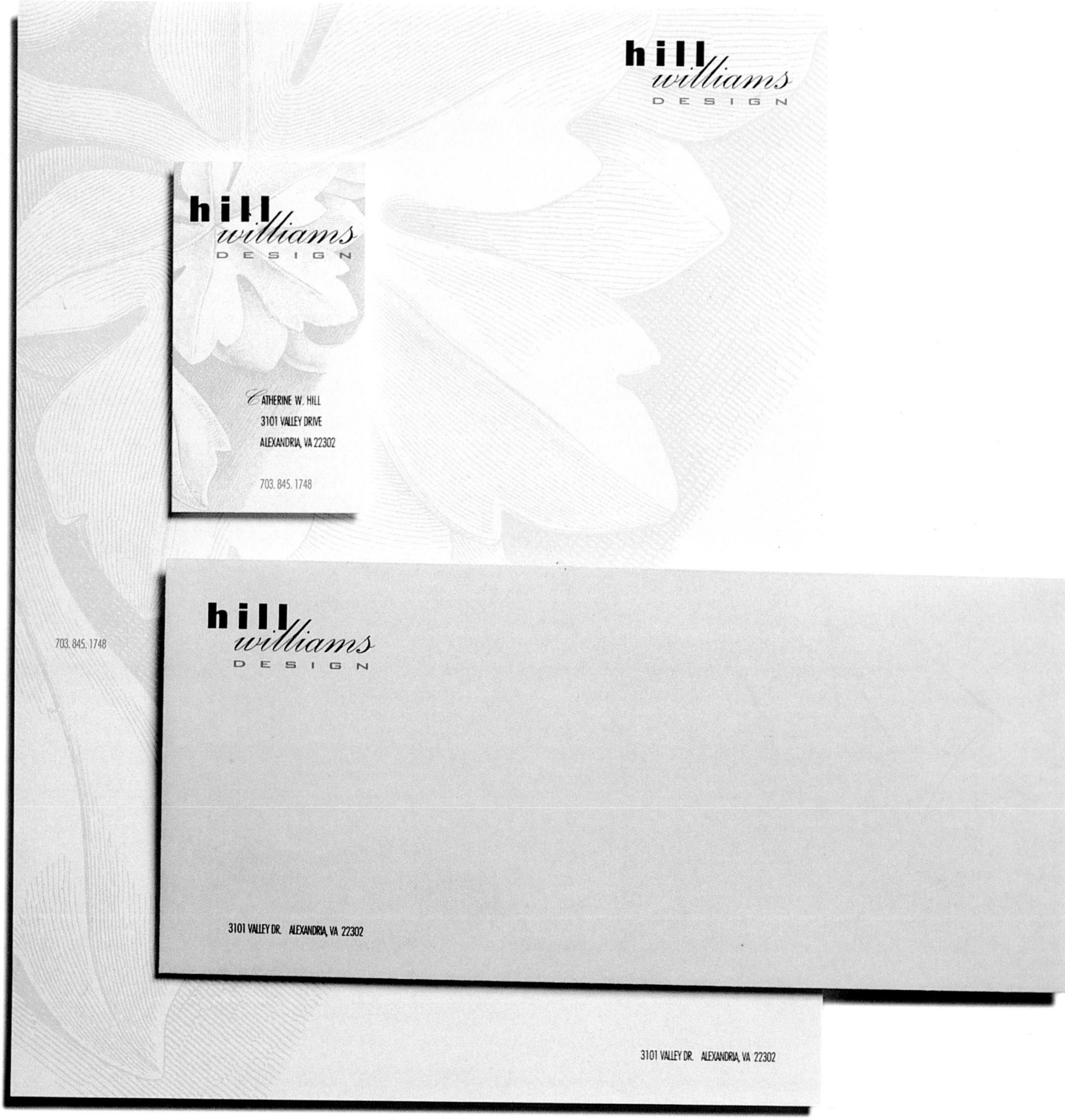

hill
williams
D E S I G N

hill
williams
D E S I G N

CATHERINE W. HILL

3101 VALLEY DRIVE

ALEXANDRIA, VA 22302

703. 845. 1748

703. 845. 1748

hill
williams
D E S I G N

3101 VALLEY DR.   ALEXANDRIA, VA 22302

3101 VALLEY DR.   ALEXANDRIA, VA 22302

DESIGN FIRM   Barbara Raab Design
ART DIRECTOR   Barbara Raab Sgouros
DESIGNER   Lee Ann Rhodes
CLIENT   Hill Williams Design
PAPER/PRINTING   Classic Crest, 2 colors

DESIGN FIRM	GrandPre and Whaley, Ltd.
ART DIRECTOR	Kevin Whaley
DESIGNER	Kevin Whaley
CLIENT	Lithoprep, Inc.
PAPER/PRINTING	Champion

DESIGN FIRM	Allan Hill
ART DIRECTOR	Allan Hill
DESIGNER	Allan Hill
CLIENT	Allan Hill
PAPER/PRINTING	Champion, Mystique Soft White

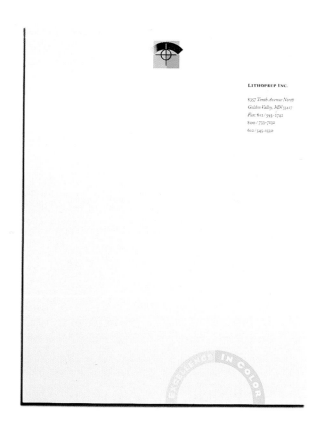

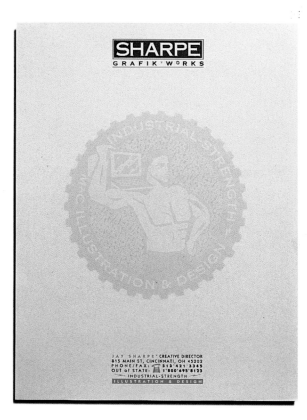

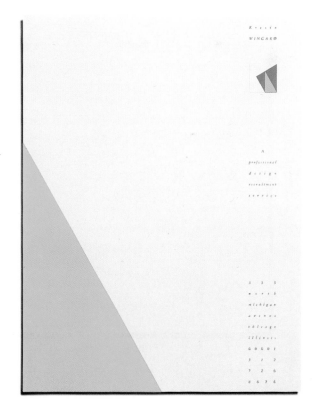

DESIGN FIRM	Sharpe Grafikworks
ART DIRECTOR	Jay Sharpe
DESIGNER	Jay Sharpe
ILLUSTRATOR	Jay Sharpe
CLIENT	Sharpe Grafikworks
PAPER/PRINTING	Frencia Speckletone

DESIGN FIRM	Ema Design
ART DIRECTOR	Thomas C. Ema
CLIENT	Kresin Wingard
PAPER/PRINTING	Kimberly Writing

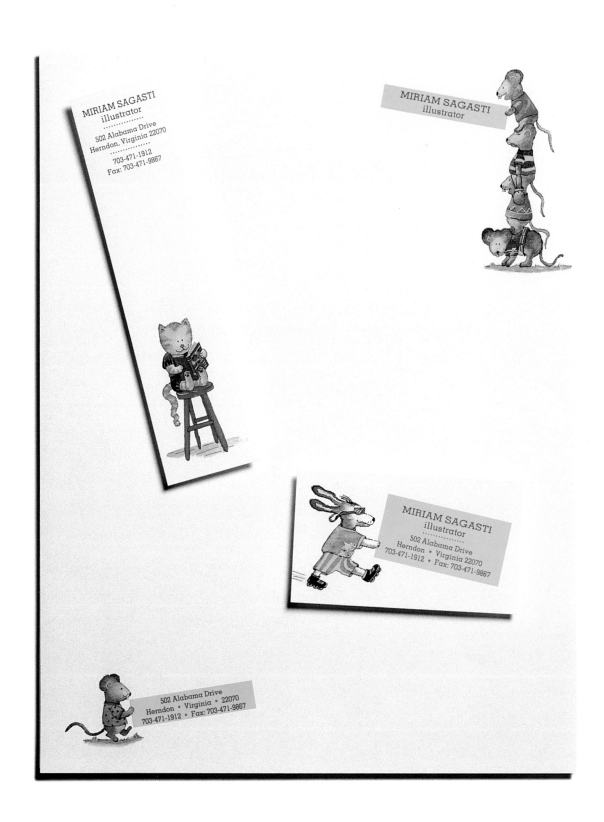

MIRIAM SAGASTI
illustrator
....
502 Alabama Drive
Herndon, Virginia 22070
....
703-471-1912
Fax: 703-471-9867

MIRIAM SAGASTI
illustrator

MIRIAM SAGASTI
illustrator
....
502 Alabama Drive
Herndon • Virginia 22070
703-471-1912 • Fax: 703-471-9867

502 Alabama Drive
Herndon • Virginia • 22070
703-471-1912 • Fax: 703-471-9867

DESIGN FIRM	Bi-design
ART DIRECTOR	Miriam Sagasti
DESIGNER	Miriam Sagasti
ILLUSTRATOR	Miriam Sagasti
CLIENT	Miriam Sagasti
PAPER/PRINTING	Classic Crest

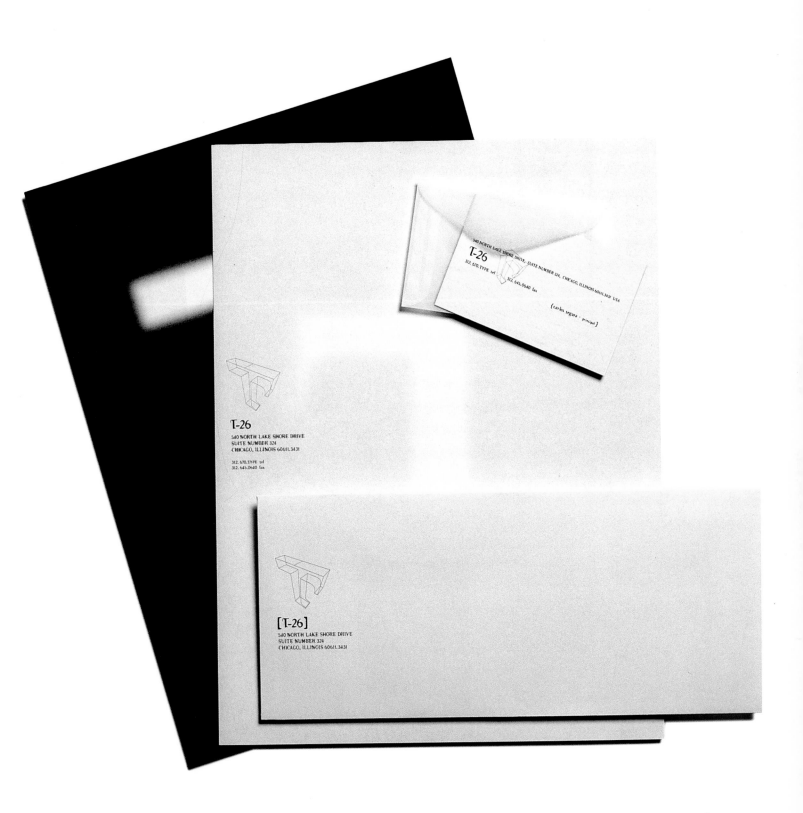

DESIGN FIRM	Segura Inc.
ART DIRECTOR	Carlos Segura
DESIGNER	Carlos Segura
ILLUSTRATOR	Carlos Segura
CLIENT	T-26
PAPER/PRINTING	Argus

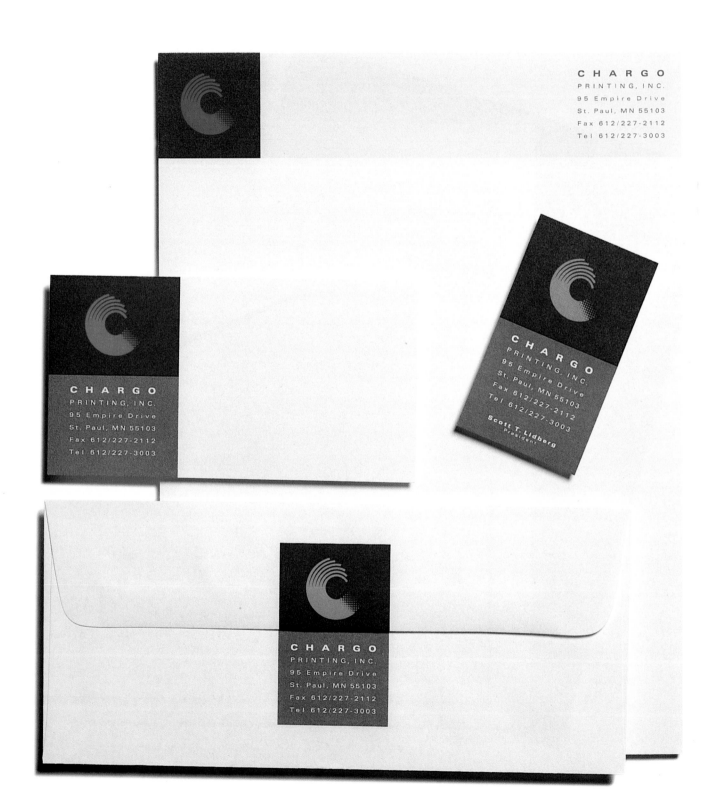

DESIGN FIRM	GrandPré and Whaley, Ltd.
ART DIRECTOR	Kevin Whaley
DESIGNER	Kevin Whaley
CLIENT	Chargo Printing, Inc.
PAPER/PRINTING	Strathmore

PRINTOLOGY

PRINTOLOGY

Stefano Introini

The Science of Impression

1291 Electric Avenue, Venice, CA 90291

310.392.1878 Fax: 310.399.5151

PRINTOLOGY

The Science of Impression

1291 Electric Avenue

Venice, CA 90291

The Science of Impression

1291 Electric Avenue

Venice, CA 90291

310.392.1878 Fax: 310.399.5151

DESIGN FIRM	Lorna Stovall Design
ART DIRECTOR	Lorna Stovall
DESIGNER	Lorna Stovall
CLIENT	Printology
PAPER/PRINTING	Simpson Evergreen

DESIGN FIRM   Segura Inc.
ART DIRECTOR   Carlos Segura
DESIGNER   Carlos Segura
CLIENT   Shulman

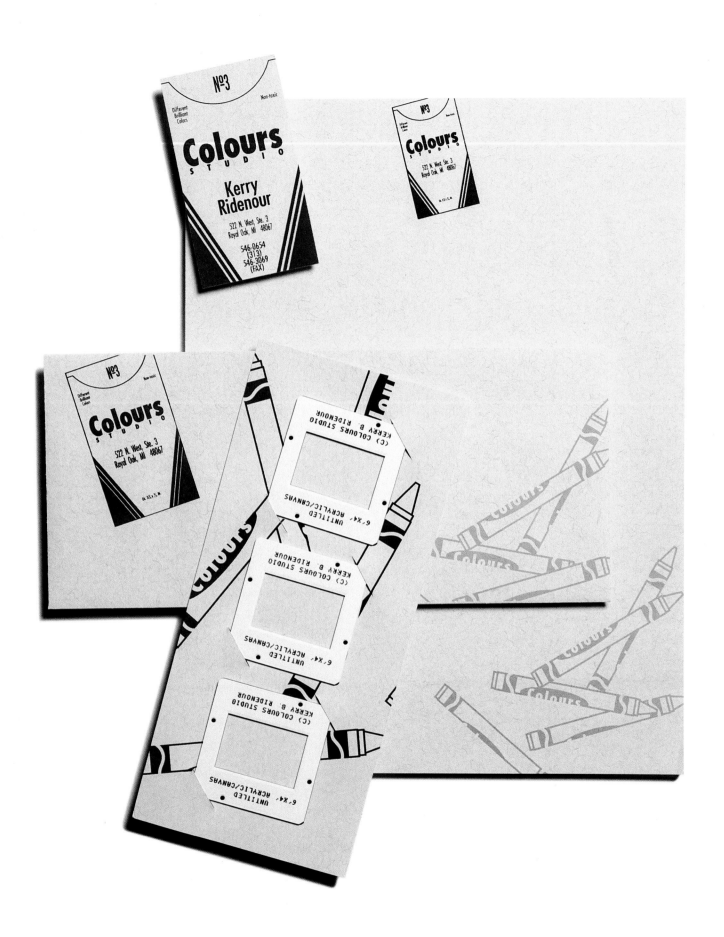

DESIGN FIRM   Ridenour Advertising
ART DIRECTOR   Kerry B. Ridenour
DESIGNER   Kerry B. Ridenour
ILLUSTRATOR   Kerry B. Ridenour
CLIENT   Colours Studio

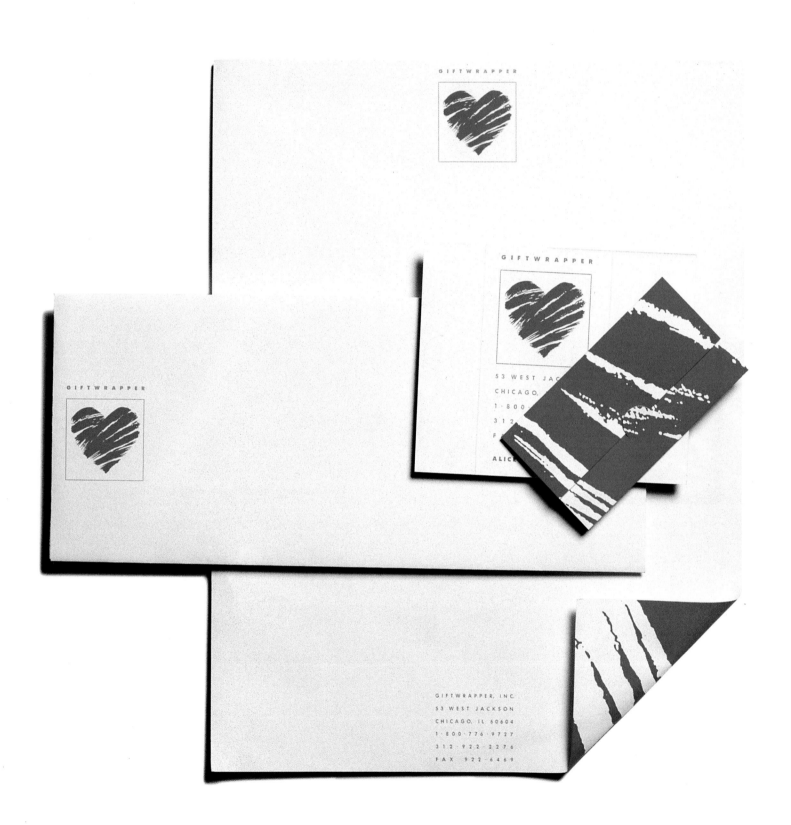

DESIGN FIRM Bartels & Company, Inc.
ART DIRECTOR David Bartels
DESIGNER Brent Wilson
ILLUSTRATOR Don Strandel
CLIENT Gift Wrapper

DESIGN FIRM	The Green House
ART DIRECTOR	Brian Green
DESIGNER	Brian Green
ILLUSTRATOR	Colin Mechan
CLIENT	Berkeley
PAPER/PRINTING	4 colors

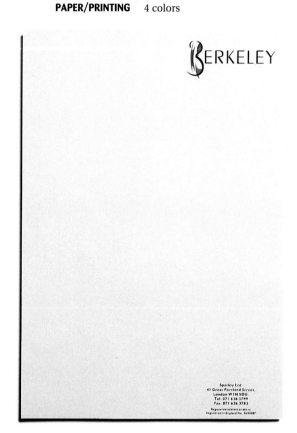

DESIGN FIRM	Bartels & Company, Inc.
ART DIRECTOR	David Bartels
DESIGNER	Brian Barclay
ILLUSTRATOR	Brian Barclay
CLIENT	Wordsworth Typography

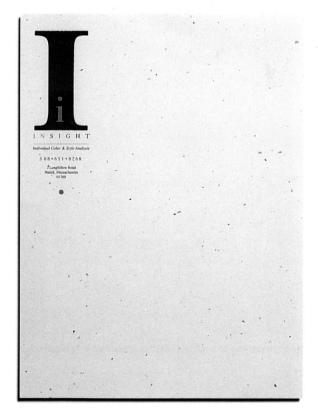

DESIGN FIRM	Patri-Keker Design
DESIGNER	Bobby Patri
CLIENT	Beth Clements-Gutcheon
PAPER/PRINTING	Evergreen cottonwood script

DESIGN FIRM	Nora Robbins
ART DIRECTOR	Nora Robbins
DESIGNER	Nora Robbins
CLIENT	Insight/Leslie Larocca
PAPER/PRINTING	Fox River Confetti/Kaliedascope

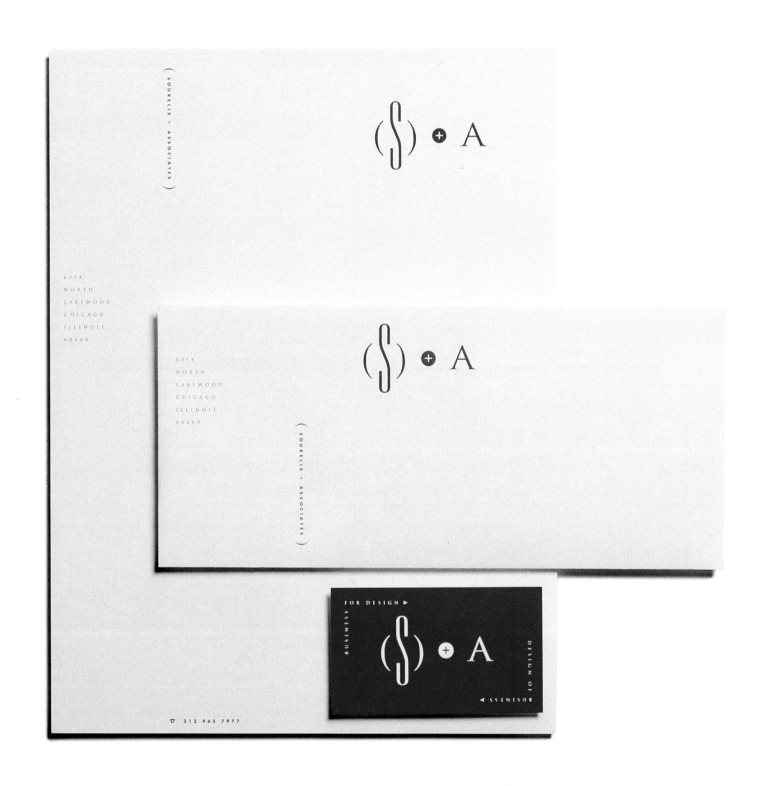

DESIGN FIRM	Mark Oldach Design
ART DIRECTOR	Mark Oldach
DESIGNER	Mark Oldach
CLIENT	Sourelis & Associates
PAPER/PRINTING	Neenah Classic Crest

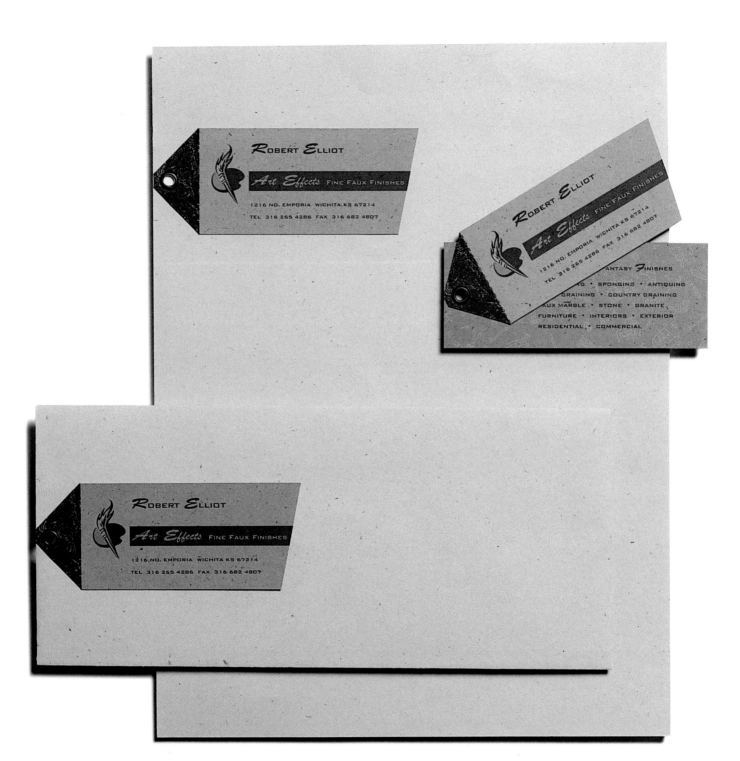

DESIGN FIRM   Love Packaging Group
ART DIRECTOR   Tracy Holdeman
DESIGNER   Tracy Holdeman, Robert Elliot
ILLUSTRATOR   Tracy Holdeman
CLIENT   Art Effects
Only the business card was printed; the client hand
rivets each card, envelope, and letterhead sheet.

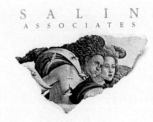

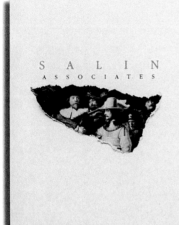

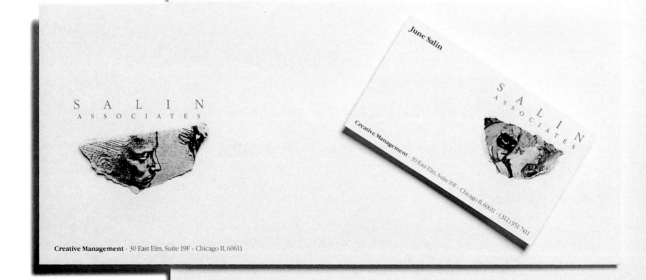

DESIGN FIRM   Jon Wells Associates
ART DIRECTOR   Jon Wells
DESIGNER   Jon Wells
CLIENT   June Salin
PAPER/PRINTING   Strathmore Writing

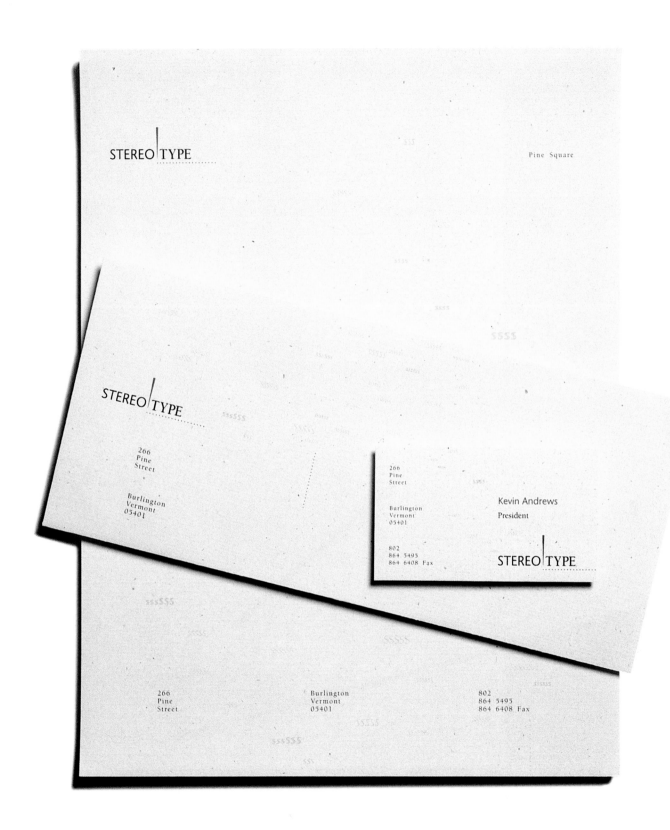

DESIGN FIRM   Creative EDGE
DESIGNER   Rick Salzman, Barbara Pitfido
CLIENT   Stereo Type
PAPER/PRINTING   Classic Laid

a h !

a h !

a h !

audrey hackman
creative director / copy
creative director

550 south gould road   columbus ohio 43209
telephone   614 231 9291   fax   614 231 1169

audrey hackman   creative director / copy

550 south gould road   columbus ohio 43209   telephone   614 231 9291   fax   614 231 1169

DESIGN FIRM	Schmeltz & Warren
ART DIRECTOR	Crit Warren
DESIGNER	Crit Warren
CLIENT	"Ah!" — Audrey Hackman
PAPER/PRINTING	Protocol

DESIGN FIRM Adele Bass & Co. Design
ART DIRECTOR Adele Bass
DESIGNER Adele Bass
ILLUSTRATOR Adele Bass
CLIENT Sharynn Bass/ Advertising Copywriter

DESIGN FIRM Earl Gee Design
ART DIRECTOR Earl Gee
DESIGNER Earl Gee, Fani Chung
ILLUSTRATOR Earl Gee
CLIENT San Francisco Arts Commission

DESIGN FIRM Segura Inc.
ART DIRECTOR Carlos Segura
DESIGNER Carlos Segura
ILLUSTRATOR Carlos Segura
CLIENT Gordon (photographer's representatives)

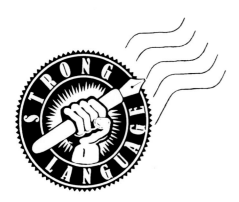

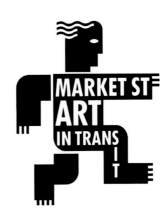

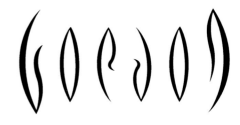

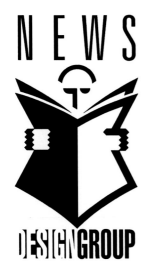

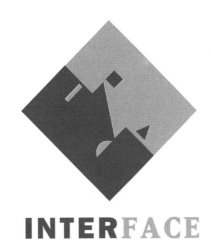

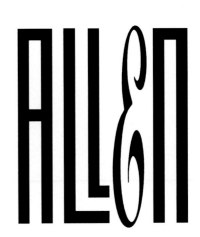

DESIGN FIRM Eilts Anderson Tracy
ART DIRECTOR Patrice Eilts
DESIGNER Patrice Eilts
ILLUSTRATOR Patrice Eilts
CLIENT News Design Group (newspaper union)

DESIGN FIRM Design Art, Inc.
ART DIRECTOR Norman Moore
DESIGNER Norman Moore
CLIENT Interface Digital Prepress

DESIGN FIRM Segura Inc.
ART DIRECTOR Carlos Segura
DESIGNER Carlos Segura
ILLUSTRATOR Carlos Segura
CLIENT Harry Allen/writer

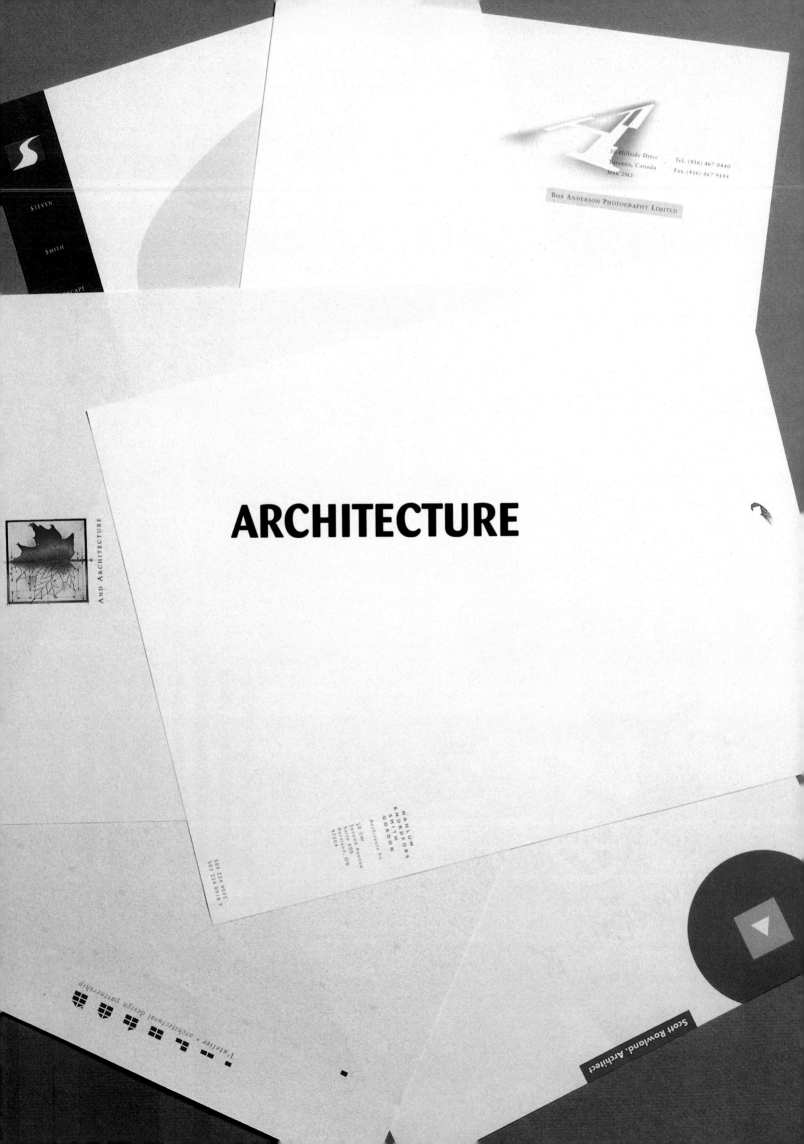

ARCHITECTURE

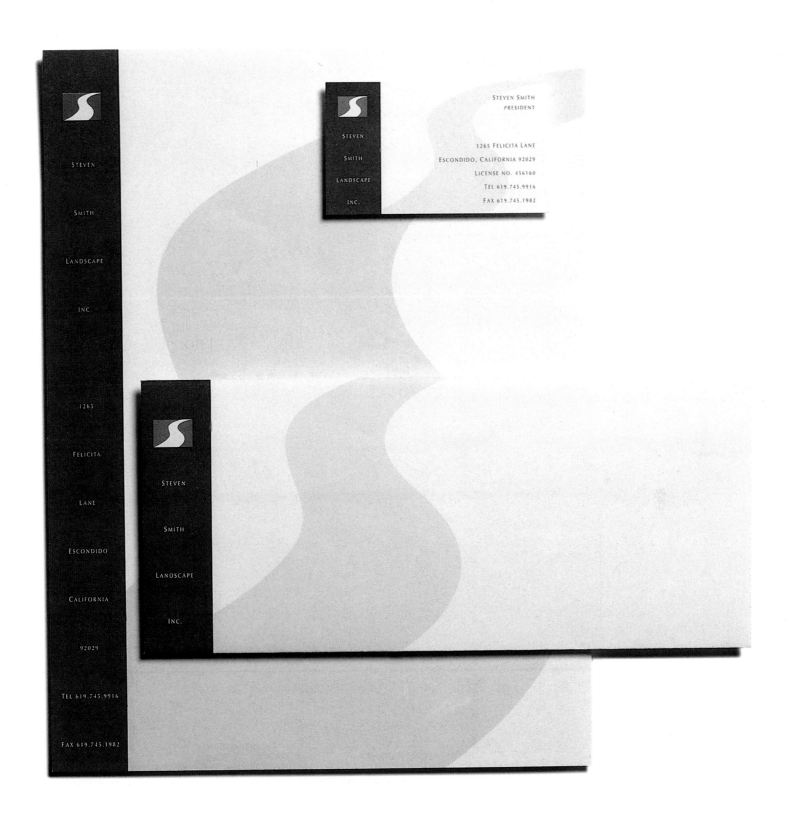

STEVEN SMITH
PRESIDENT

1265 FELICITA LANE
ESCONDIDO, CALIFORNIA 92029
LICENSE NO. 456160
TEL 619.745.9916
FAX 619.745.1982

STEVEN
SMITH
LANDSCAPE
INC.

1265
FELICITA
LANE
ESCONDIDO
CALIFORNIA
92029
TEL 619.745.9916
FAX 619.745.1982

STEVEN
SMITH
LANDSCAPE
INC.

DESIGN FIRM   Beauchamp Design
ART DIRECTOR   Michele Beauchamp
DESIGNER   Michele Beauchamp
CLIENT   Steve Smith Landscape Inc.
PAPER/PRINTING   Evergreen

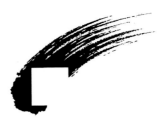

MAHLUM
&NORDFORS
SMITH
GORDON

50 SW
Second Avenue
Suite 600
Portland, OR
97204

Darrell W. Turner
architect

MAHLUM
&NORDFORS
McKINLEY
GORDON

2505
Third Avenue
Suite 219
Seattle, WA
98121

206 441 4151
206 441 0478 F

MAHLUM
&NORDFORS
SMITH
GORDON

Architects PC

50 SW
Second Avenue
Suite 600
Portland, OR
97204

503 224 4032
503 224 0918 F

DESIGN FIRM	Hornall Anderson Design Works
ART DIRECTOR	Jack Anderson
DESIGNER	Jack Anderson, Scott Eggers, Leo Raymundo
CLIENT	Mahlum & Nordfors McKinley Gordon
PAPER/PRINTING	Monadnock Astro Lite, embossed

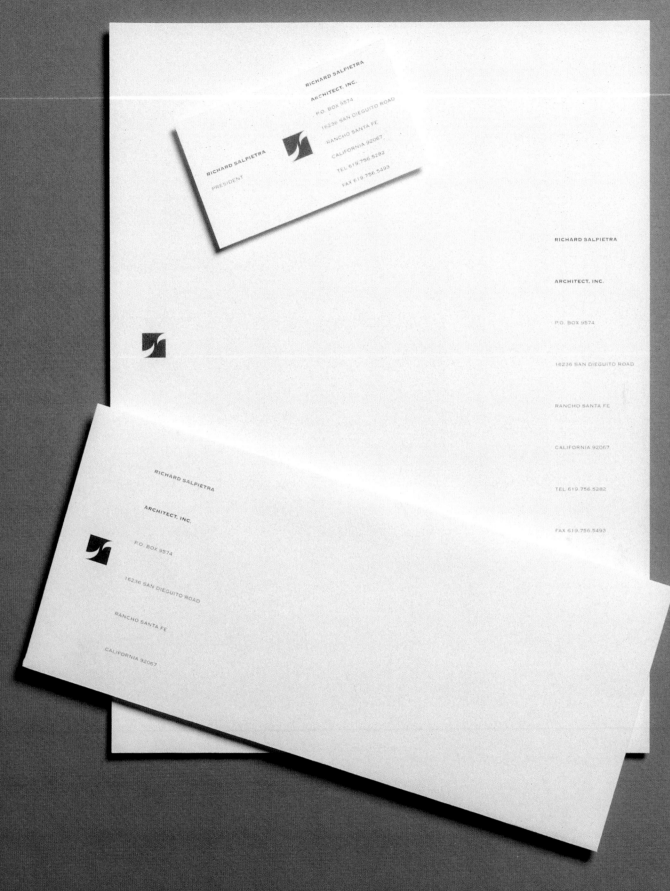

DESIGN FIRM	Beauchamp Design
ART DIRECTOR	Michele Beauchamp
DESIGNER	Michele Beauchamp
CLIENT	Richard Salpietra Architect, Inc.
PAPER/PRINTING	Classic Crest

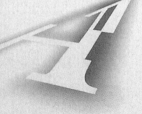

50 Hillside Drive
Toronto, Canada
M4K 2M2

Tel. (416) 467 0440
Fax.(416) 467 9195

Bob Anderson Photography Limited

Bob Anderson Photography Limited

50 Hillside Drive
Toronto, Canada
M4K 2M2

Tel. (416) 467 0440
Fax.(416) 467 9195

Bob Anderson Photography Limited

50 Hillside Drive
Toronto, Canada
M4K 2M2

DESIGN FIRM	Eskind Waddell
ART DIRECTOR	Malcolm Waddell
DESIGNER	Nicola Lyon
CLIENT	Bob Anderson Photography Ltd.
PAPER/PRINTING	Strathmore Script

DESIGN FIRM	Choplogic
ART DIRECTOR	Walter McCord, Mary Cawein
DESIGNER	Walter McCord, Mary Cawein
ILLUSTRATOR	Walter McCord, Mary Cawein
CLIENT	Argabrite Architects
PAPER/PRINTING	Monadnock, 1 color

DESIGN FIRM	William Field Design
ART DIRECTOR	Willy Field
DESIGNER	Willy Field
ILLUSTRATOR	Peter Marquez
CLIENT	Turner, Marquez & Romero
PAPER/PRINTING	Environment

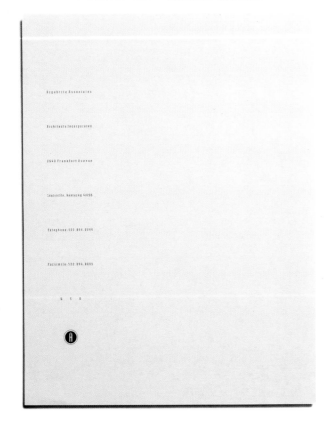

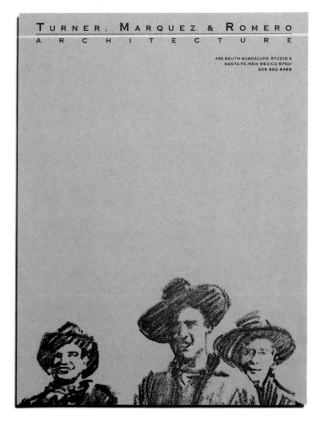

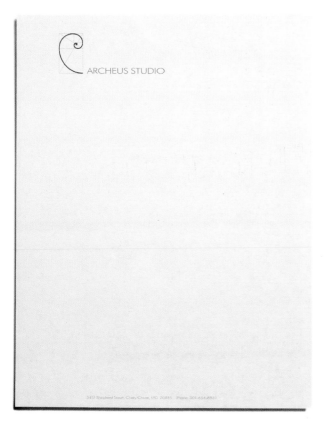

DESIGN FIRM	Musikar Design
ART DIRECTOR	Sharon R. Musikar
DESIGNER	Sharon R. Musikar, Lynn Iadarola
ILLUSTRATOR	Sharon R. Musikar
CLIENT	Archeus Studio
PAPER/PRINTING	Gilbert Writing, 2 colors

DESIGN FIRM	Bartels & Company, Inc.
ART DIRECTOR	David Bartels
DESIGNER	Mark Illig
ILLUSTRATOR	Mark Illig
CLIENT	The Lawrence Group

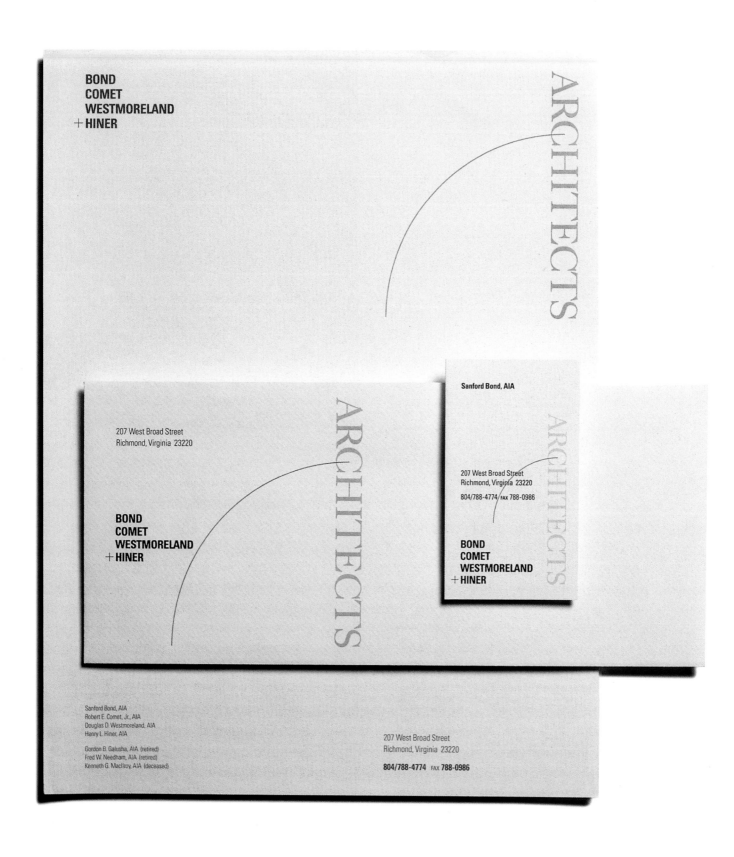

DESIGN FIRM Communication Design, Inc.
ART DIRECTOR Robert Meganck
DESIGNER Tim Priddy, Bil Cullen
CLIENT Bond Comet Westmoreland & Hiner Architects
PAPER/PRINTING Dillard

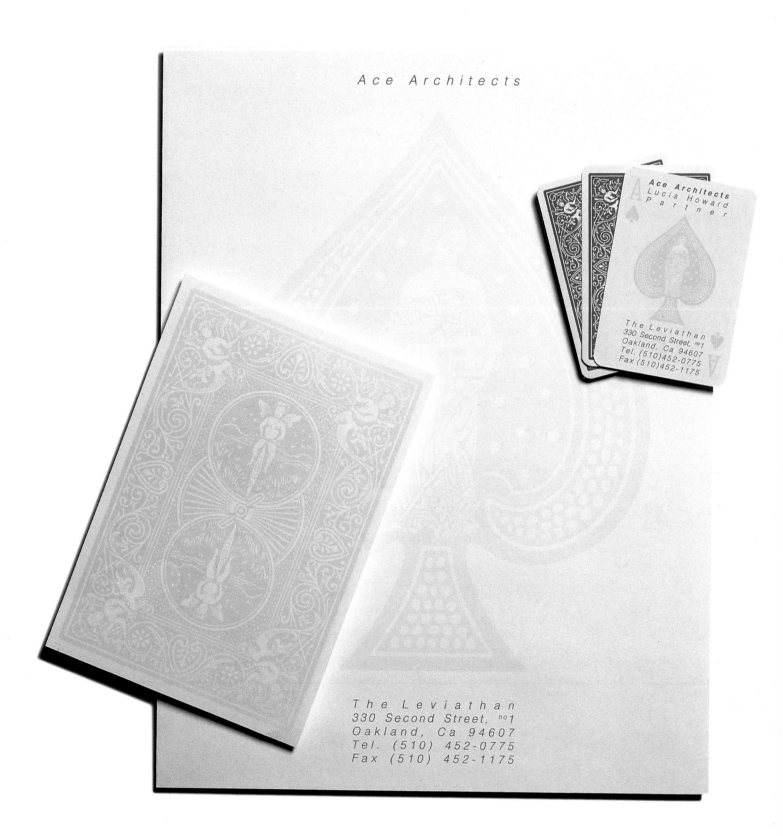

DESIGN FIRM   Ace Architects by Judith Oaus
ILLUSTRATOR   Judith Oaus
CLIENT   Ace Architects
PAPER/PRINTING   Ampersand

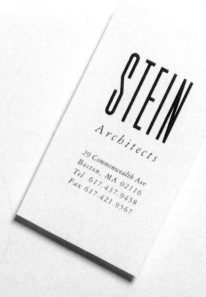

DESIGN FIRM	Clifford Selbert Design
ART DIRECTOR	Clifford Selbert, Robin Perkins
DESIGNER	Robin Perkins
CLIENT	Stein Architects
PAPER/PRINTING	Strathmore Starwhite Vicksburg, 3 colors

De stichting heeft tot doel het bevorderen van de ontwikkeling van de architectuur in de ruimste zin van het woord en het scheppen van voorwaarden voor de realisatie van projecten met een hoge architectonische kwaliteit in Nederland **Stimuleringsfonds voor Architectuur**

Datum

Uw kenmerk

Ons kenmerk

Betreft

Schouwburgplein 30-34

3012 CL Rotterdam

telefoon (010) 433 05 25

fax (010) 413 66 66

KvK Rotterdam S 133717

Bank: Crediet en Effecten Bank

Postbus 85100, 3508 AC Utrecht

Rekeningnummer: 69.98.59.336

Girorekening C en E Bank: 75651

Schouwburgplein 30-34, 3012 CL Rotterdam

De stichting heeft tot doel het bevorderen van de ontwikkeling van de architectuur in de ruimste zin van het woord en het scheppen van voorwaarden voor de realisatie van projecten met een hoge architectonische kwaliteit in Nederland **Stimuleringsfonds** voor Architectuur

Stimuleringsfonds voor Architectuur
Antwoordnummer 3525
3000 WB Rotterdam

kan ongefrankeerd worden verzonden

DESIGN FIRM Proforma Rotterdam
DESIGNER Ciaran O'Gaora
CLIENT Stimuleringsfonds voor Architectuur
PAPER/PRINTING Strathmore Writing Wove

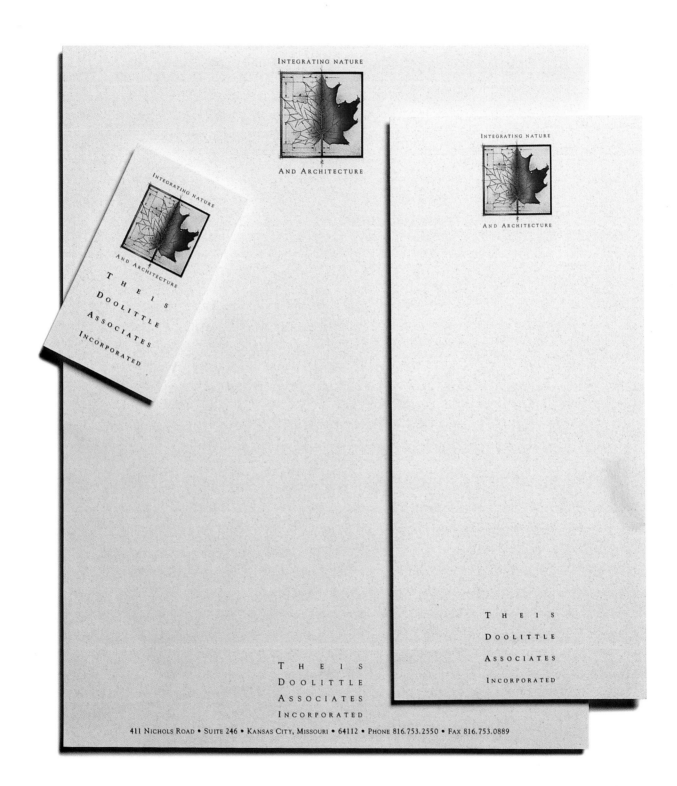

INTEGRATING NATURE

AND ARCHITECTURE

THEIS
DOOLITTLE
ASSOCIATES
INCORPORATED

411 NICHOLS ROAD • SUITE 246 • KANSAS CITY, MISSOURI • 64112 • PHONE 816.753.2550 • FAX 816.753.0889

DESIGN FIRM Eilts Anderson Tracy
ART DIRECTOR Patrice Eilts
DESIGNER Patrice Eilts
ILLUSTRATOR Michael Weaver
CLIENT Theis Doolitle Architects & Landscape Architects
PAPER/PRINTING Passport

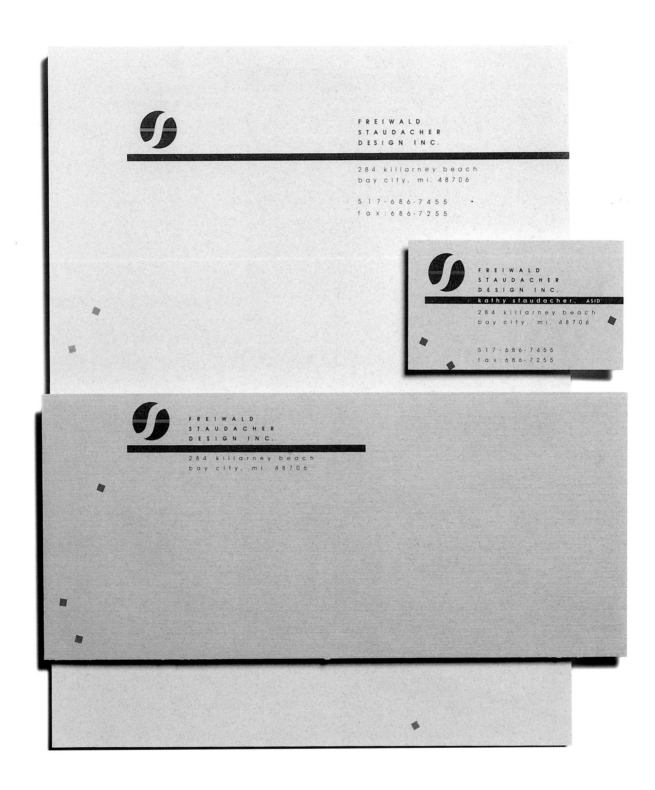

DESIGN FIRM	Heart Graphic Design
ART DIRECTOR	Clark Most
DESIGNER	Clark Most
CLIENT	Freiwald/Standecher Design Inc.
PAPER/PRINTING	Classic Linen

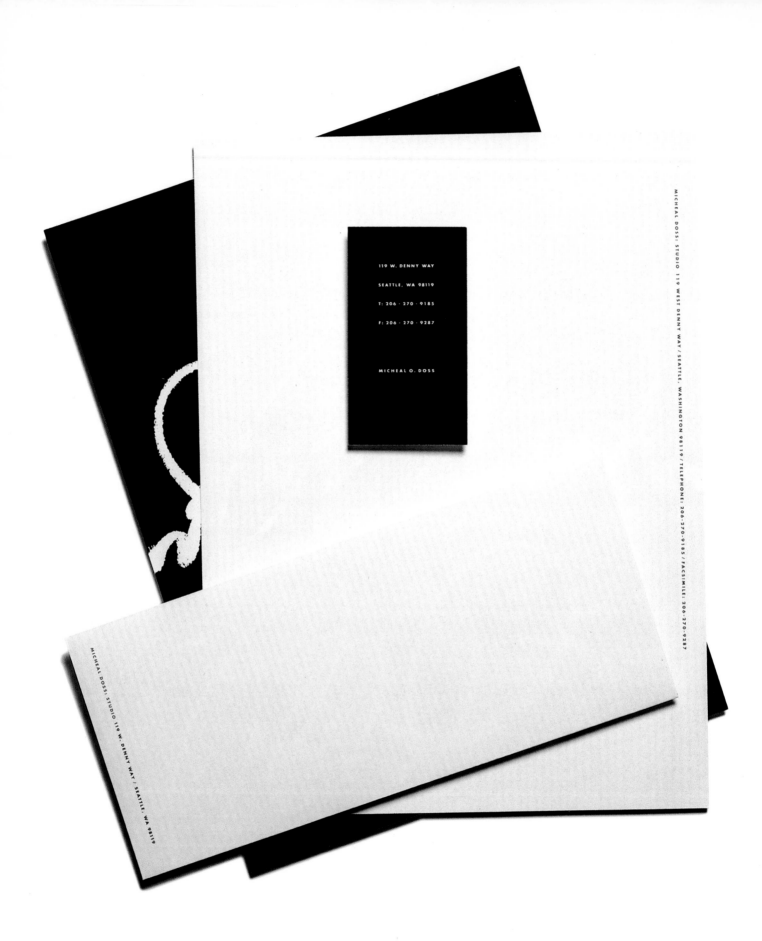

DESIGN FIRM	Hornall Anderson Design Works
ART DIRECTOR	Jack Anderson
DESIGNER	Jack Anderson
CLIENT	Micheal Doss

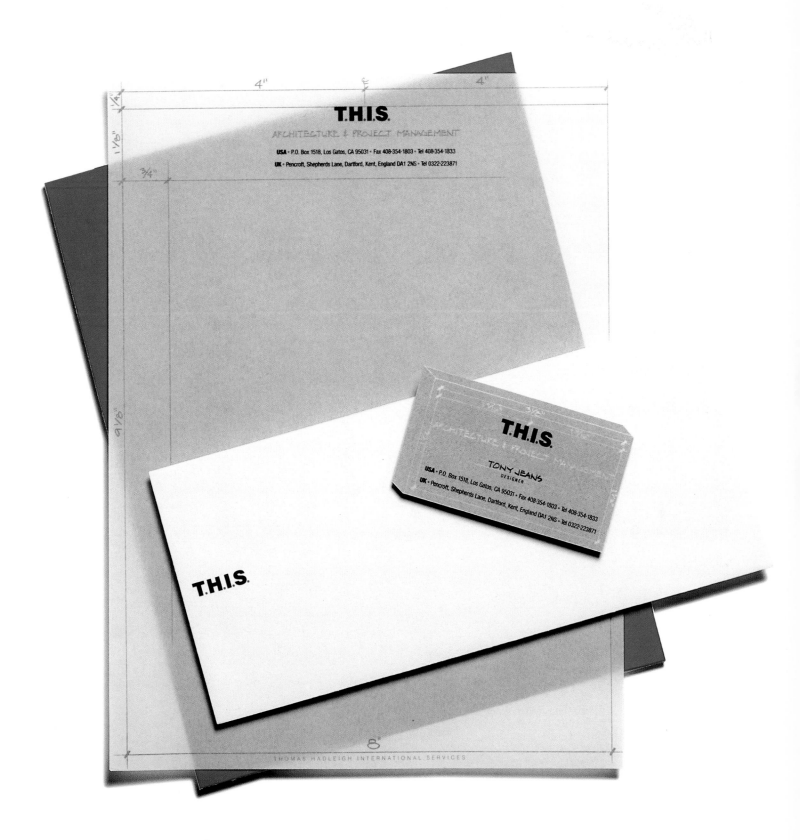

DESIGN FIRM   THARP DID IT
DESIGNER   Rick Tharp, Jana Heer
CLIENT   Thoma Hadley International Services
PAPER/PRINTING   Gilbert Paper

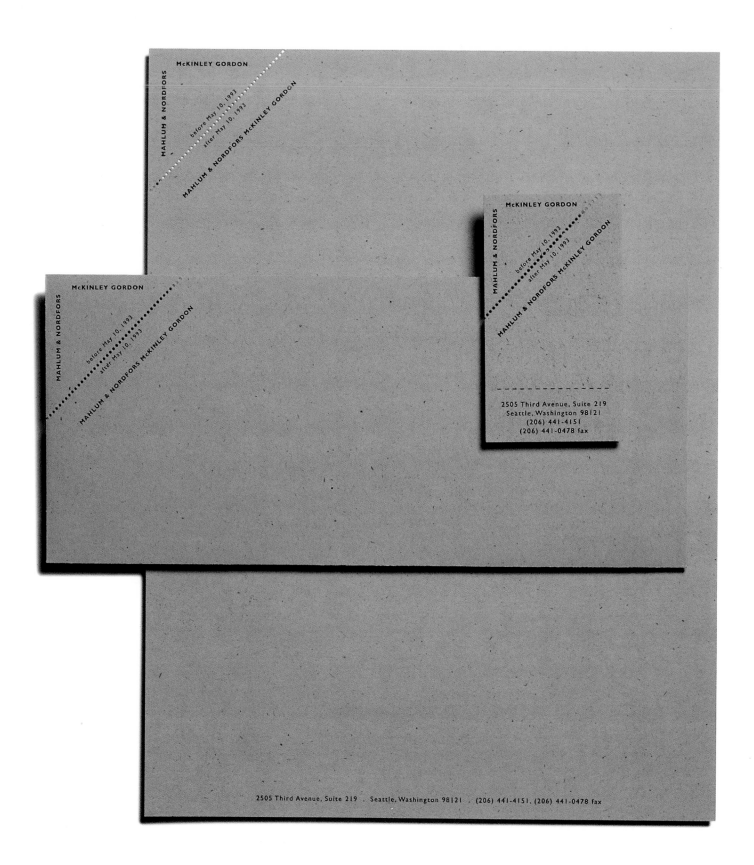

DESIGN FIRM   Hornall Anderson Design Works
ART DIRECTOR   Jack Anderson
DESIGNER   Jack Anderson, Scott Eggers, Leo Raymundo
CLIENT   Mahlum & Nordfors McKinley Gordon
PAPER/PRINTING   French Speckletone, perforation

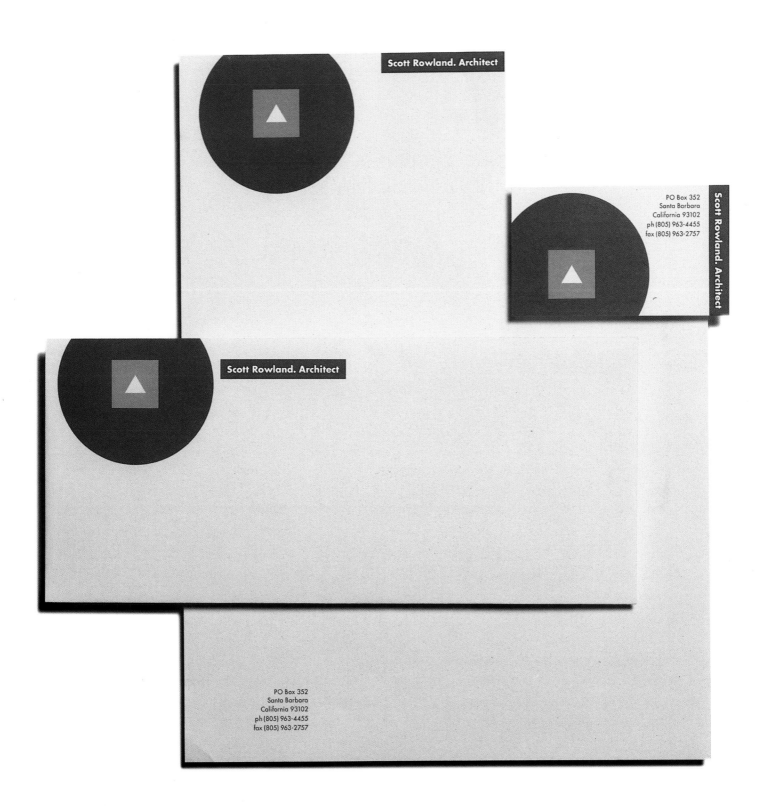

DESIGN FIRM	Puccinelli Design
ART DIRECTOR	Keith Puccinelli
DESIGNER	Keith Puccinelli, Heidi Palladino
ILLUSTRATOR	Keith Puccinelli
CLIENT	Scott Rowland
PAPER/PRINTING	Cranes Crest, to minimize the effects of the watermark on the paper, the designer underprinted opaque white beneath the image.

l'atelier • architectural design partnership

l'atelier • architectural design partnership

l'atelier • architectural design partnership

ralph c. ortiz

113 east st. joseph street • arcadia ca 91006 • 818 446 9400

113 east st. joseph street • arcadia ca 91006 • 818 446 9400 • fax 818 446 9533

DESIGN FIRM Adele Bass & Co. Design
ART DIRECTOR Adele Bass
DESIGNER Adele Bass
ILLUSTRATOR Adele Bass
CLIENT L'aterlier
PAPER/PRINTING Kraft Speckletone, 2 PMS

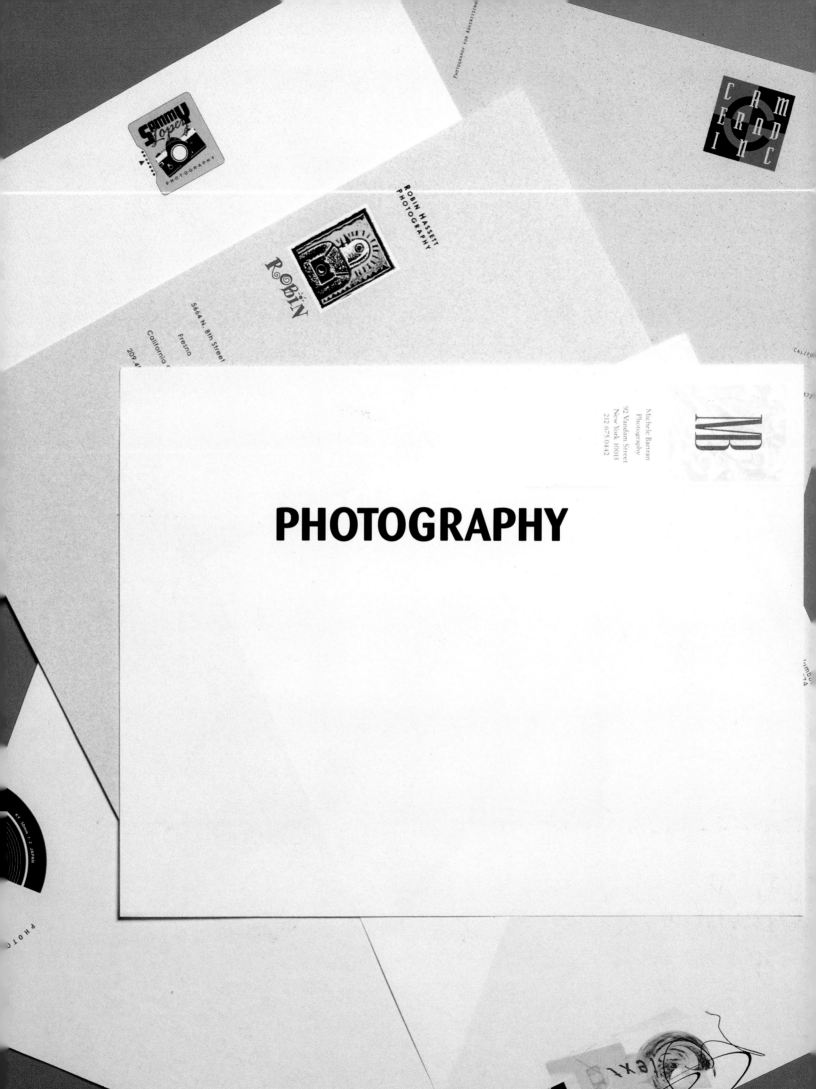

PHOTOGRAPHY

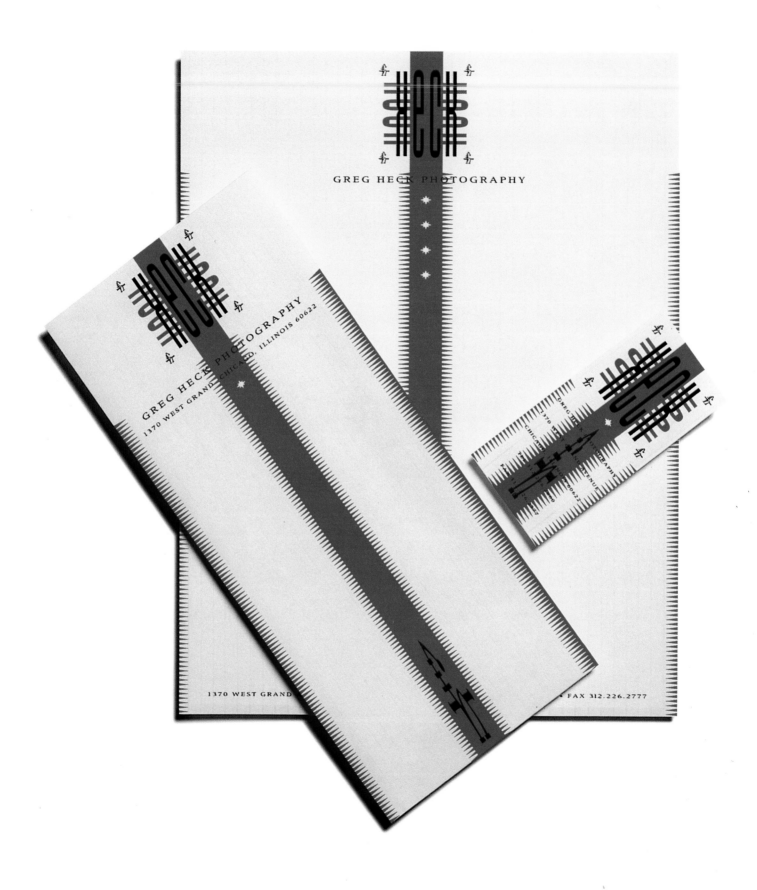

DESIGN FIRM	Segura Inc.
ART DIRECTOR	Carlos Segura
DESIGNER	Carlos Segura
ILLUSTRATOR	Carlos Segura
CLIENT	Greg Heck Photography
PAPER/PRINTING	Argus

DESIGN FIRM   Hawley & Armian Marketing/Design
DESIGNER   Karen Emond
CLIENT   Keitaro Yoshioka/Photographer
PAPER/PRINTING   Strathmore Writing

DESIGN FIRM	Mike Quon Design Office
ART DIRECTOR	Mike Quon, Art Kane
DESIGNER	Mike Quon
ILLUSTRATOR	Mike Quon
CLIENT	Art Kane/Photography

DESIGN FIRM	The Design Associates
ART DIRECTOR	Victor Cheong
DESIGNER	Victor Cheong, Philip Sven
CLIENT	Kenny Ip Photography
PAPER/PRINTING	Gilbert

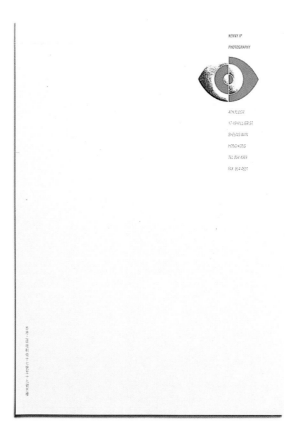

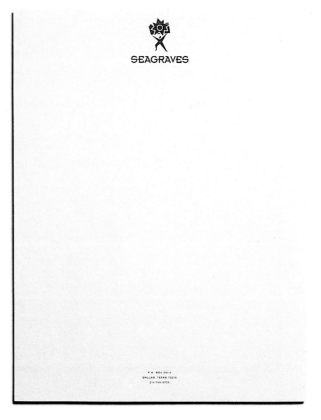

DESIGN FIRM	Walsh and Associates, Inc.
ART DIRECTOR	Miriam Lisco
DESIGNER	Michael Stearns
ILLUSTRATOR	Michael Stearns
CLIENT	Browne Production Group
PAPER/PRINTING	Classic Crest

DESIGN FIRM	Focus 2
ART DIRECTOR	Todd Hart, Shawn Freeman
DESIGNER	Todd Hart
ILLUSTRATOR	Todd Hart
CLIENT	Richard Seagraves
PAPER/PRINTING	Speckletone

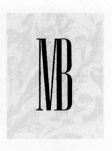

Michele Bartran
Photography
92 Vandam Street
New York 10013
212.675.0442

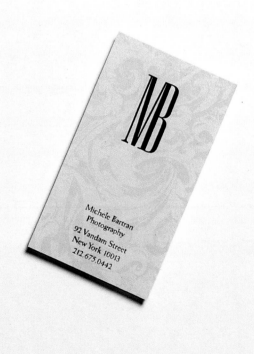

Michele Bartran
Photography
92 Vandam Street
New York 10013
212.675.0442

DESIGN FIRM   Cheryl Waligory Design
ART DIRECTOR   Cheryl Waligory
DESIGNER   Cheryl Waligory
CLIENT   Michele Bartran Photography
PAPER/PRINTING   Strathmore Wove, 2 colors

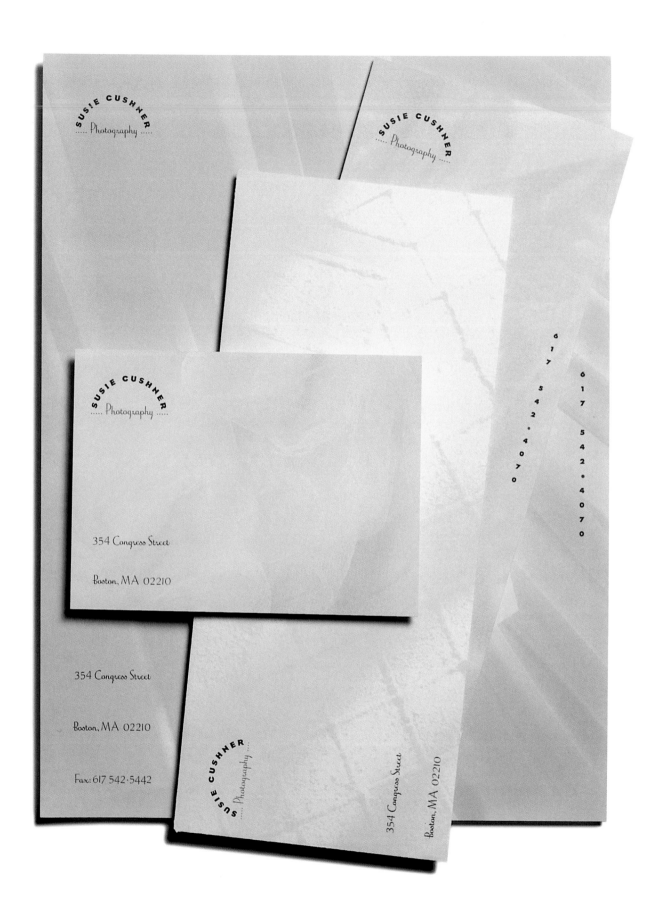

DESIGN FIRM   Clifford Selbert Design
ART DIRECTOR   Melanie Lowe
DESIGNER   Melanie Lowe
CLIENT   Susie Cushner Photography
PAPER/PRINTING   Strathmore

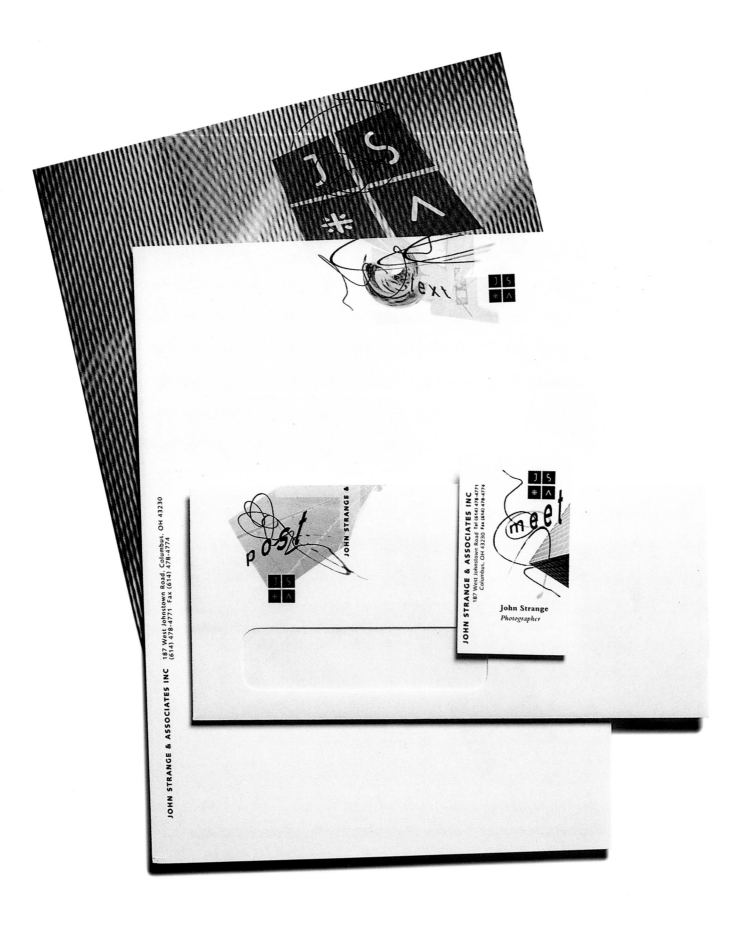

DESIGN FIRM	Schmeltz & Warren
ART DIRECTOR	Crit Warren
DESIGNER	Crit Warren
PHOTOGRAPHY	John Strange
PHOTO MANIPULATIONS	Crit Warren
CLIENT	John Strange & Associates
PAPER/PRINTING	Gilbert Esse

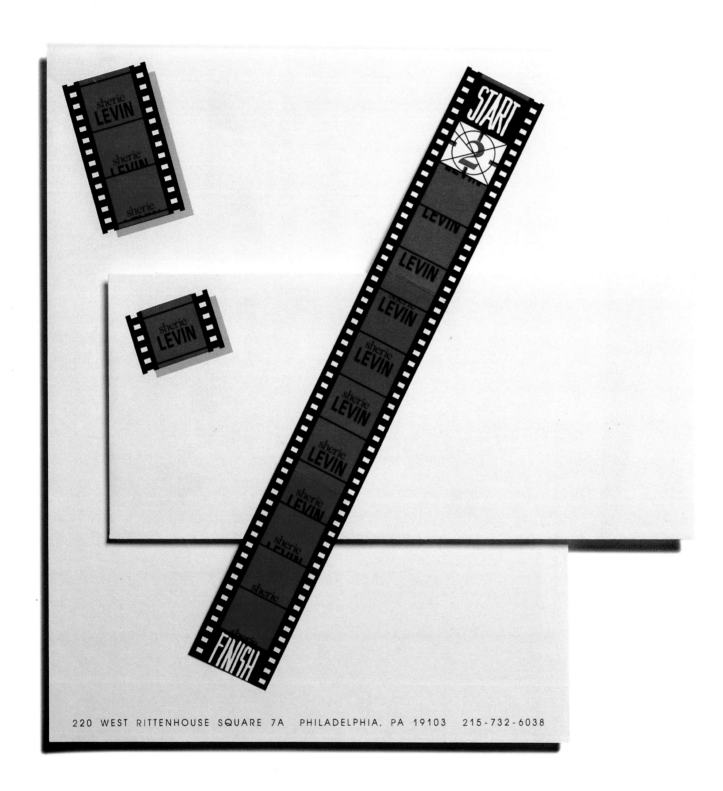

220 WEST RITTENHOUSE SQUARE 7A   PHILADELPHIA, PA 19103   215-732-6038

DESIGN FIRM   Peter Hermesmann
DESIGNER   Peter Hermesmann
CLIENT   Sherie Levin

ROBIN HASSETT
PHOTOGRAPHY

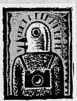

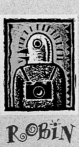

ROBIN

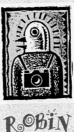

ROBIN

ROBIN HASSETT
PHOTOGRAPHY

5664 N. 8th Street
Fresno
California 93710
209.485.7343

DESIGN FIRM	Shields Design
ART DIRECTOR	Charles Shields
DESIGNER	Charles Shields
ILLUSTRATOR	Charles Shields
CLIENT	Robin Hassett Photography
PAPER/PRINTING	Neenah Classic Crest

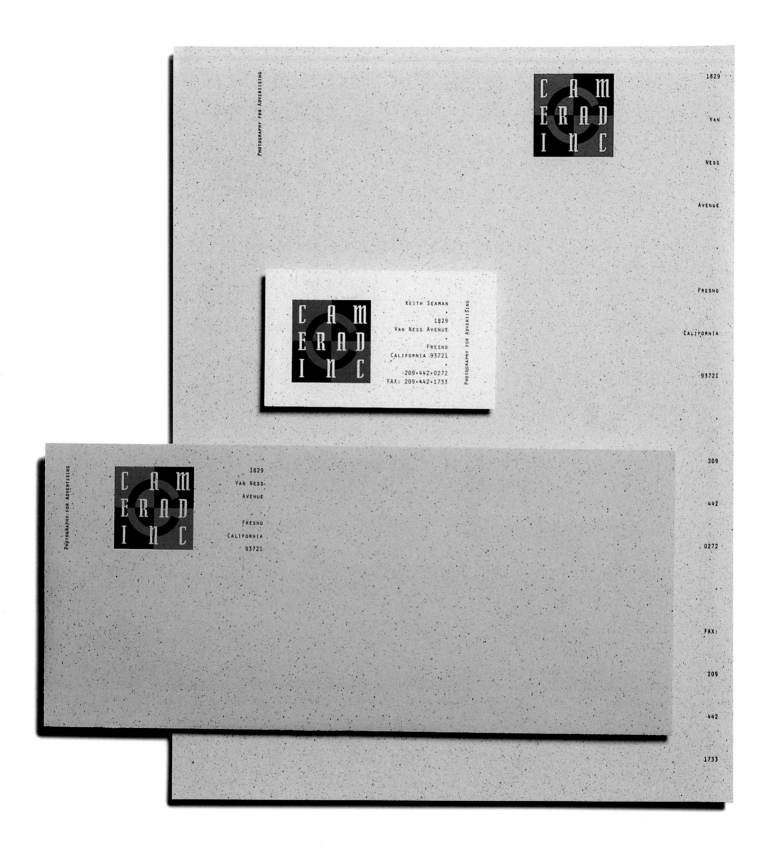

DESIGN FIRM	Shields Design
ART DIRECTOR	Charles Shields
DESIGNER	Charles Shields
CLIENT	Camarad Photography
PAPER/PRINTING	Simpson Quest

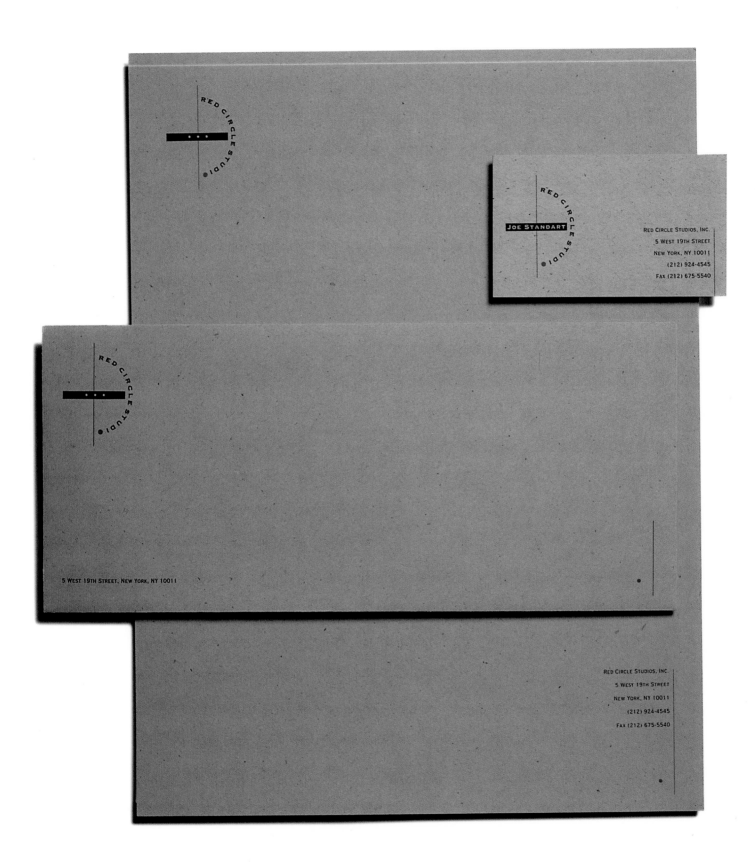

DESIGN FIRM	Platinum Design
ART DIRECTOR	Vickie Peslak, Sandy Quinn
DESIGNER	Sandy Quinn
ILLUSTRATOR	Sandy Quinn
CLIENT	Red Circle Studio
PAPER/PRINTING	French Speckle Tone

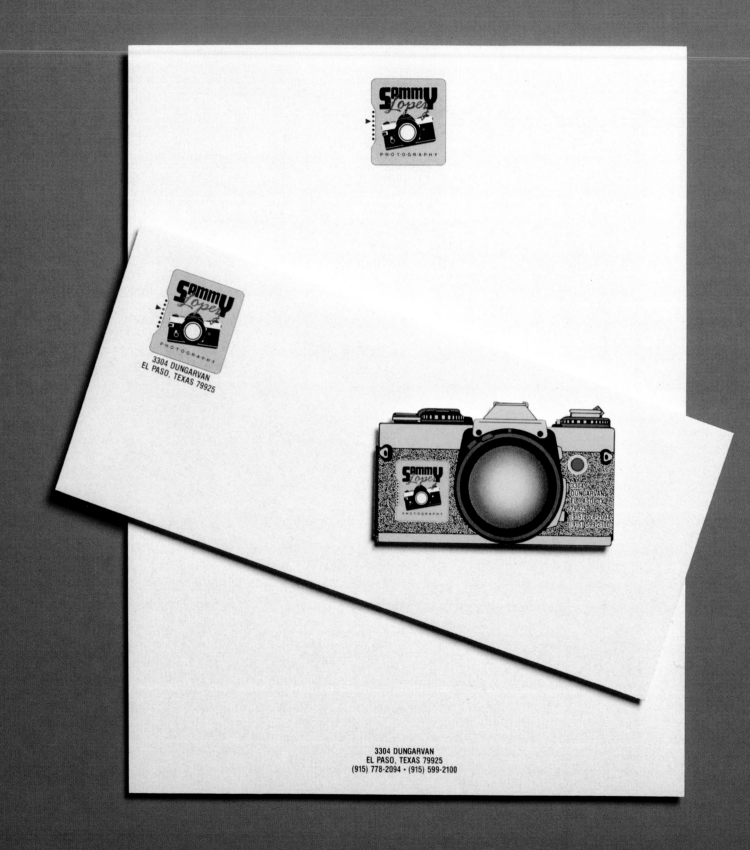

DESIGN FIRM	Albert Juarez Design & Illustration
ART DIRECTOR	Albert Juarez
DESIGNER	Albert Juarez
ILLUSTRATOR	Albert Juarez
CLIENT	Sammy Lopez Photography
PAPER/PRINTING	Gainsborough Silver Stock, 2 colors

DESIGN FIRM	Segura Inc.
ART DIRECTOR	Carlos Segura
DESIGNER	Carlos Segura
ILLUSTRATOR	Carlos Segura
CLIENT	Heimo Photograpy

DESIGN FIRM	Segura Inc.
ART DIRECTOR	Carlos Segura
DESIGNER	Carlos Segura
ILLUSTRATOR	Carlos Segura
CLIENT	Guy Hurka Photography

DESIGN FIRM	Eilts Anderson Tracy
ART DIRECTOR	Jan Tracy
DESIGNER	Jan Tracy
ILLUSTRATOR	Jan Tracy
CLIENT	Steve Fuller, Photographer

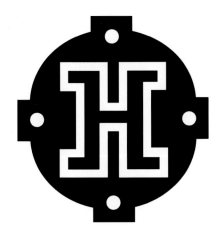

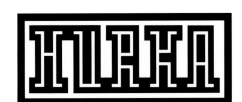

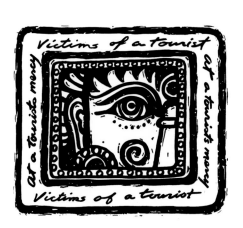

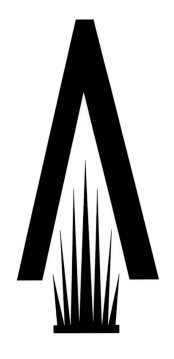

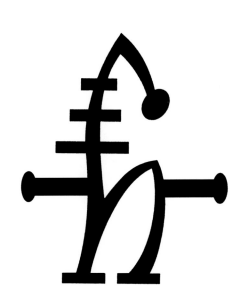

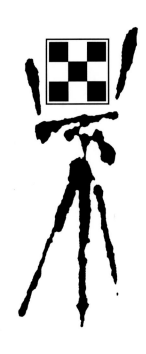

DESIGN FIRM	Segura Inc.
ART DIRECTOR	Carlos Segura
DESIGNER	Carlos Segura
ILLUSTRATOR	Carlos Segura
CLIENT	Anthony Arcievo Photography

DESIGN FIRM	Segura Inc.
ART DIRECTOR	Carlos Segura
DESIGNER	Carlos Segura
ILUSTRATOR	Carlos Segura
CLIENT	Heck Photography

DESIGN FIRM	Hornall Anderson Design Works
ART DIRECTOR	Jack Anderson
DESIGNER	Jack Anderson, Debra Hampton, Mary Chin Hutchison
ILLYSTRATOR	Debra Hampton
CLIENT	Rod Ralston Photography

GRANDPRE & WHALEY LTD.

475 Cleveland Ave. N., Suite 222

Saint Paul, Minnesota 55104

Facsimile 612 / 645-2430

Telex 15-3463

S H R

SHR Perceptual Management
8700 E. Via de Ventura, Suite 100
Scottsdale, AZ 85258
Tel: (602) 483-3700
Fax: (602) 483-3675

INNOVATIVE SEARCH GROUP

PROFESSIONAL
SERVICES

Kid Marketing Group

DDB Needham Worldwide

IMAGE group

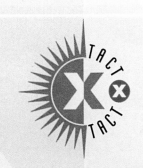

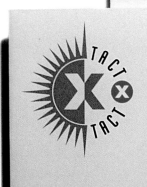

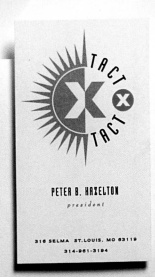

PETER B. HAZELTON
president

316 SELMA ST. LOUIS, MO 63119
314-961-3194

316 SELMA ST. LOUIS, MO 63119

316 SELMA ST. LOUIS, MO 63119 314-961-3194

DESIGN FIRM   Bartels & Company, Inc.
ART DIRECTOR   David Bartels
DESIGNER   Bill Gantner
ILLUSTRATOR   Bill Gantner
CLIENT   Tact-X

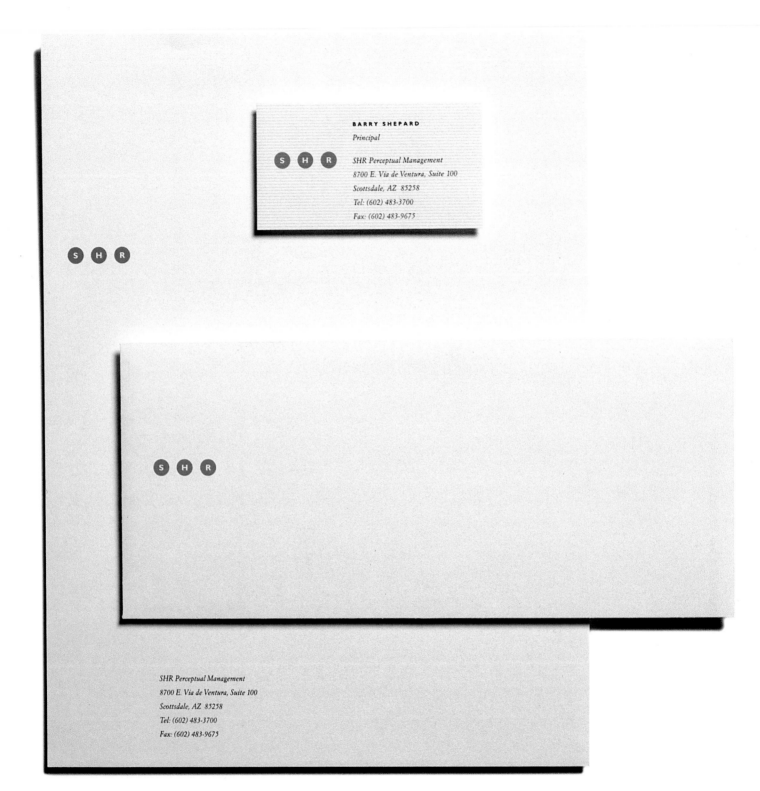

DESIGN FIRM SHR Perceptual Management
ART DIRECTOR Barry Shepard
DESIGNER Nathan Joseph
CLIENT SHR Perceptual Management
PAPER/PRINTING Simpson Starwhite Vicksburg

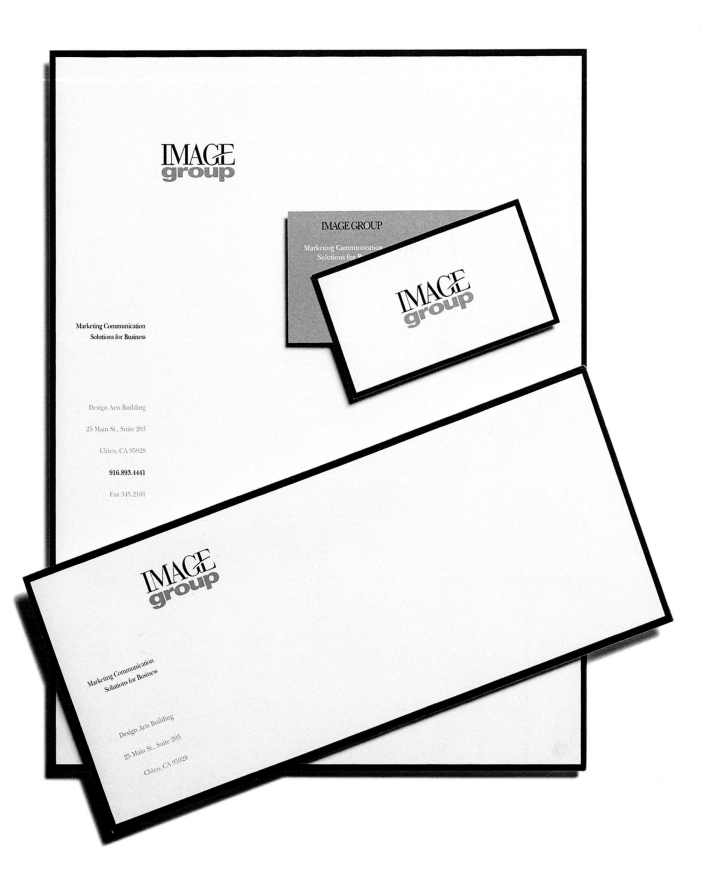

DESIGN FIRM   Image Group
ART DIRECTOR   Charles Osborn
DESIGNER   Charles Osborn, David Zavala, Eric Sanchez
CLIENT   Image Group
PAPER/PRINTING   Concept

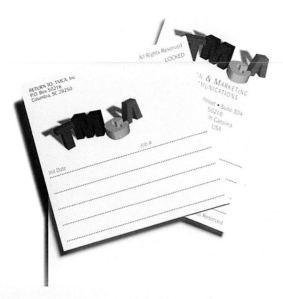

RETURN TO: TMCA, Inc.
P.O. Box 50216
Columbia, SC 29250

Job #

Init Date

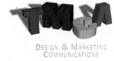

DESIGN & MARKETING
COMMUNICATIONS

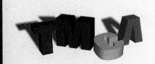

DESIGN & MARKETING
COMMUNICATIONS

P.O. Box 50216
Columbia • South Carolina
29250-0216 USA

Tim McKeever
President/Creative Director

DESIGN & MARKETING
COMMUNICATIONS

TIM MCKEEVER COMMUNICATION ARTS, INC.
2231 Devine Street • Suite 304 • P.O. Box 50216
Columbia • South Carolina • 29250-0216 USA
☎ 803/256-3010   ✎ 803/252-0424

TIM MCKEEVER COMMUNICATION ARTS, INC.
2231 Devine Street • Suite 304 • P.O. Box 50216
Columbia • South Carolina • 29250-0216 USA
☎ 803/256-3010   ✎ 803/252-0424

DESIGN FIRM TMCA, Inc.
ART DIRECTOR Tim McKeever
DESIGNER Tim McKeever
CLIENT TMCA, Inc.
PAPER/PRINTING Neenah Classic Crest, Avon Brilliant White, 4 colors

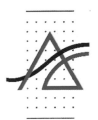

STRATEGIC IMPACT

182-186
Blues Point Road
McMahons Point
NSW 2060
Telephone
(02) 954 5400
Facsimile
(02) 923 1270

STRATEGIC IMPACT

182-186 Blues Point Road
McMahons Point NSW 2060
Telephone (02) 954 5400
Facsimile (02) 923 1270

Brian Purdey *Director*

STRATEGIC IMPACT

With Compliments   182-186 Blues Point Road McMahons Point NSW 2060 Telephone (02) 954 5400 Facsimile (02) 923 1270

A division of Purdey & Associates Pty Limited A.C.N. 003 214 542

DESIGN FIRM	Jenssen Design Pty. Limited
ART DIRECTOR	David Jenssen
DESIGNER	David Jenssen
ILLUSTRATOR	Karen Lloyd-Jones
CLIENT	Strategic Impact
PAPER/PRINTING	Conservation White Laid

INNOVATIVE SEARCH GROUP

isg

JOANNE GIUDICELLI

isg

innovative search group
901 mariner's island blvd.
suite 235
san mateo, ca 94404
fax 415-574-8620

415 / 574-7335

INNOVATIVE SEARCH GROUP

isg

901 mariner's island blvd.
suite 235
san mateo, ca 94404

415 / 369-1215

DESIGN FIRM	Dan Frazier Design
ART DIRECTOR	Dan Frazier
DESIGNER	Dan Frazier
CLIENT	Innovative Search Group
PAPER/PRINTING	Strathmore Writing

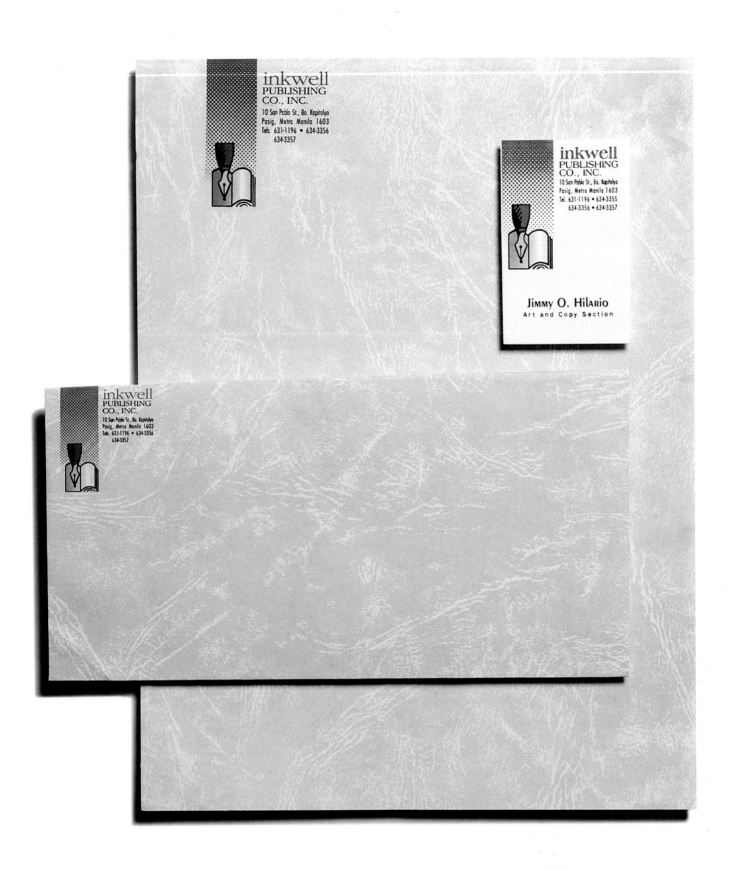

DESIGN FIRM	Jim O. Hilario
DESIGNER	Jim O. Hilario
ILLUSTRATOR	Jim O. Hilario
CLIENT	Inkwell Publishing Co., Inc.
PAPER/PRINTING	Bookpaper, Classic Laid

FĪNELĪNE

COMMUNICATIONS

GROUP

FĪNELĪNE

COMMUNICATIONS

GROUP

MARCIA FERNALD
PARTNER

348 PARK STREET EAST
NORTH READING, MA 01864
TEL: 508.664.3579
FAX: 508.664.3692

FĪNELĪNE

COMMUNICATIONS

GROUP

348 PARK STREET EAST
NORTH READING, MA 01864

348 PARK STREET EAST
NORTH READING, MA 01864
TEL: 508.664.3579
FAX: 508.664.3692

DESIGN FIRM	i4 Design
DESIGNER	Bevery Carter
ILLUSTRATOR	Janet Mumford
CLIENT	Fineline Communications
PAPER/PRINTING	Graphika Lineal

DESIGN FIRM	Walsh and Associates, Inc.
ART DIRECTOR	Miriam Lisco
DESIGNER	Miriam Lisco
CLIENT	Concord Mortgage Corporation, Inc.
PAPER/PRINTING	Classic Crest

DESIGN FIRM	Thomas Hillman Design
ART DIRECTOR	Thomas Hillman
DESIGNER	Thomas Hillman
ILLUSTRATOR	Thomas Hillman
CLIENT	Radical Radio
PAPER/PRINTING	Strathmore Renewal

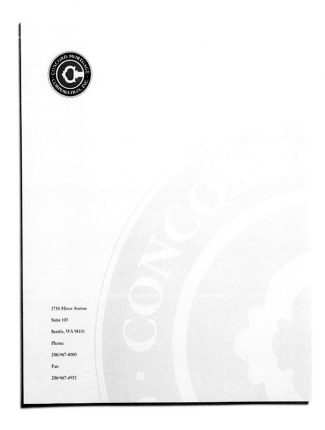

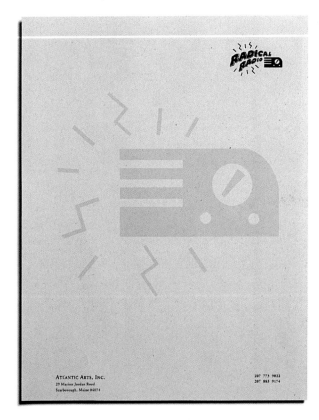

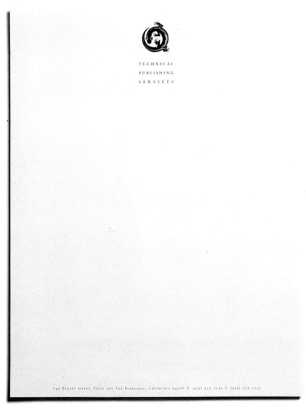

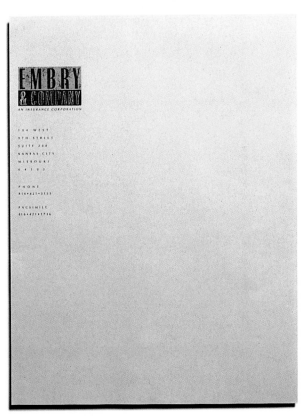

DESIGN FIRM	Jim Ales Design
ART DIRECTOR	Jim Ales
DESIGNER	Jim Ales
ILLUSTRATOR	Tim Clark
CLIENT	Technical Publishing Services
PAPER/PRINTING	Strathmore

DESIGN FIRM	Eilts Anderson Tracy
ART DIRECTOR	Jan Tracy
DESIGNER	Jan Tracy
ILLUSTRATOR	Jan Tracy
CLIENT	Embry & Company
PAPER/PRINTING	Evergreen

GATTORNA STRATEGY

Gattorna Strategy
Consultants Pty Ltd
Inc in NSW
1 James Place North Sydney
NSW 2060 Australia
Tel: (02) 959 3899
Fax: (02) 959 3990

131 Rokeby Road
Subiaco
WA 6008 Australia
Tel: (09) 381 3580
Fax: (09) 382 2519

708C Swanson Road
Swanson
PO Box 83163 Edmonton
Auckland 8 New Zealand
Tel: (09) 833 9991
Fax: (09) 833 9992

33 South Montilla
San Clemente
CA 92672
USA
Tel: (714) 498 9440
Fax: (714) 492 1152

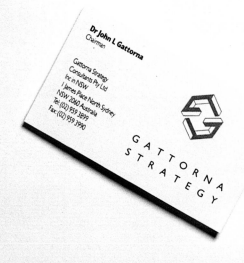

DESIGN FIRM	Jenssen Design Pty. Limited
ART DIRECTOR	David Jenssen
DESIGNER	David Jenssen
ILLUSTRATOR	David Jenssen, Yahyeh Abouloukme
CLIENT	Gattorna Strategy Consultants Pty. Ltd.
PAPER/PRINTING	Strathmore Writing, Bright White Laid

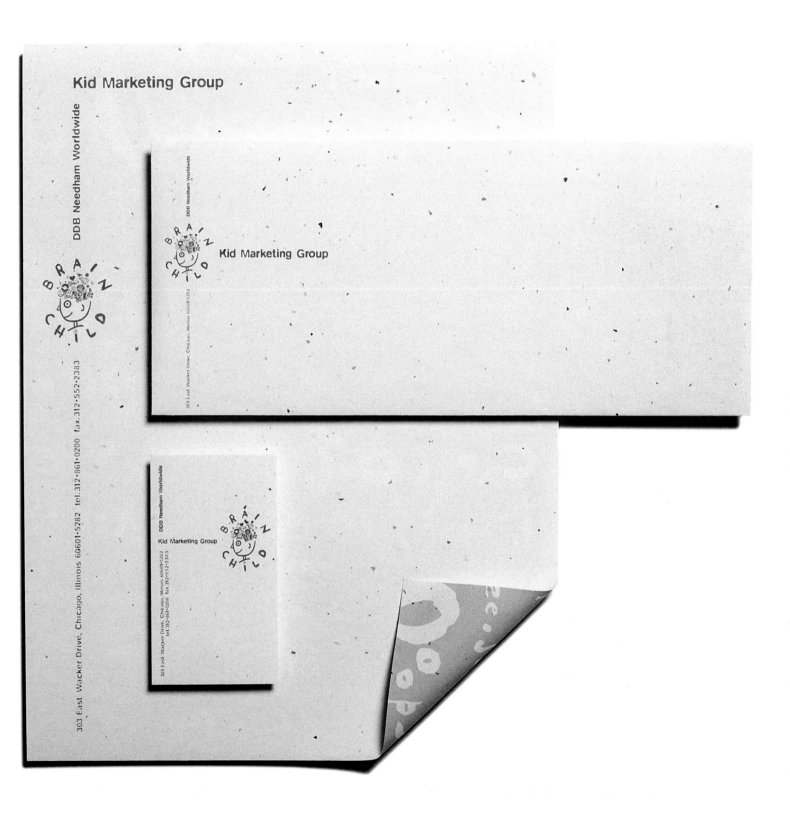

DESIGN FIRM Segura Inc.
ART DIRECTOR Carlos Segura
DESIGNER Carlos Segura
ILLUSTRATOR John Stepping
CLIENT Brain Child
PAPER/PRINTING Argus

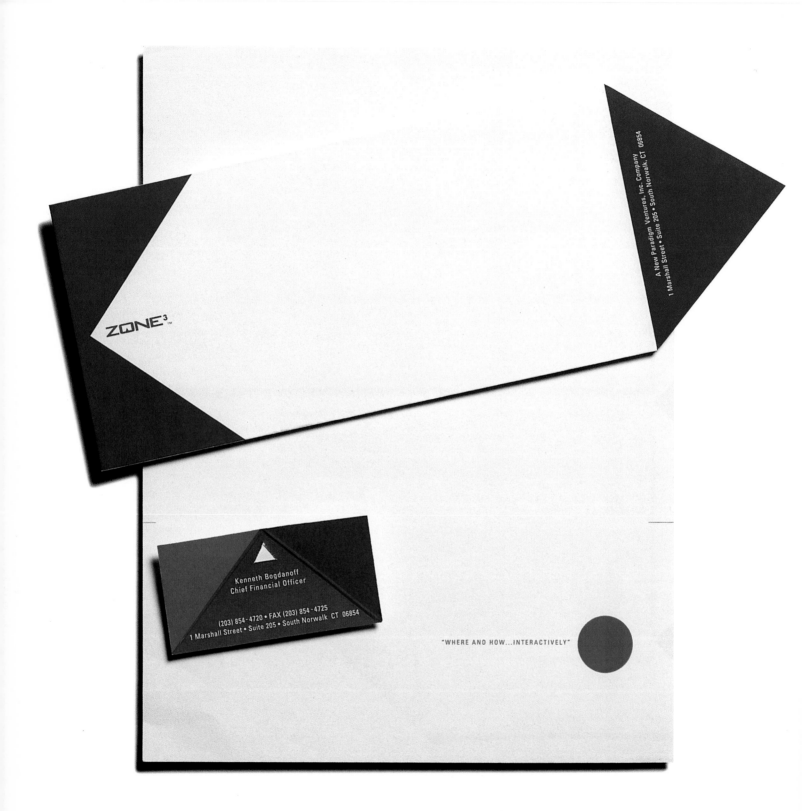

DESIGN FIRM	Ultimo Inc.
ART DIRECTOR	Clare Ultimo
DESIGNER	Joanne Obarowski, Clare Ultimo
CLIENT	Zone 3
PAPER/PRINTING	Finch Paper

Lois Bensen, Media Buyer

EvansHardy+Young INC.

829 De La Vina Street, Santa Barbara, CA 93101 USA
fax (805) 564-4279, tel (805) 963-5841

EvansHardy+Young INC.

2049 Century Park East, Ste. 1200, Los Angeles, CA 90067 USA

EvansHardy+Young INC.

829 De La Vina Street, Santa Barbara, CA 93101 USA, fax (805) 564-4279, tel (805) 963-5841

DESIGN FIRM	Puccinelli Design
ART DIRECTOR	Keith Puccinelli
DESIGNER	Keith Puccinelli, Heidi Palladino
ILLUSTRATOR	Keith Puccinelli
CLIENT	Evans, Hardy & Young
PAPER/PRINTING	Gilbert Neo

DESIGN FIRM	O&J Design, Inc.
ART DIRECTOR	Andrzej J. Olejniczak
DESIGNER	Andrzej J. Olejniczak
CLIENT	Corporate Communication Group
PAPER/PRINTING	Starwhite Vicksburg/4 colors

DESIGN FIRM	Heart Graphic Design
ART DIRECTOR	Clark Most
DESIGNER	Joan Most
CLIENT	English Training Consultants
PAPER/PRINTING	Cottonwood/Evergreen

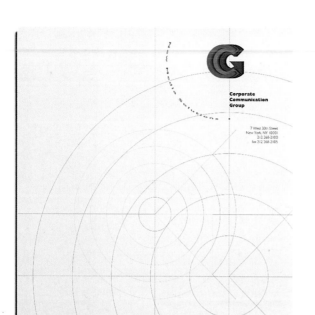

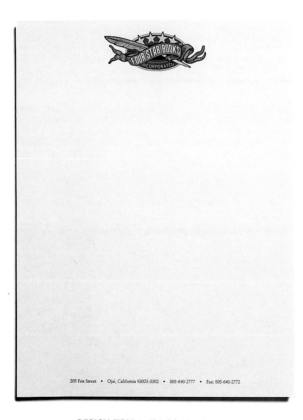

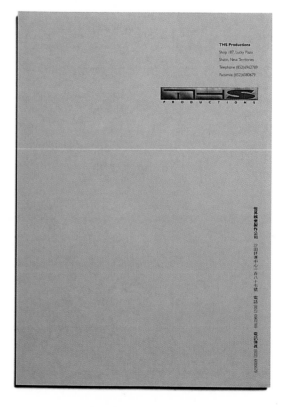

DESIGN FIRM	Shields Design
ART DIRECTOR	Charles Shields
DESIGNER	Charles Shields
CLIENT	The Ken Roberts Company/ Four Star Books
PAPER/PRINTING	Neenah Classic Crest

DESIGN FIRM	The Design Associates
ART DIRECTOR	Victor Cheong
DESIGNER	Victor Cheong, Philip Sven
CLIENT	THS Productions
PAPER/PRINTING	Conqueror, foil stamp

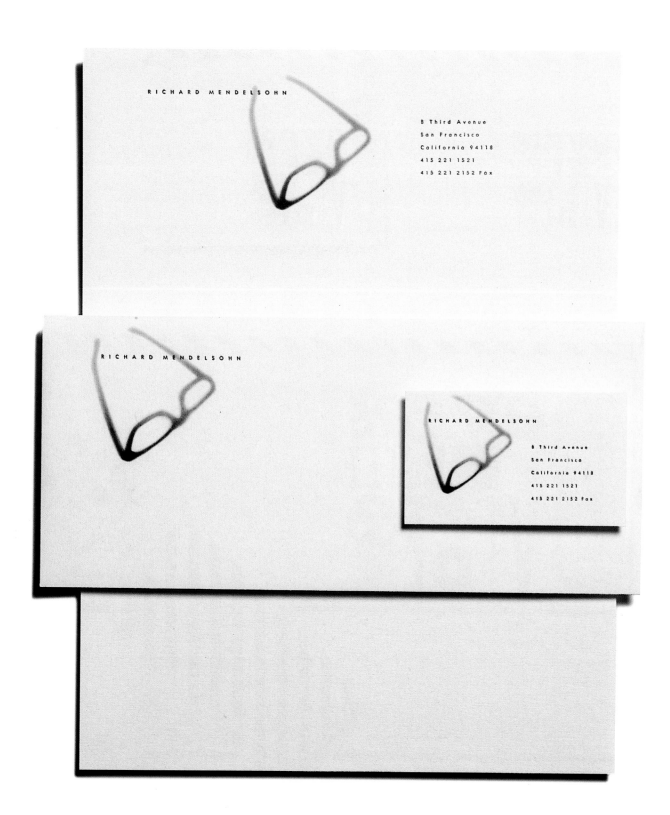

DESIGN FIRM   Debra Nichols Design
ART DIRECTOR   Debra Nichols
DESIGNER   Debra Nichols, Kelan Smith
ILLUSTRATOR   Mark Schroeder
CLIENT   Richard Mendelsohn

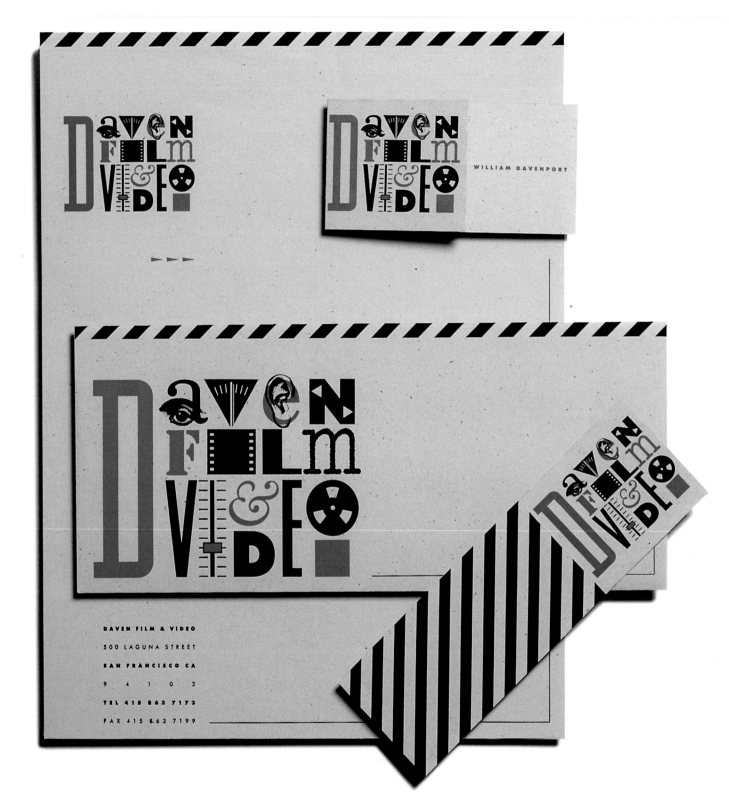

DESIGN FIRM   Earl Gee Design
ART DIRECTOR   Earl Gee
DESIGNER   Earl Gee
ILLUSTRATOR   Earl Gee
CLIENT   Daven Film & Video
PAPER/PRINTING   Speckletone Natural text

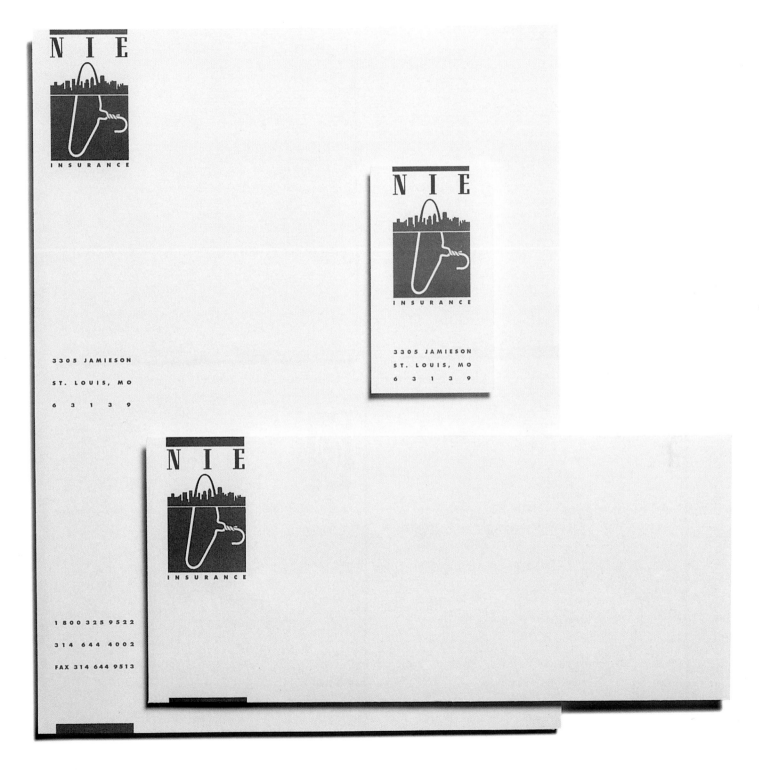

DESIGN FIRM Bartels & Company, Inc.
ART DIRECTOR David Bartels
DESIGNER Aaron Segall
ILLUSTRATOR Aaron Segall
CLIENT NIE Insurance

DESIGN FIRM	Smith Group Communications
ART DIRECTOR	Thom Smith, Gregg Frederickson
DESIGNER	Thom Smith, Gregg Frederickson
ILLUSTRATOR	Gregg Frederickson
CLIENT	Lightman & Associates
PAPER/PRINTING	Protocol Writing

DESIGN FIRM	Source/Inc.
ART DIRECTOR	Michael Livolsi
DESIGNER	Source Staff
CLIENT	Source/Inc.
PAPER/PRINTING	Strathmore Writing

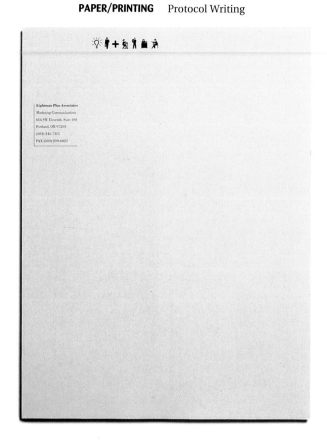

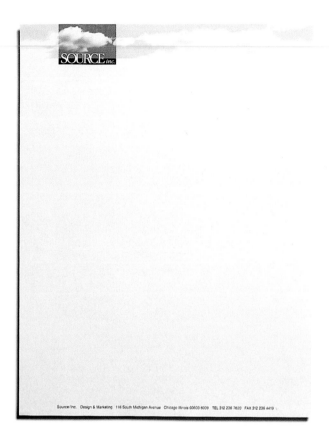

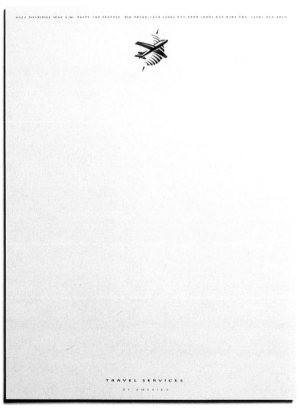

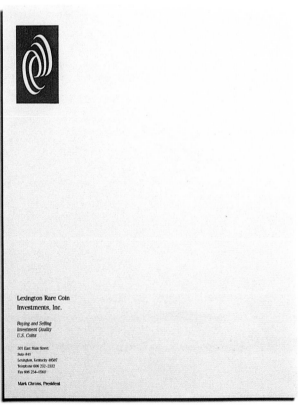

DESIGN FIRM	Hornall Anderson Design Works
ART DIRECTOR	Jack Anderson
DESIGNER	Jack Anderson, David Bates, Mary
ILLUSTRATOR	Hermes, Julia LaPine
CLIENT	Yutaka Sasaki
PAPER/PRINTING	Travel Services of America
	Simpson Environment

DESIGN FIRM	Ellen Kendrick Creative, Inc.
ART DIRECTOR	Ellen K. Spalding
DESIGNER	Ellen K. Spalding
ILLUSTRATOR	Ellen K. Spalding
CLIENT	Lexington Rare Coin Investments, Inc.
PAPER/PRINTING	Simpson Gainsborough black and metallic
	green registered to sculptured brass die

BROOKS MARKETING LTD.
475 Cleveland Avenue N., Suite 315
Saint Paul, Minnesota 55104
Fax: 612 / 645-5250
Tel: 612 / 645-1282

BROOKS MARKETING LTD.
475 Cleveland Avenue N., Suite 315
Saint Paul, Minnesota 55104

MICHAEL BROOKS   **BROOKS MARKETING LTD.**
475 Cleveland Avenue N., Suite 315
Saint Paul, Minnesota 55104
Fax: 612 / 645-5250
Tel: 612 / 645-1282

DESIGN FIRM	GrandPré and Whaley, Ltd.
ART DIRECTOR	Kevin Whaley
DESIGNER	Kevin Whaley
CLIENT	Brooks Marketing, Ltd.
PAPER/PRINTING	Strathmore

I N T E R M A T I O N

INTERMATION

DOUGLAS ADAMS

PRESIDENT

P.O. BOX 2107

REDMOND, WA. 98073-2107

PHONE 206 883 1271

FAX 206 861 1501

P.O. BOX 2107

REDMOND, WA. 98073-2107

PHONE 206 883 1271

FAX 206 869 2613

DESIGN FIRM	Hornall Anderson Design Works
ART DIRECTOR	Jack Anderson
DESIGNER	Jack Anderson, Julia LaPine, Jill Bustamante
CLIENT	Intermation
PAPER/PRINTING	Monadnock Astro Lite White, embossed

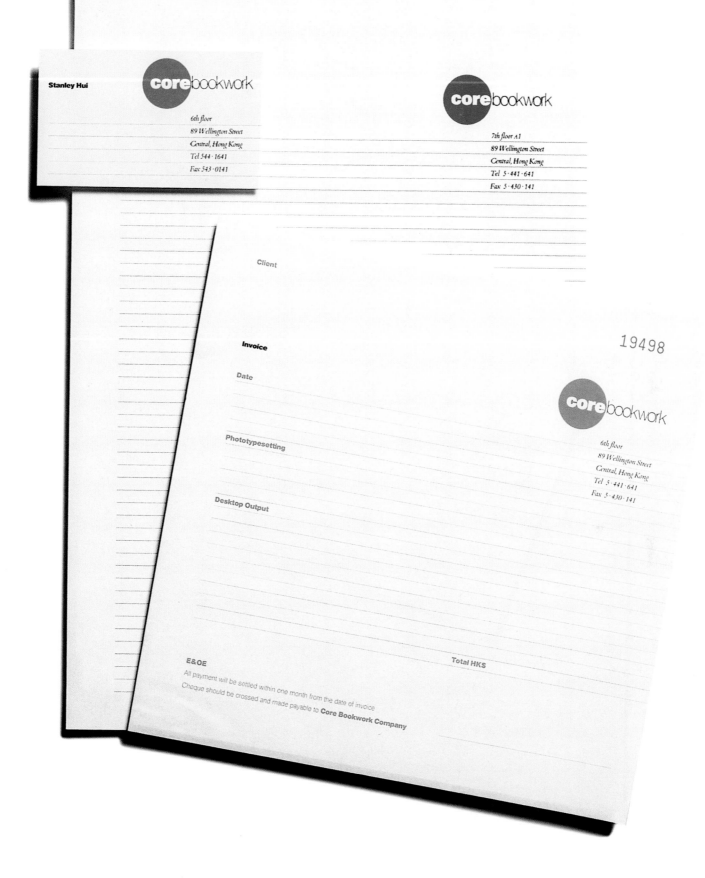

DESIGN FIRM	The Design Associates
ART DIRECTOR	Victor Cheong
DESIGNER	Victor Cheong, Philip Sven
CLIENT	Corebookwork Company
PAPER/PRINTING	Conqueror

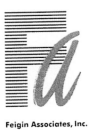

Feigin Associates, Inc.

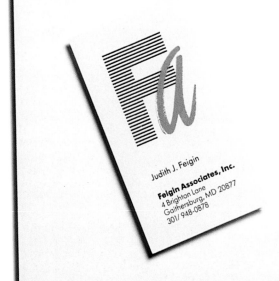

Judith J. Feigin
Feigin Associates, Inc.
4 Brighton Lane
Gaithersburg, MD 20877
301/ 948-0878

4 Brighton Lane
Gaithersburg, MD 20877
301-840-9813
fax 301-869-1759

DESIGN FIRM	Musikar Design
ART DIRECTOR	Sharon R. Musikar
DESIGNER	Sharon R. Musikar
ILLUSTRATOR	Sharon R. Musikar
CLIENT	Feigin Associates, Inc.
PAPER/PRINTING	Classic Crest, 2 colors

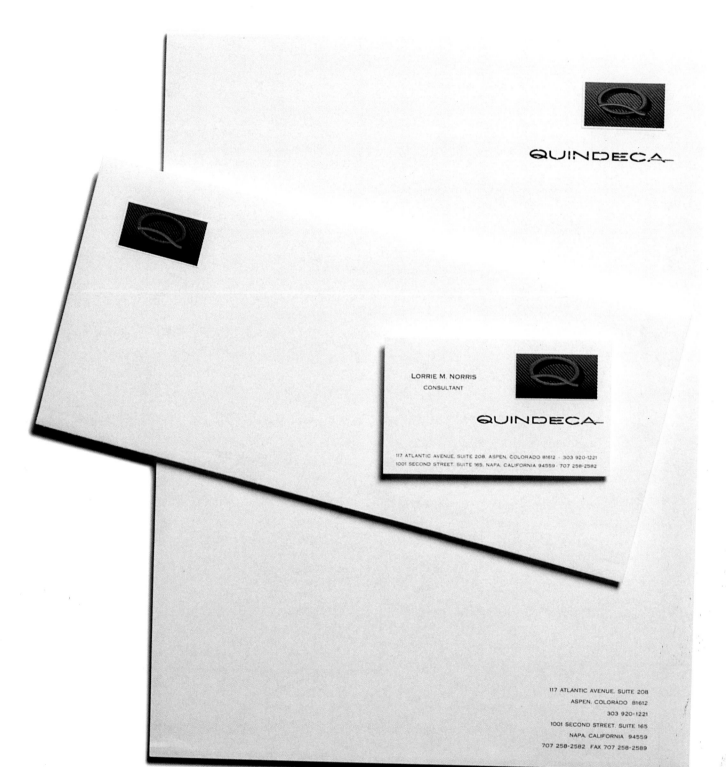

DESIGN FIRM	Ortega Design Studio
ART DIRECTOR	Joann Ortega, Susann Ortega
DESIGNER	Susann Ortega, Joann Ortega
ILLUSTRATOR	Susann Ortega
TYPE DESIGN	Joann Oretga
CLIENT	Quindeca Corporation
PAPER/PRINTING	Enhance, foil stamp, emboss/deboss

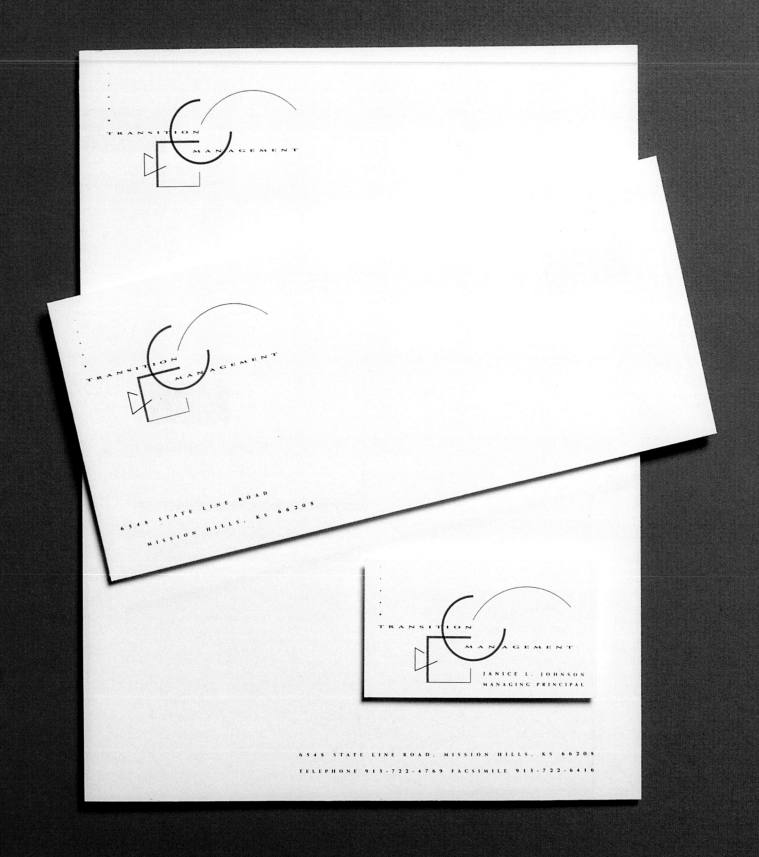

DESIGN FIRM	Eilts Anderson Tracy
ART DIRECTOR	Jan Tracy
DESIGNER	Jan Tracy
ILLUSTRATOR	Jan Tracy
CLIENT	Transition Management
PAPER/PRINTING	Vicksburg/Instyprints

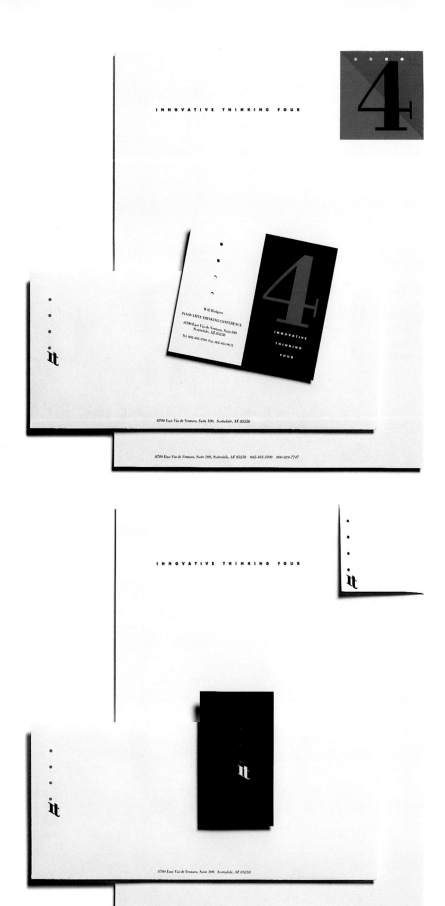

DESIGN FIRM   SHR Perceptual Management
ART DIRECTOR   Barry Shepard
DESIGNER   Mike Shanks
CLIENT   SHR Perceptual Management
PAPER/PRINTING Curtis Brightwater Aretsian

DESIGN FIRM	Bruce Yelaska Design	DESIGN FIRM	Fountainhead Graphics	DESIGN FIRM	Lipson Alport Glass & Associates
ART DIRECTOR	Bruce Yelaska	ART DIRECTOR	William A. Donabedian	ART DIRECTOR	Jeff Rich
DESIGNER	Bruce Yelaska	DESIGNER	William A. Donabedian	DESIGNER	Keith Shupe
CLIENT	Consumer Direct Access	ILLUSTRATOR	William A. Donabedian	CLIENT	Coregis
		CLIENT	Veale & Associates, Inc.		

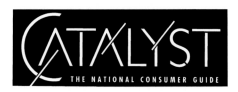

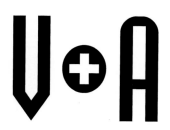

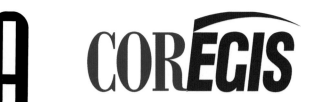

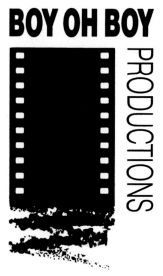

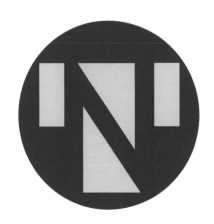

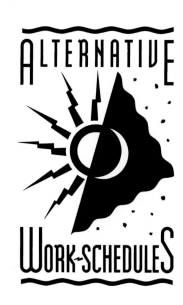

DESIGN FIRM	Riley Design Associates	DESIGN FIRM	Design Art, Inc.	DESIGN FIRM	Rickabaugh Graphics
ART DIRECTOR	Daniel Riley	ART DIRECTOR	Norman Moore	ART DIRECTOR	Mark Krumel
DESIGNER	Daniel Riley	DESIGNER	Norman Moore	DESIGNER	Mark Krumel
ILLUSTRATOR	Daniel Riley	CLIENT	Tim Neece Management	ILLUSTRATOR	Tony Meuser
CLIENT	Boy Oh Boy Productions			CLIENT	Huntington Banks

DESIGN FIRM	The Weller Institute for the Cure of Design, Inc.
ART DIRECTOR	Don Weller
DESIGNER	Don Weller
ILLUSTRATOR	Don Weller
CLIENT	Western Exposure

DESIGN FIRM	Schowalter² Design
ART DIRECTOR	Toni Schowalter
DESIGNER	Ilene Price, Toni Schowalter
CLIENT	Green Point Bank

DESIGN FIRM	Adam, Filippo & Associates
ART DIRECTOR	Robert A. Adam
DESIGNER	Sharon L. Bretz, Barbara Peak Long
CLIENT	Tuscarora Inc.

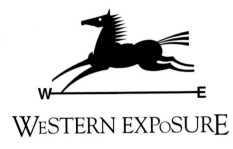

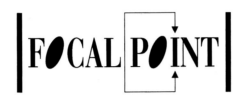

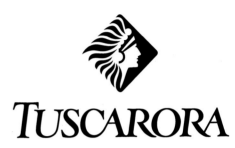

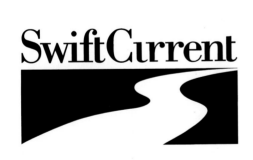

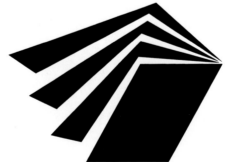

DESIGN FIRM	Palmquist & Palmquist Design
ART DIRECTOR	Kurt & Denise Palmquist
DESIGNER	Kurt & Denise Palmquist
CLIENT	Swiftcurrent (film and video production company)

DESIGN FIRM	MacVicar Design & Communications
ART DIRECTOR	John Vance
DESIGNER	William A. Gordon
CLIENT	Newsletter Services, Inc.

DESIGN FIRM	Schowalter² Design
ART DIRECTOR	Toni Schowalter
DESIGNER	Ilene Price, Toni Schowalter
CLIENT	Towers Perrin

DESIGN FIRM	Lambert Design Studio	**DESIGN FIRM**	Aslan Grafix	**DESIGN FIRM**	TW Design
ART DIRECTOR	Christie Lambert	**ART DIRECTOR**	Tracy Grubbs	**DESIGNER**	Jordan Patsios
DESIGNER	Joy Cathey	**DESIGNER**	Tracy Grubbs	**CLIENT**	MARCAM
CLIENT	Ideas & Solutions	**CLIENT**	Argadine Publishing		Corporation

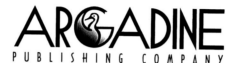

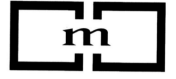

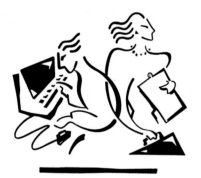

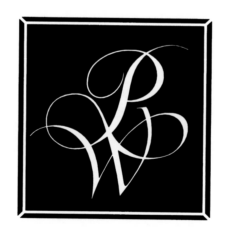

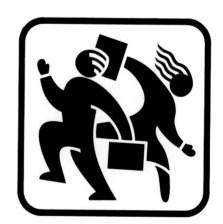

DESIGN FIRM	Riley Design Associates	**DESIGN FIRM**	Lambert Design Studio	**DESIGN FIRM**	Vaughn Wedeen Creative
ART DIRECTOR	Daniel Riley	**ART DIRECTOR**	Christie Lambert	**ART DIRECTOR**	Steve Wedeen
DESIGNER	Daniel Riley	**DESIGNER**	Christie Lambert, Joy Cathey	**DESIGNER**	Lisa Graff
ILLUSTRATOR	Daniel Riley	**ILLUSTRATOR**	Joy Cathey	**ILLUSTRATOR**	Lisa Graff
CLIENT	Hiring Resources	**CLIENT**	ProjectWorks	**COMPUTER PRODUCTION**	Chip Wyly
				CLIENT	Stratecom

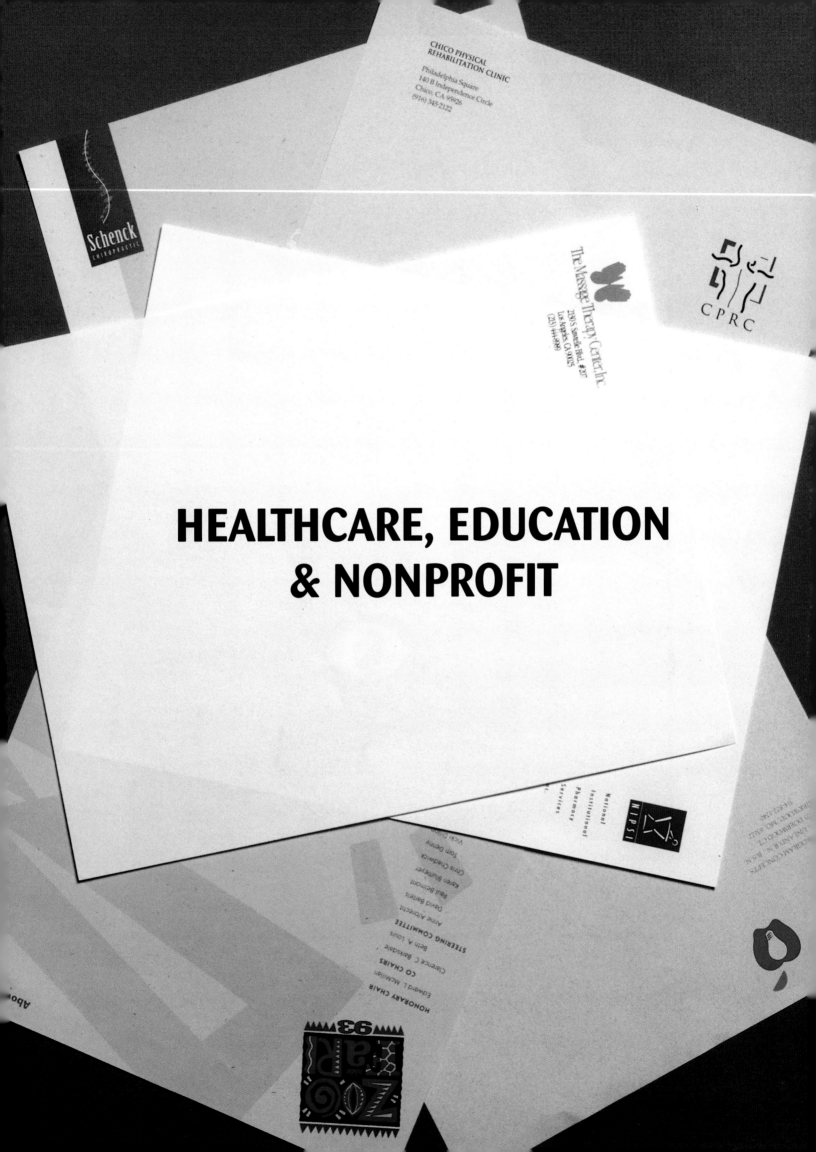

CHICO PHYSICAL
REHABILITATION CLINIC

Philadelphia Square
140 B Independence Circle
Chico, CA 95926
(916) 345-2122

Schenck
CHIROPRACTIC

The Message Therapy Center Inc.
2150 S. Sawtelle Blvd. #207
Los Angeles, CA 90025
(213) 444-8990

CPRC

HEALTHCARE, EDUCATION & NONPROFIT

National
Institutional
Pharmacy
Services

NIPSI

Vicki Dulin
Tom Denny
Chris Chadwick
Karen Blumberg
Paul Belmont
David Barrett
Anne Albrecht
STEERING COMMITTEE
Beth A. Louis
Clarence C. Barnsdale
CO CHAIRS
Edward L. McMillan
HONORARY CHAIR

'93

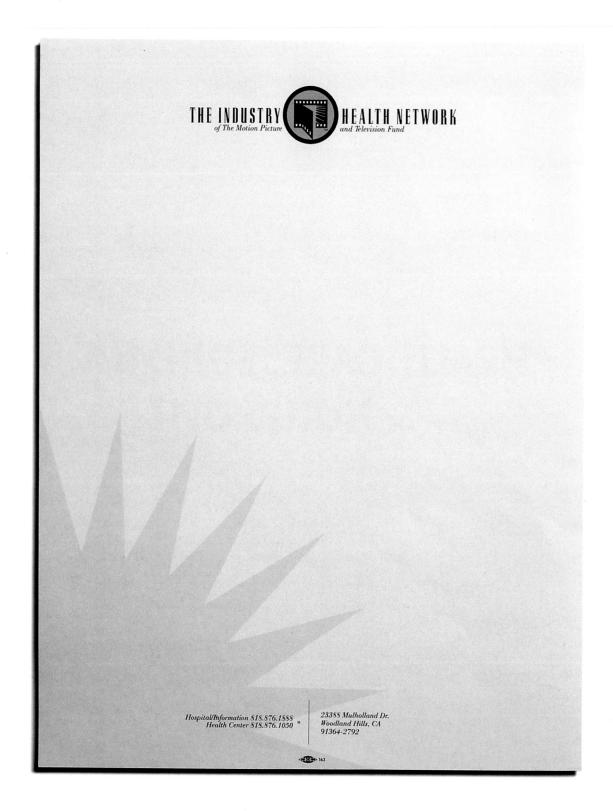

THE INDUSTRY **HEALTH NETWORK**
of The Motion Picture *and Television Fund*

Hospital/Information 818.876.1888
Health Center 818.876.1050 ™

23388 Mulholland Dr.
Woodland Hills, CA
91364-2792

DESIGN FIRM	Vrontikis Design Office
ART DIRECTOR	Petrula Vrontikis
DESIGNER	Kim Sage
CLIENT	MPTF Industry Health Network
PAPER/PRINTING	Classic Crest Solar White

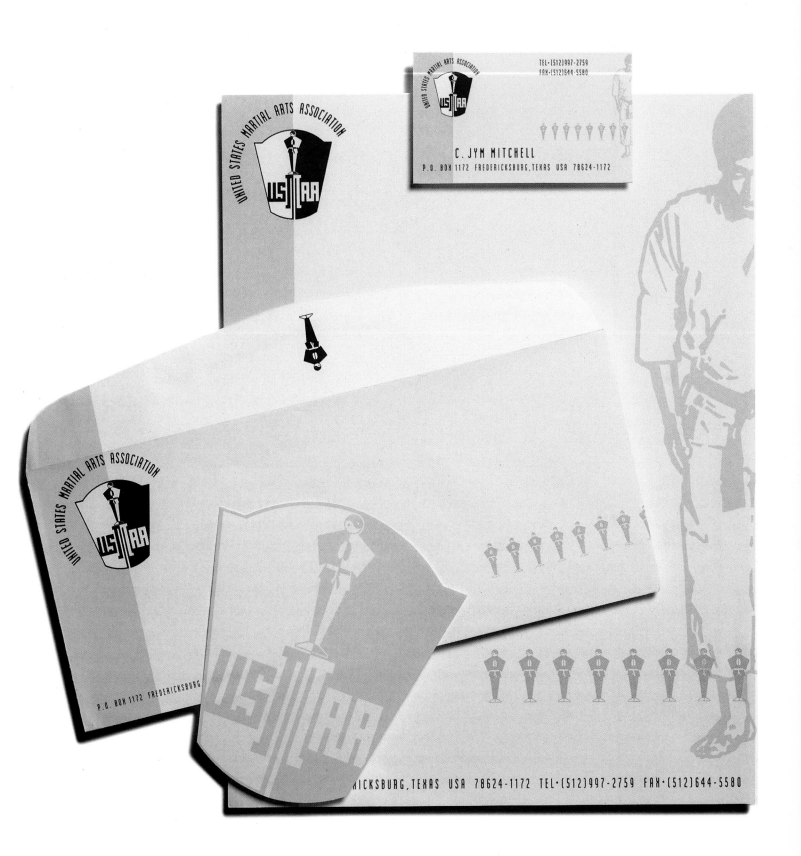

DESIGN FIRM	Romeo Empire Design
ART DIRECTOR	Vincent Romeo
DESIGNER	Vincent Romeo
ILLUSTRATOR	Vincent Romeo
CLIENT	United States Martial Arts Association
PAPER/PRINTING	Mohawk Superfine

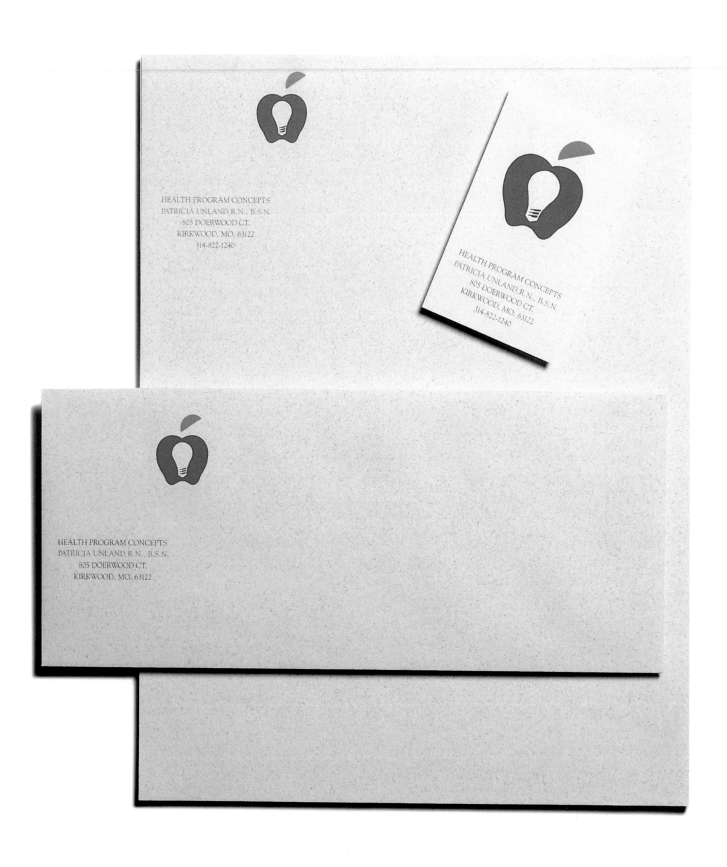

DESIGN FIRM	Bartels & Company, Inc.
ART DIRECTOR	David Bartels
DESIGNER	Chuck Hart
ILLUSTRATOR	Chuck Hart
CLIENT	Health Program Concepts

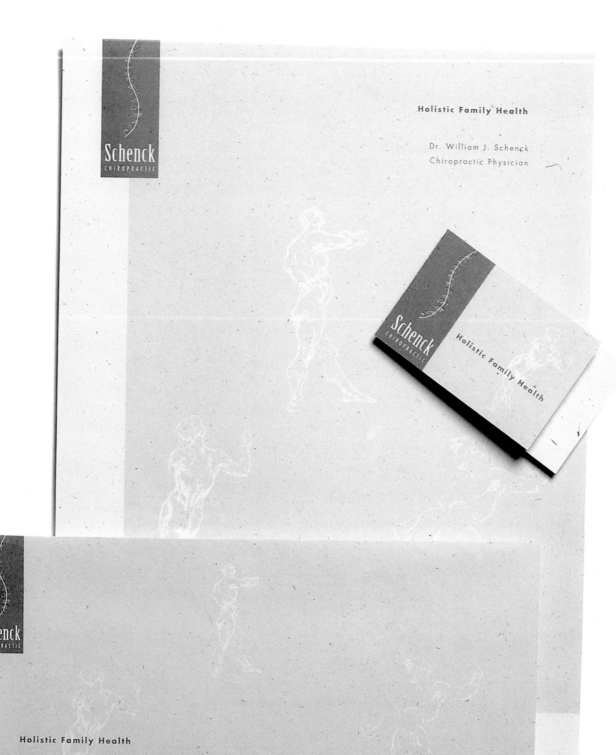

DESIGN FIRM   Creative EDGE
DESIGNER   Rick Salzman, Barbara Pitfido
CLIENT   Schenck Chiropractic
PAPER/PRINTING   Strathmore Renewal

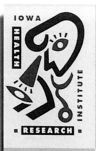

FAX 432-7713

(515) 432-7700

P.O. BOX 367

BOONE, IOWA 50036

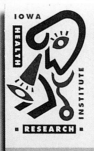

P.O. BOX 367

BOONE, IOWA 50036

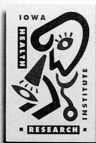

DR. SHEILA MCGUIRE

MEDICAL SCIENTIST

P.O. BOX 367

BOONE, IOWA 50036

(515) 432-7700

FAX 432-7713

DESIGN FIRM   Sayles Graphic Design
ART DIRECTOR   John Sayles
DESIGNER   John Sayles
ILLUSTRATOR   John Sayles
CLIENT   Iowa Health Research Institute
PAPER/PRINTING   James River, Graphika Vellum White, 2 colors

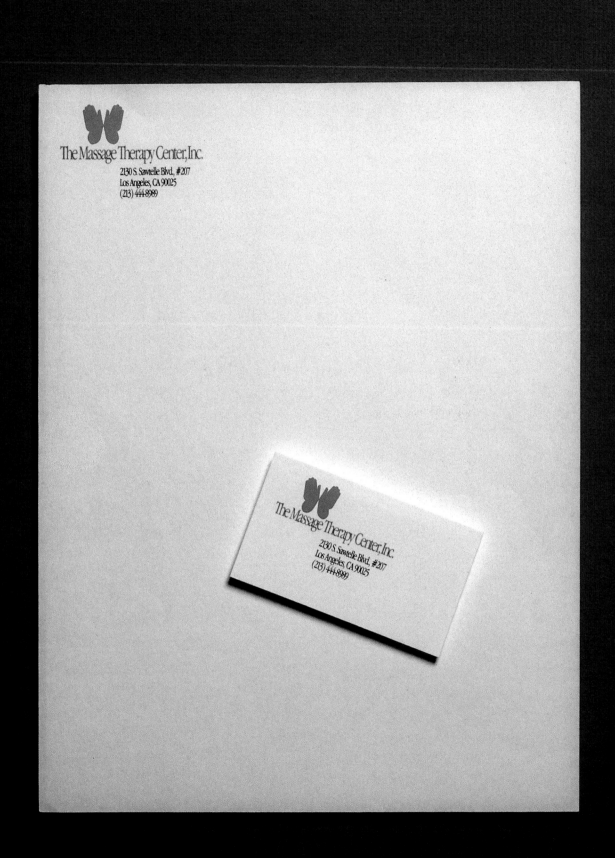

DESIGN FIRM   Ilan Geva & Friends
ART DIRECTOR   Ilan Geva
DESIGNER   Ilan Geva
CLIENT   The Massage Therapy Center

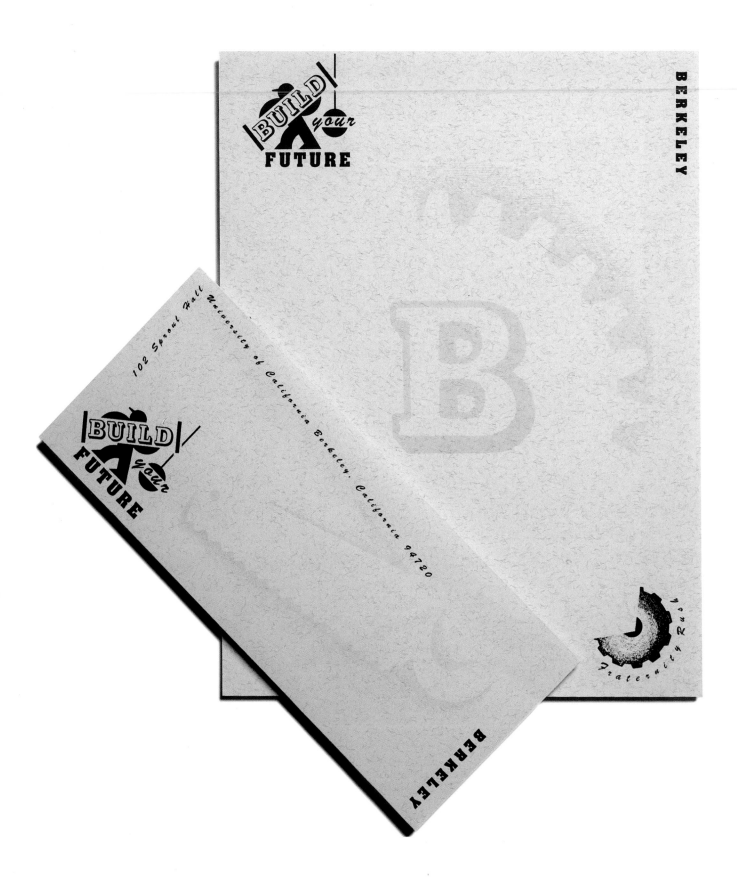

DESIGN FIRM	Sayles Graphic Design
ART DIRECTOR	John Sayles
DESIGNER	John Sayles
ILLUSTRATOR	John Sayles
CLIENT	University of California, Berkeley
PAPER/PRINTING	James River, Tuscan Terra Gray, 2 colors

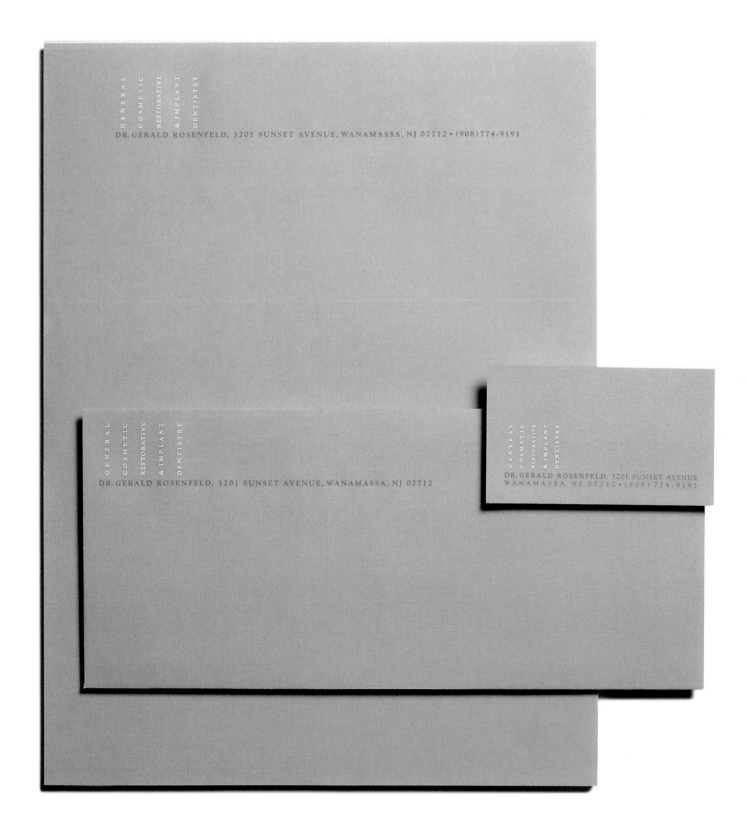

GENERAL COSMETIC RESTORATIVE & IMPLANT DENTISTRY

DR. GERALD ROSENFELD, 3201 SUNSET AVENUE, WANAMASSA, NJ 07712 • (908) 774-9191

DESIGN FIRM	The Marketing & Design Group
ART DIRECTOR	Howard Levy
DESIGNER	Howard Levy
CLIENT	Dr. Gerald Rosenfeld, Dentist
PAPER/PRINTING	Neenah Classic, linen-engraved in 2 colors

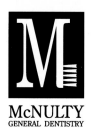

McNULTY
GENERAL DENTISTRY

Brian P. McNulty, DDS
2416 W. Sugar Creek Rd.
Charlotte, North Carolina
28262

Office: 704-596-3186
Residence: 704-547-8889

*Quality Dental Care for
Adults and Children.*

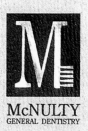

McNULTY
GENERAL DENTISTRY

DESIGN FIRM	Turner Design
ART DIRECTOR	Bert Turner
DESIGNER	Bert Turner
ILLUSTRATOR	Bert Turner
CLIENT	Dr. Brian McNulty
PAPER/PRINTING	Simpson Gainsborough Silver

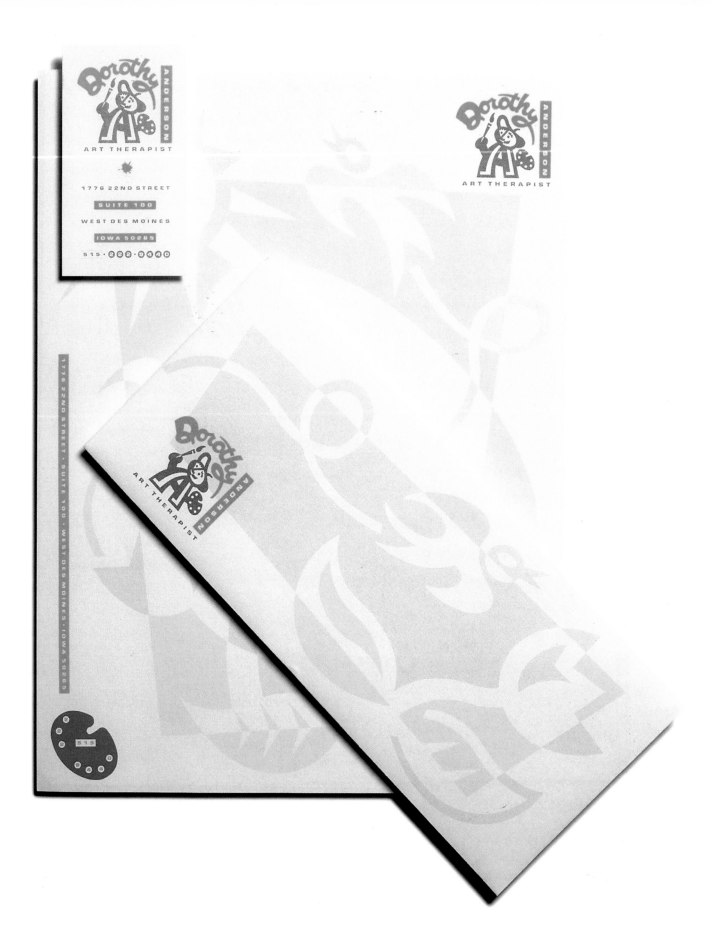

DESIGN FIRM   Sayles Graphic Design
ART DIRECTOR   John Sayles
DESIGNER   John Sayles
ILLUSTRATOR   John Sayles
CLIENT   Dorothy Anderson, Art Therapist
PAPER/PRINTING   Gilbert Paper, White, 2 colors

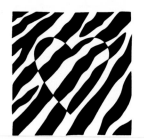

Friends Of The Zoo

Friends of the
Washington Park Zoo

4001 S.W. Canyon Road
Portland, OR 97221-2799
(503) 226-1561
FAX (503) 226-6836

Friends Of The Zoo

Friends of the
Washington Park Zoo

4001 S.W. Canyon Road
Portland, OR 97221-2799
(503) 226-1561
FAX (503) 226-6836

Margie Mee Pate
Executive Director

"Caring Now for
the Future of Life"

Friends Of The Zoo

Friends of the
Washington Park Zoo

4001 S.W. Canyon Road
Portland, OR 97221-2799

"Caring Now for the Future of Life"

"Caring Now for the Future of Life"

DESIGN FIRM	Smith Group Communications
ART DIRECTOR	Gregg Frederickson
DESIGNER	Lena James
ILLUSTRATOR	Lena James
CLIENT	Friends of the Zoo
PAPER/PRINTING	Classic Crest

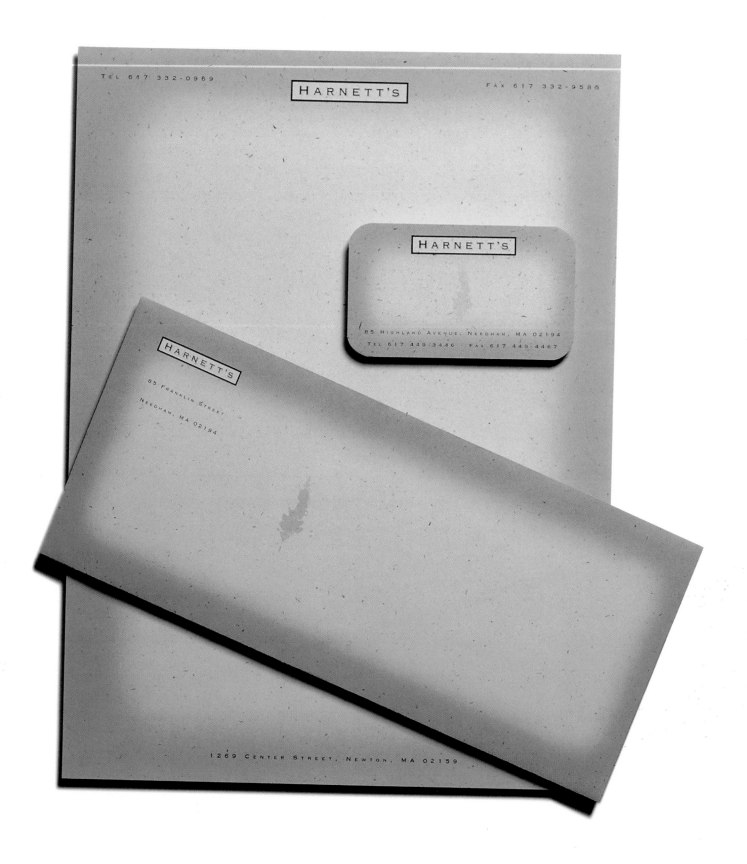

DESIGN FIRM   Clifford Selbert Design
ART DIRECTOR   Melanie Lowe
DESIGNER   Melanie Lowe
CLIENT   Harnett's
PAPER/PRINTING   Champion Benefit

National

Institutional

Pharmacy

Services

Inc.

7619 S. University

Suite B

Lubbock, TX 79423

806 · 745 · 0271

Fax: 806 · 748 · 1712

National
Institutional
Pharmacy
Services
Inc.

April Bonds, R.Ph.
Pharmacy Manager

12758 Cimarron Path
Suite 126
San Antonio, TX 78249
210 · 690 · 0607
Fax: 210 · 694 · 0998
800 · 793 · 0607

National

Institutional

Pharmacy

Services

Inc.

DESIGN FIRM	Vaughn Wedeen Creative
ART DIRECTOR	Rick Vaughn
DESIGNER	Dan Flynn
CLIENT	National Institutional Pharmacy Service Inc.
PAPER/PRINTING	Starwhite Vicksburg Archiva

CHICO PHYSICAL
REHABILITATION CLINIC

Philadelphia Square
140 B Independence Circle
Chico, CA 95926
(916) 345·2122

CPRC

CHICO PHYSICAL
REHABILITATION CLINIC

Philadelphia Square
140 B Independence Circle
Chico, CA 95926

CPRC

CHICO PHYSICAL
REHABILITATION CLINIC

Cheri Rolandelli
Exercise Physiologist

Philadelphia Square
140 B Independence Circle
Chico, CA 95926
(916) 345·2122

CPRC

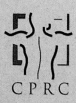

DESIGN FIRM	Image Group
ART DIRECTOR	David Zavala, Eric Sanchez
DESIGNER	David Zavala, Eric Sanchez
ILLUSTRATOR	David Zavala, Eric Sanchez
CLIENT	Child Physical Rehabilitation Clinic
PAPER/PRINTING	Classic Linen

DESIGN FIRM	Handler Design Ltd.
ART DIRECTOR	Bruce Handler
DESIGNER	Bruce Handler
ILLUSTRATOR	Ray Ringston III
CLIENT	Martial Arts Institute of America
PAPER/PRINTING	Strathmore Bond

DESIGN FIRM	Image Group
ART DIRECTOR	David Zavala, Eric Sanchez
DESIGNER	David Zavala, Eric Sanchez
ILLUSTRATOR	David Zavala
CLIENT	Assistance Dog Institute
PAPER/PRINTING	Concept

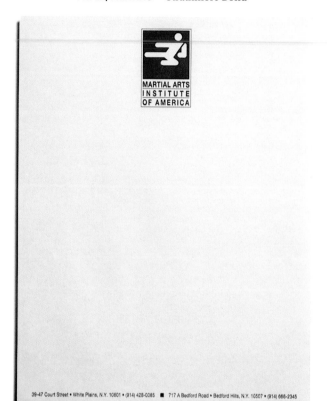

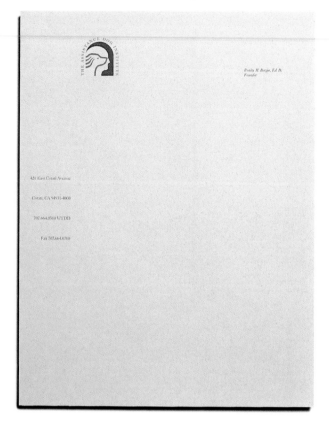

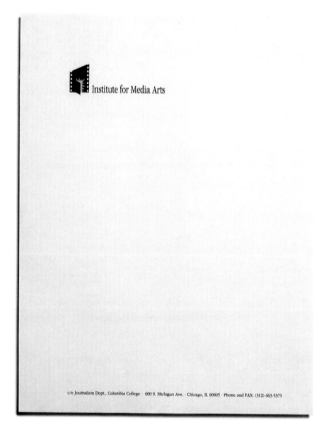

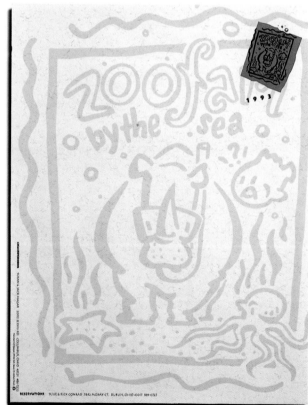

DESIGN FIRM	Jon Wells Associates
DESIGNER	Jon Wells
ILLUSTRATOR	Institute for Media Arts
CLIENT	Curtis Brightwater

DESIGN FIRM	Integrate Inc.
ART DIRECTOR	Stephen Quinn
DESIGNER	Darryl Levering
ILLUSTRATOR	Darryl Levering
CLIENT	Columbus Zoo

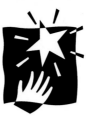

Community Partnership
of Santa Clara County

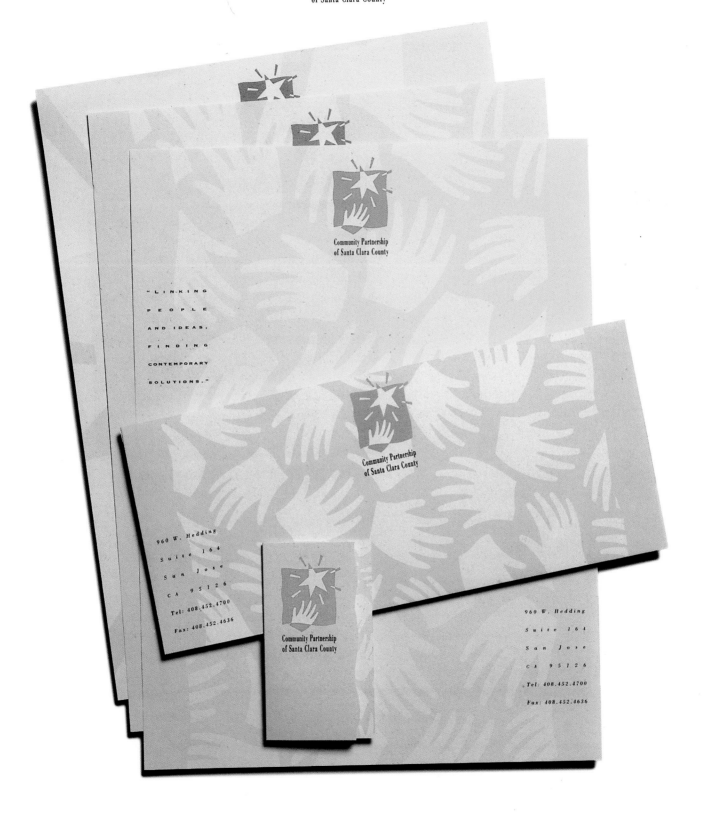

DESIGN FIRM Earl Gee Design
ART DIRECTOR Fani Chung
DESIGNER Fani Chung
ILLUSTRATOR Earl Gee, Fani Chung
CLIENT Community Partnership of Santa Clara County
PAPER/PRINTING Speckletone Cream text

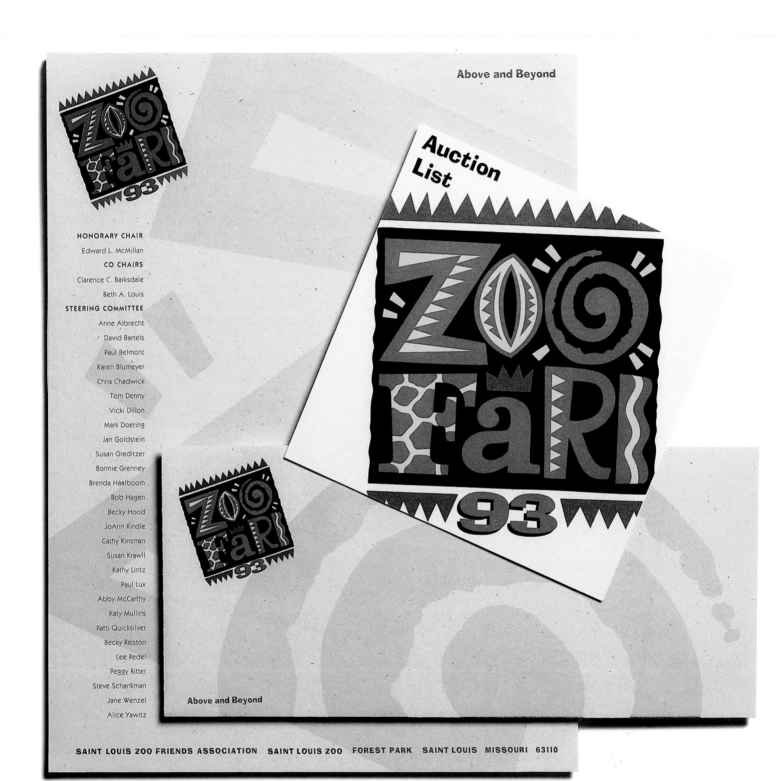

Above and Beyond

Auction List

HONORARY CHAIR
Edward L. McMillan
CO CHAIRS
Clarence C. Barksdale
Beth A. Louis
STEERING COMMITTEE
Anne Albrecht
David Bartels
Paul Belmont
Karen Blumeyer
Chris Chadwick
Tom Denny
Vicki Dillon
Mark Doering
Jan Goldstein
Susan Greditzer
Bonnie Grenney
Brenda Haalboom
Bob Hagen
Becky Hood
JoAnn Kindle
Cathy Kinsman
Susan Krawll
Kathy Lintz
Paul Lux
Abby McCarthy
Katy Mullins
Patti Quicksilver
Becky Ralston
Lee Redel
Peggy Ritter
Steve Schankman
Jane Wenzel
Alice Yawitz

Above and Beyond

SAINT LOUIS ZOO FRIENDS ASSOCIATION   SAINT LOUIS ZOO   FOREST PARK   SAINT LOUIS   MISSOURI   63110

DESIGN FIRM	Bartels & Company
ART DIRECTOR	David Bartels
DESIGNER	Brian Barclay
ILLUSTRATOR	Brian Barclay
CLIENT	St. Louis Zoo/Zoofari '93

Pittsburgh Public Theater
ASSOCIATION

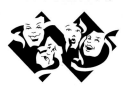

Pittsburgh Public Theater
ASSOCIATION

Allegheny Square
Pittsburgh, PA 15212-5349
412 323-8200 Ext. 207
Fax 412 323-8550

DESIGN FIRM Adam, Filippo & Associates
ART DIRECTOR Robert A. Adam
DESIGNER Adam, Filippo & Associates
CLIENT Pittsburgh Public Theater Association

Australian Institute of Spatial
Information Sciences and Technology

Panorama Avenue Bathurst
PO Box 143 Bathurst NSW Australia 2795
Telephone (61) 063 32 8250
Facsimile (61) 063 31 8095

Australian Institute of Spatial
Information Sciences and Technology

Panorama Avenue Bathurst
PO Box 143 Bathurst NSW Australia 2795
Telephone (063) 32 8200
Facsimile (063) 32 8366
Int. Prefix (61 - 63)

With Compliments

Australian Institute of Spatial
Information Sciences and Technology
Panorama Avenue Bathurst
PO Box 143 Bathurst NSW Australia 2795
Telephone (063) 32 8408
Private (063) 37 5310
Facsimile (063) 32 8366
Int. Prefix (61 - 63)

David L. Mills
Manager

DESIGN FIRM	Jenssen Design Pty. Limited
ART DIRECTOR	David Jenssen
DESIGNER	David Jenssen, Karen Lloyd Jones
ILLUSTRATOR	Karen Lloyd Jones
CLIENT	Australian Institute of Spatial Information Sciences and Technology
PAPER/PRINTING	Conqueror Laid White

DESIGN FIRM	Schowalter² Design
ART DIRECTOR	Toni Schowalter
DESIGNER	Toni Schowalter
CLIENT	Judy Freedman, Yoga Instructor

DESIGN FIRM	MacVicar Design & Communications
ART DIRECTOR	John Vance
DESIGNER	William A. Gordon
CLIENT	Association of Universities for Research in Astronomy, Inc.

DESIGN FIRM	Adam Filippo & Associates
ART DIRECTOR	Robert A. Adam, Ralph James Russini
DESIGNER	Sharon L. Bretz, Barbara Peak Long
CLIENT	Forbes Health System

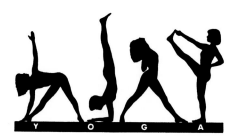

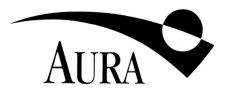

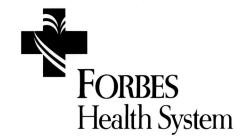

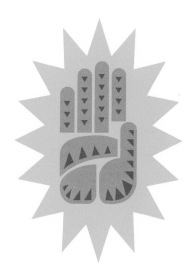

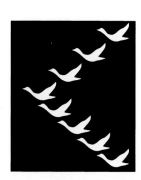

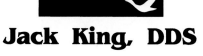

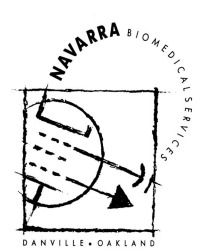

DESIGN FIRM	The Weller Institute for the Cure of Design, Inc.
ART DIRECTOR	Don Weller
DESIGNER	Don Weller
ILLUSTRATOR	Don Weller
CLIENT	Todd Ware Massage

DESIGN FIRM	Turner Design
ART DIRECTOR	Bert Turner
DESIGNER	Bert Turner
ILLUSTRATOR	Bert Turner
CLIENT	Jack King, D.D.S.

DESIGN FIRM	Riley Design Associates
ART DIRECTOR	Daniel Riley
DESIGNER	Daniel Riley
ILLUSTRATOR	Daniel Riley
CLIENT	Navarra Biomedical Services

DESIGN FIRM	Luis Fitch Diseño
ART DIRECTOR	Luis Fitch
DESIGNER	Luis Fitch
CLIENT	Ohio Heart Association

DESIGN FIRM	Design Art, Inc.
ART DIRECTOR	Norman Moore
DESIGNER	Norman Moore
CLIENT	Humanitas Foundation

DESIGN FIRM	Design Art, Inc.
ART DIRECTOR	Norman Moore
DESIGNER	Norman Moore
CLIENT	Beverly Glen Play Group

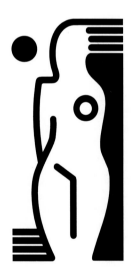

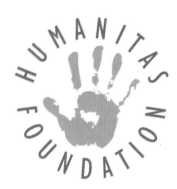

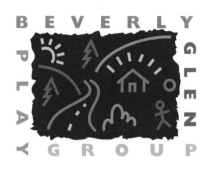

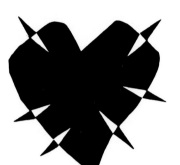

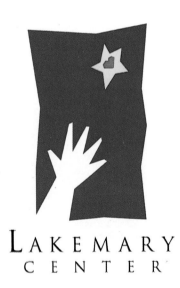

LAKEMARY
CENTER

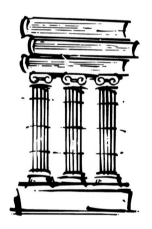

Friends of the
Wilmington Library

DESIGN FIRM	Sommese Design
ART DIRECTOR	Kristin Sommese
DESIGNER	Kristin Sommese
ILLUSTRATOR	Kristin Sommese
CLIENT	Penn State Panhellenic Council, "Women's Awareness Week"

DESIGN FIRM	Eilts Anderson Tracy
ART DIRECTOR	Patrice Eilts
DESIGNER	Patrice Eilts
ILLUSTRATOR	Patrice Eilts
CLIENT	Lakemary Center

DESIGN FIRM	Delmarva Power Corp. Comm.
ART DIRECTOR	Christy Macintyre
DESIGNER	John Alfred
ILLUSTRATOR	Wayne Parmenter
CLIENT	Wilmington Library

DESIGN FIRM Ramona Hutko
Design
ART DIRECTOR Ramona Hutko
DESIGNER Ramona Hutko
CLIENT American Red Cross,
Rochester Chapter

DESIGN FIRM Richard Danne &
Associates Inc.
ART DIRECTOR Richard Danne
DESIGNER Gayle Shimoun,
Richard Danne
CLIENT American Academy
on Physician and
Patient

DESIGN FIRM The Great American
Logo Company
ART DIRECTOR Gregg Frederickson
DESIGNER Gregg Frederickson
CLIENT Ewing Institute of
Therapeutic Massage

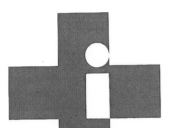

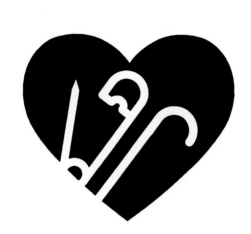

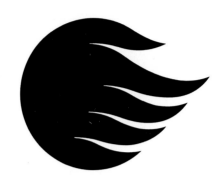

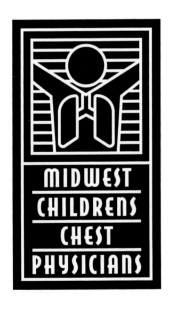

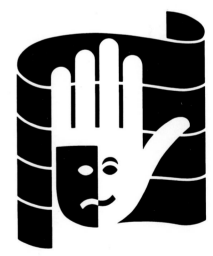

DESIGN FIRM New Idea Design Inc.
DESIGNER Ron Boldt
ILLUSTRATOR Ron Boldt
CLIENT Midwest Children's
Chest Physicians

DESIGN FIRM Schowalter² Design
ART DIRECTOR Toni Schowalter
DESIGNER Ilene Price, Toni
Schowalter
ILLUSTRATOR Ilene Price, Toni
Schowalter
CLIENT Towers Perrin

DESIGN FIRM Frank D'Astolfo
Design
ART DIRECTOR Frank D'Astolfo
DESIGNER Frank D'Astolfo
CLIENT Visual and
Performing Arts,
Rutgers University,
New Jersey

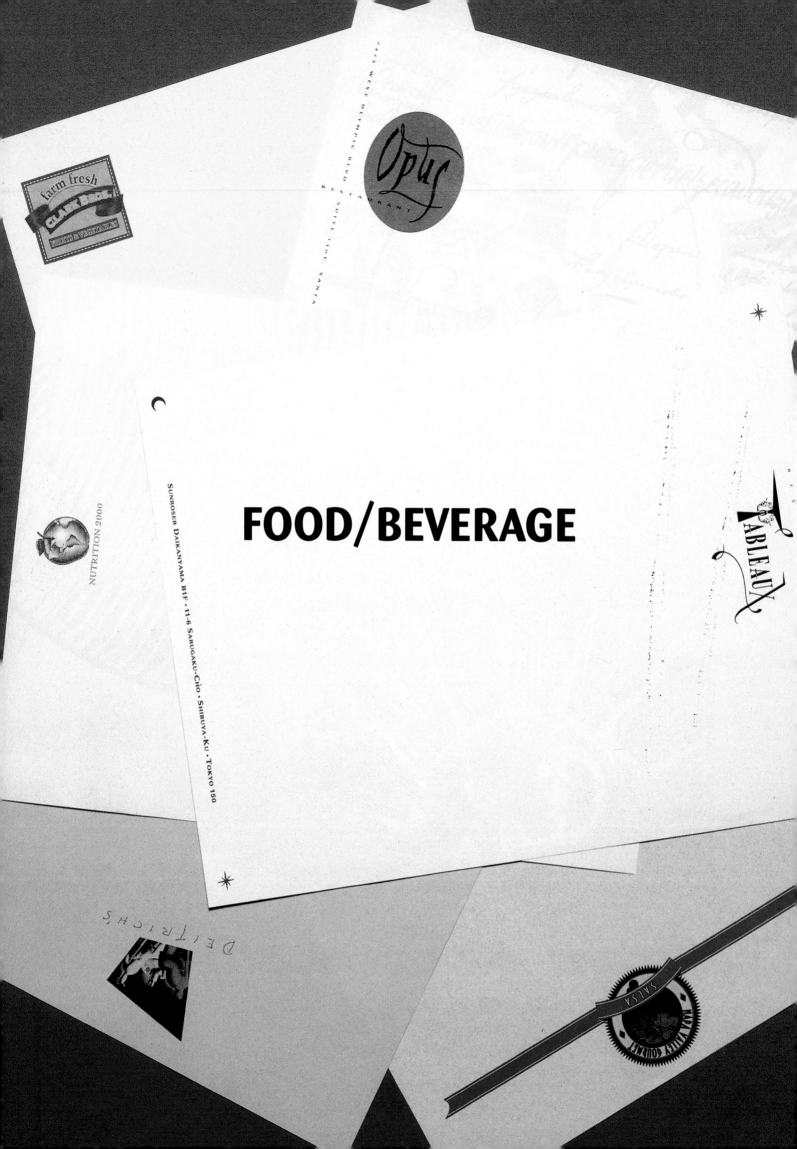

FOOD/BEVERAGE

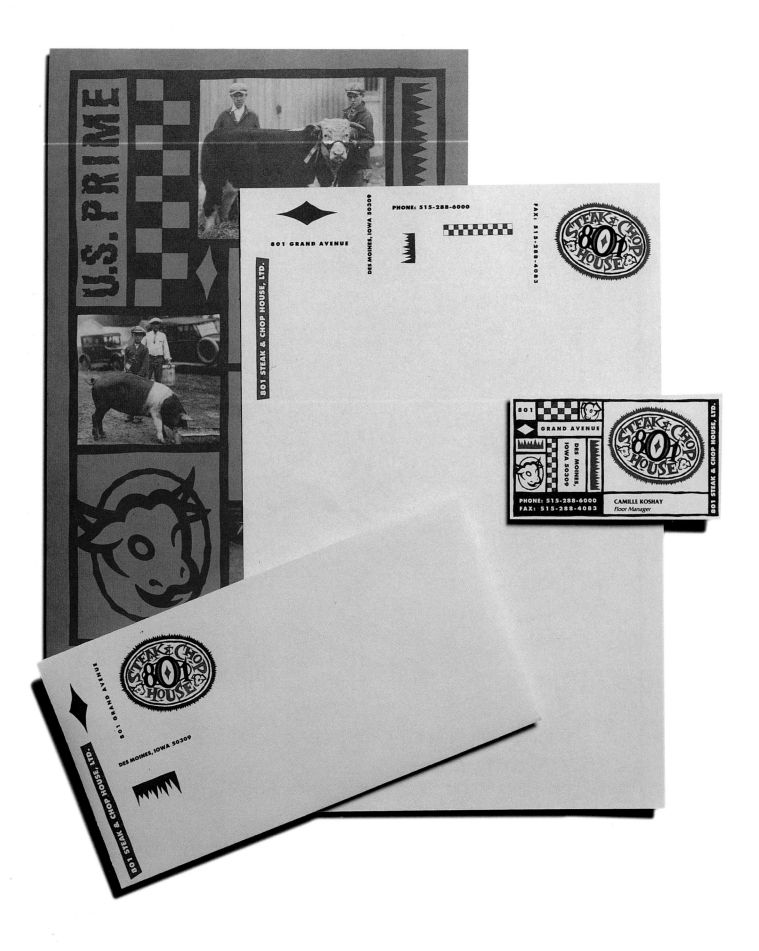

DESIGN FIRM   Sayles Graphic Design
ART DIRECTOR   John Sayles
DESIGNER   John Sayles
ILLUSTRATOR   John Sayles
CLIENT   801 Steak & Chop House
PAPER/PRINTING   James River, Retreeve Tan, 2 colors

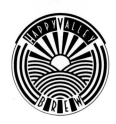

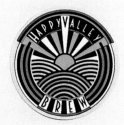

HAPPY VALLEY BREWERY, 2570 BOULEVARD OF THE GENERALS, BUILDING 100, SUITE 122, NORRISTOWN, PA 19403 (215) 630-8710, FAX 215-630-8134

DESIGN FIRM   Sommese Design
ART DIRECTOR   Lanny Sommese, Kristin Sommese
DESIGNER   Kristin Sommese
ILLUSTRATOR   Lanny Sommese
CLIENT   Happy Valley Brew
PAPER/PRINTING   Classic Linen

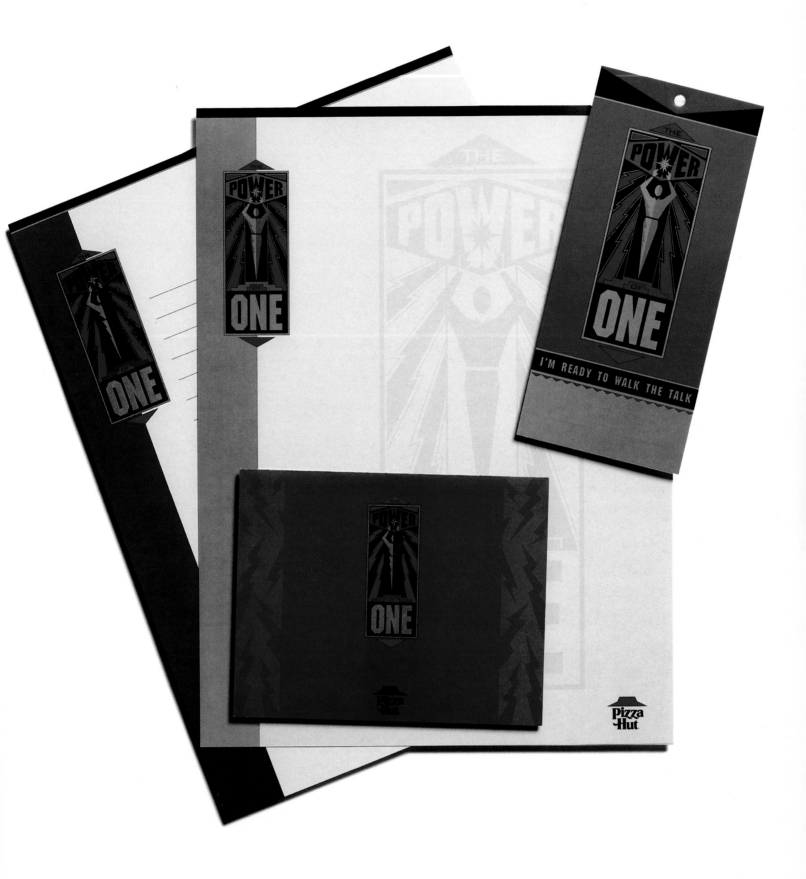

DESIGN FIRM Creative Services by Pizza Hut
ART DIRECTOR Lisa Voss, Lori Cox
DESIGNER Lisa Voss
ILLUSTRATOR Lisa Voss
CLIENT Pizza Hut
PAPER/PRINTING Mead offset enamel, metallic purple and gold

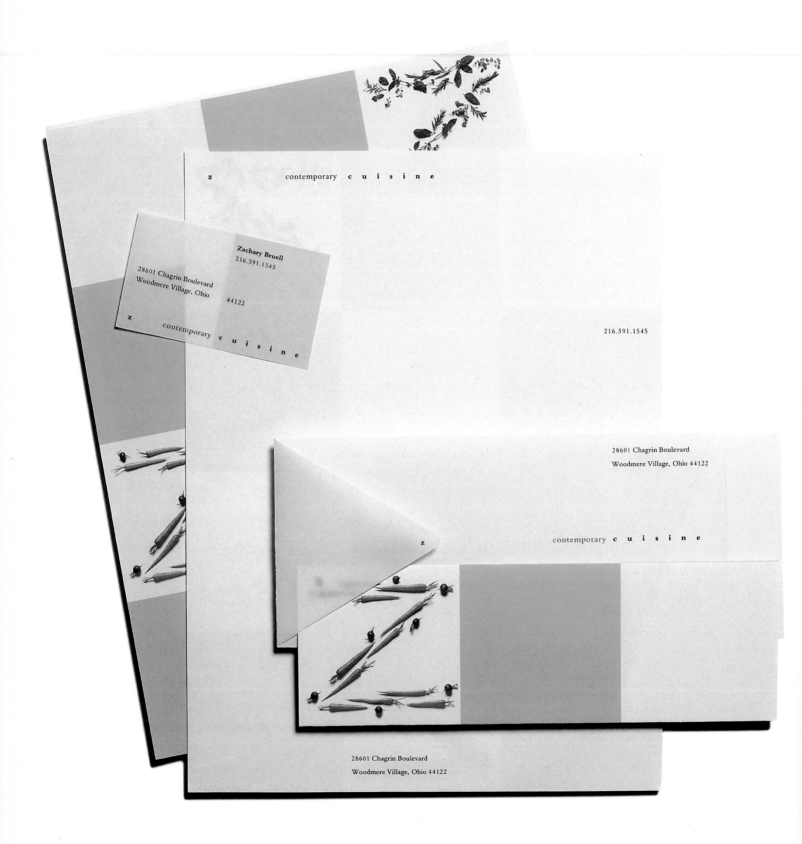

z   contemporary **c u i s i n e**

Zachary Bruell
216.591.1545

28601 Chagrin Boulevard
Woodmere Village, Ohio

44122

z   contemporary **c u i s i n e**

216.591.1545

28601 Chagrin Boulevard
Woodmere Village, Ohio 44122

z   contemporary **c u i s i n e**

28601 Chagrin Boulevard
Woodmere Village, Ohio 44122

DESIGN FIRM	Nesnadny & Schwartz
ART DIRECTOR	Joyce Nesnadny, Mark Schwartz
DESIGNER	Joyce Nesnadny
CLIENT	Z Contemporary Cuisine
PAPER/PRINTING	Crane's (letterhead), Neenah (envelope, 2/2)

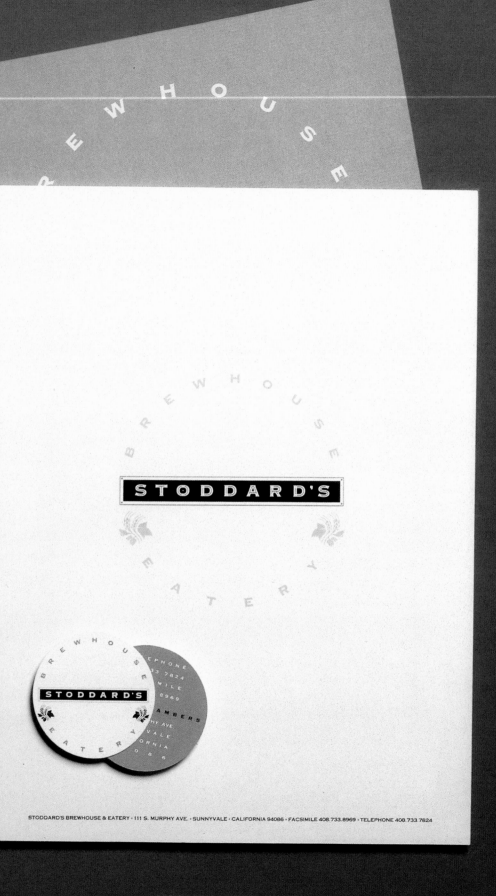

DESIGN FIRM   THARP DID IT
ART DIRECTOR   Rick Tharp
DESIGNER   Sandy Russell, Colleen Sullivan, Rick Tharp
CLIENT   Stoddard's Brewhouse & Eatery
PAPER/PRINTING   Simpson

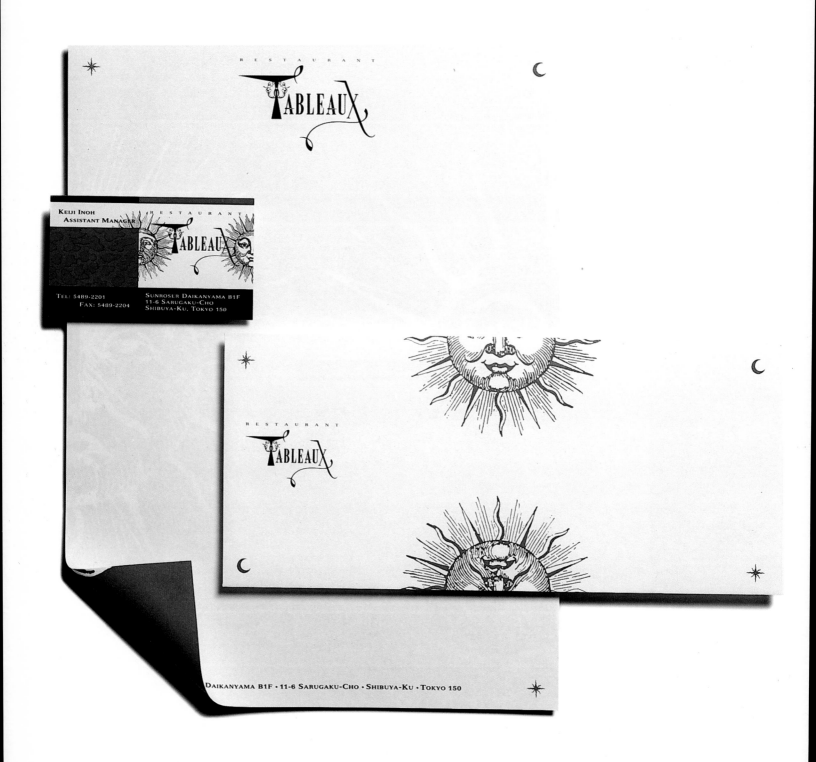

DESIGN FIRM   Vrontikis Design Office
ART DIRECTOR   Petrula Vrontikis
DESIGNER   Kim Sage
CLIENT   Tableaux
PAPER/PRINTING   Classic Crest Solar White

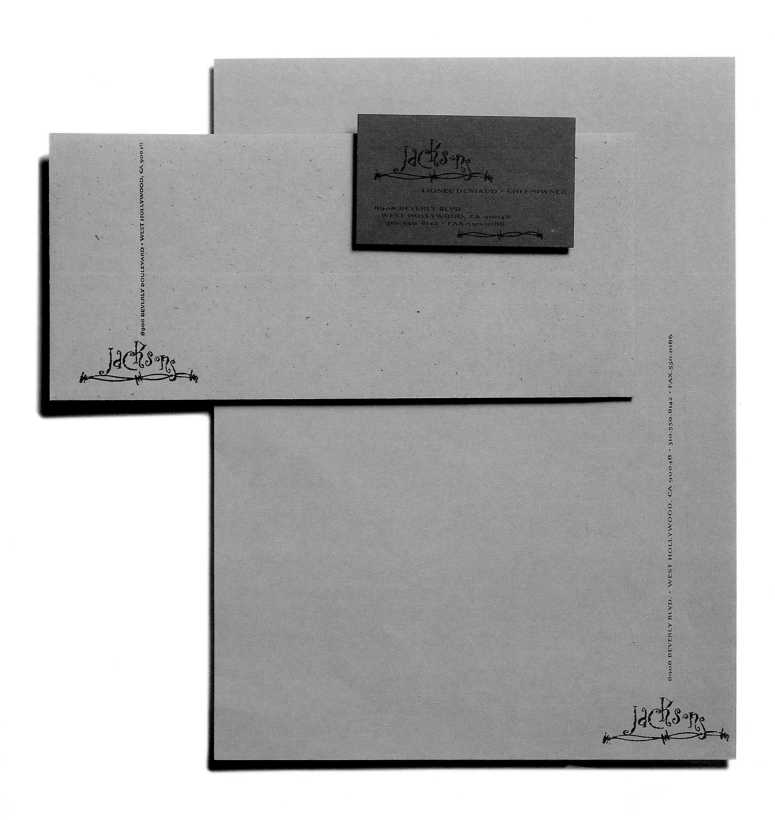

DESIGN FIRM	Vrontikis Design Office
ART DIRECTOR	Petrula Vrontikis
DESIGNER	Kim Sage
CLIENT	Jacksons
PAPER/PRINTING	French Durotone

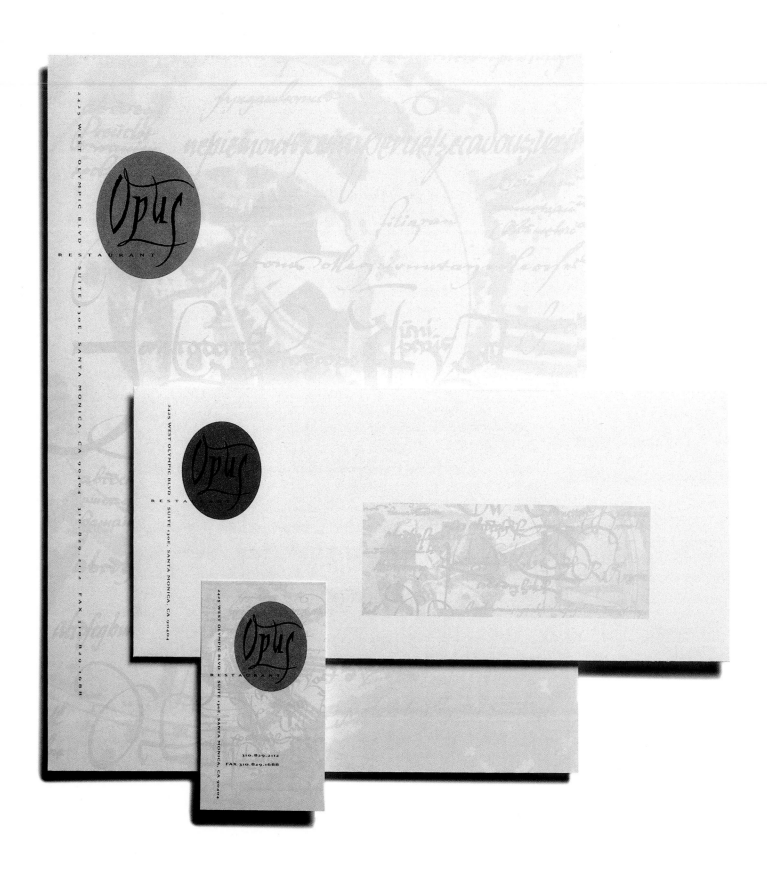

DESIGN FIRM   Let Her Press
ART DIRECTOR   Heather Van Haaften, Lorna Stovall
DESIGNER   Lorna Stovall, Heather Van Haaften
CLIENT   L'Orfe/Opus Restaurant
PAPER/PRINTING   Starwhite Vicksberg

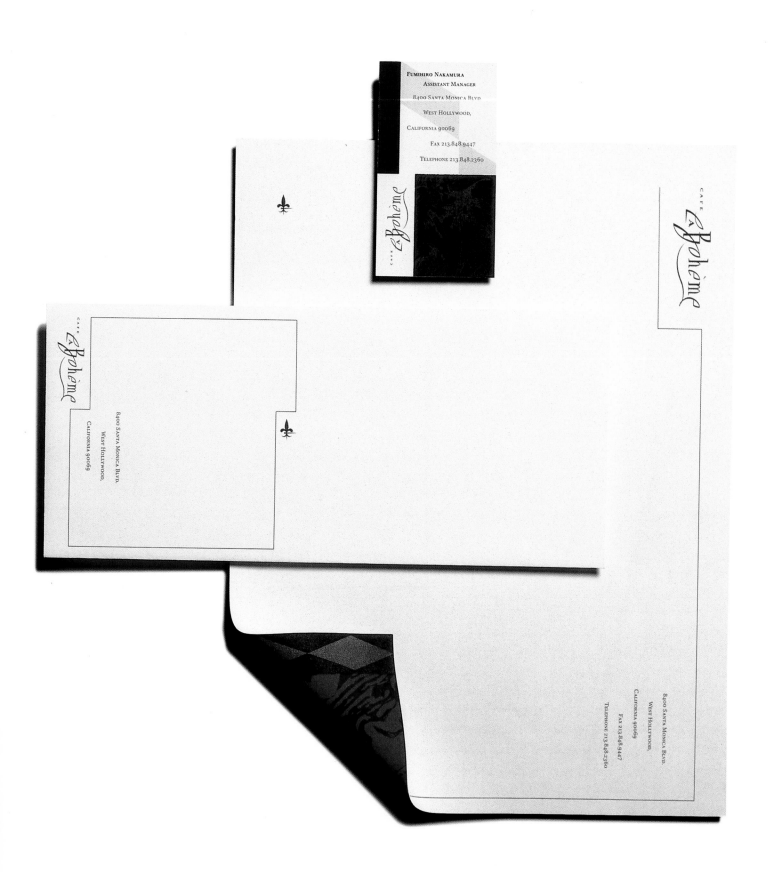

DESIGN FIRM Vrontikis Design Office
ART DIRECTOR Petrula Vrontikis
DESIGNER Kim Sage, Lorna Stovall
CLIENT Café La Boheme
PAPER/PRINTING Simpson Starwhite Vicksburg

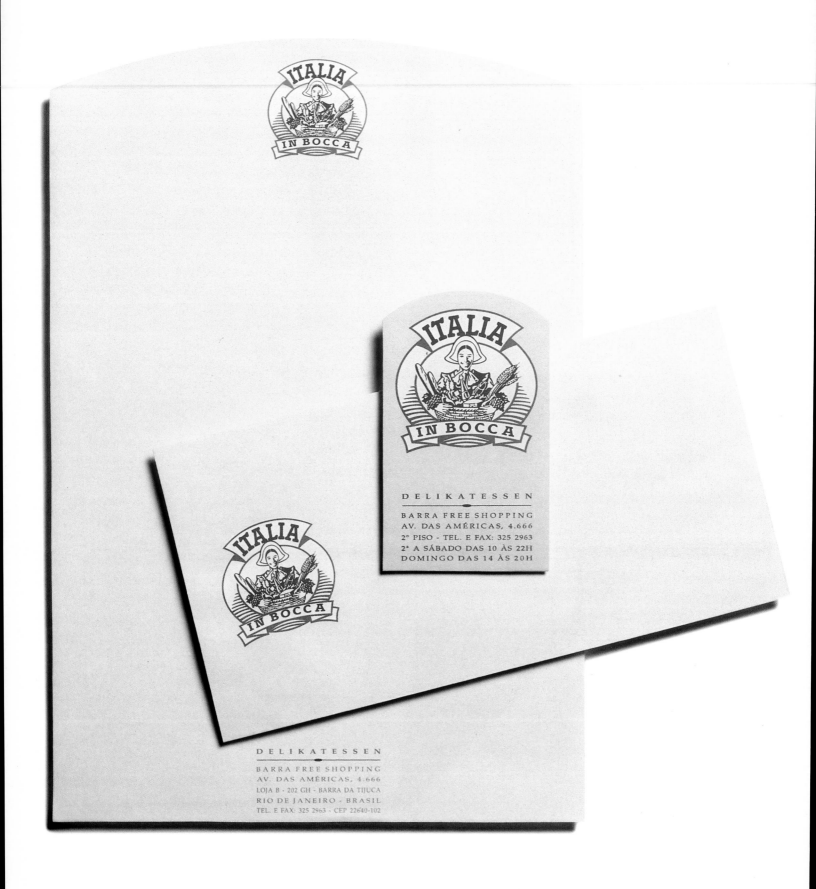

DESIGN FIRM	Animus Comunicacaō
ART DIRECTOR	Rique Nitzsche
DESIGNER	Rique Nitzsche, Felicio Torres
ILLUSTRATOR	Antonino Homobono
CLIENT	Italia in Bocca
PAPER/PRINTING	Alta Alvura (letterhead and envelope), Opaline (Business card)

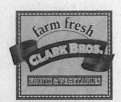

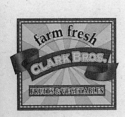

☞ **Office**

5 Concourse Parkway

Suite 3100

Atlanta, Georgia

30328

☞ **Office**

5 Concourse Parkway

Suite 3100

Atlanta, Georgia

30328

☎ (404) 804-5830

🌿 **Farm**

Route 6

Moultrie, Georgia

31768

☎ (912) 985-1444

☞ **Office**
5 Concourse Parkway
Suite 3100
Atlanta, Georgia 30328
☎ (404) 804-5830

🌿 **Farm**
Route 6
Moultrie, Georgia 31768
☎ (912) 985-1444

Bryan V. Clark

DESIGN FIRM   Coker Golley Ltd.
ART DIRECTOR   Frank Golley, June Coker
DESIGNER   Julia Mahood
CLIENT   Clark Brothers

Joan Deccio Wickham
Food Stylist & Culinary Instructor

Joan Deccio Wickham
Food Stylist & Culinary Instructor

P.O. Box 442
Vashon, WA
98070
206-463-3647
Fax 206-463-9223

Joan Deccio Wickham
Food Stylist & Culinary Instructor
P.O. Box 442
Vashon, WA
98070

P.O. Box 442

Vashon, WA

98070

206-463-3647

Fax 206-463-9223

DESIGN FIRM	Walsh and Associates, Inc.
ART DIRECTOR	Miriam Lisco
DESIGNER	Katie Dolejsi
CLIENT	Joan Deccio Wickham

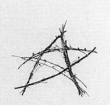

STARS
·OAKVILLE
CAFE

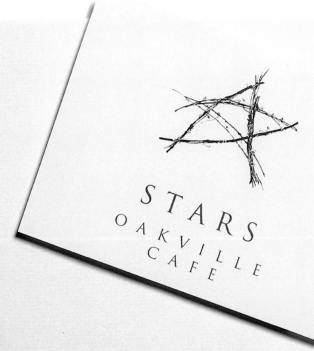

STARS
OAKVILLE
CAFE

7848 St. Helena Highway 29
P.O. Box 410
Oakville, California 94562
reservations 707-944-8905
fax 707-944-0469

StarTeam, Ltd.
tel 415-897-7560
fax 415-897-8191

Stars Restaurant
tel 415-861-7827
fax 415-861-6706

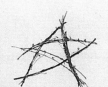

STARS
OAKVILLE
CAFE

DESIGN FIRM	Debra Nichols Design
ART DIRECTOR	Debra Nichols
DESIGNER	Debra Nichols, Roxanne Malek
CLIENT	Stars Restaurant

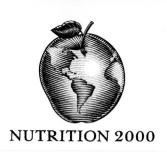

NUTRITION 2000

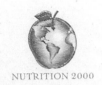

NUTRITION 2000

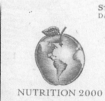

STEVEN G. HASTINGS
Director of Marketing

136 Chesterfield
Industrial Blvd

Chesterfield
Missouri 63005

Tel: 314.537.9715
Fax: 314.537.0137

NUTRITION 2000

NUTRITION 2000

136 Chesterfield Industrial Blvd · Chesterfield. Missouri 63005 · Tel: 314.537.9715 Fax: 314.537.0137

DESIGN FIRM   Reliv, Inc.

ART DIRECTOR   Jay Smith

DESIGNER   Jay Smith

ILLUSTRATOR   Cindy Wrobel

CLIENT   Nutrition 2000

PAPER/PRINTING   Hopper Proterra, 3 PMS

DESIGN FIRM	Stephen Divoky
ART DIRECTOR	Stephen Divoky
DESIGNER	Stephen Divoky
CLIENT	Traditions Catering

DESIGN FIRM	Schowalter² Design
ART DIRECTOR	Toni Schowalter
DESIGNER	Ilene Price, Toni Schowalter
ILLUSTRATOR	Ilene Price, Toni Schowalter
CLIENT	Anne Semmes
PAPER/PRINTING	Strathmore Writing

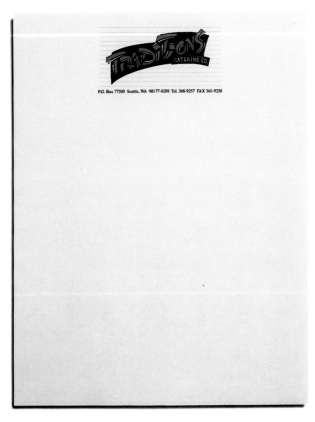

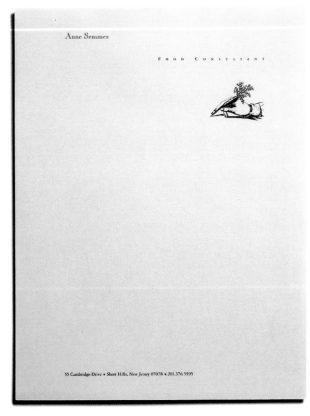

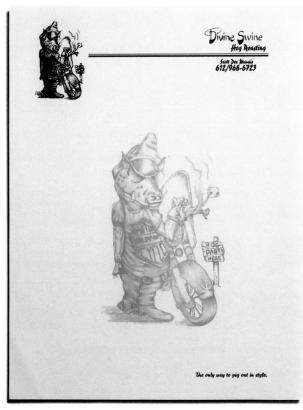

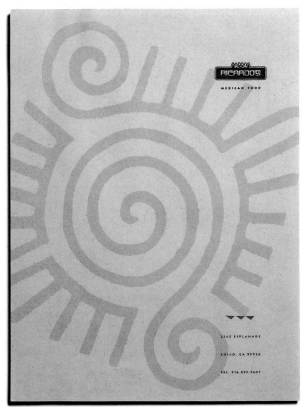

DESIGN FIRM	Designs N Logos
ART DIRECTOR	Douglas Martini
DESIGNER	Douglas Martini
ILLUSTRATOR	Douglas Martini
CLIENT	Divine Swine
PAPER/PRINTING	Classic Linen, White Enamel

DESIGN FIRM	Image Group
ART DIRECTOR	David Zavala
DESIGNER	David Zavala
CLIENT	Ricardo's Restaurant
PAPER/PRINTING	Strathmore Renewal

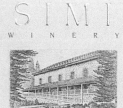

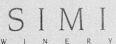

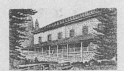

SIMI
W I N E R Y

POST OFFICE BOX 698 • HEALDSBURG, CALIFORNIA 95448

SIMI
W I N E R Y

STEPHANIE DUCKHORN
MARKETING ASSISTANT

16275 HEALDSBURG AVE.
POST OFFICE BOX 698
HEALDSBURG, CA 95448

(707) 433-6981 TEL.
(707) 433-6253 FAX

16275 HEALDSBURG AVENUE • POST OFFICE BOX 698 • HEALDSBURG, CALIFORNIA 95448 • TEL (707) 433-6981 • FAX (707) 433-6253

DESIGN FIRM	Ortega Design Studio
ART DIRECTOR	Susann Ortega, Joann Ortega
DESIGNER	Susann Ortega
ILLUSTRATOR	Robert Swartly
CLIENT	Simi Winery
PAPER/PRINTING	Enhance

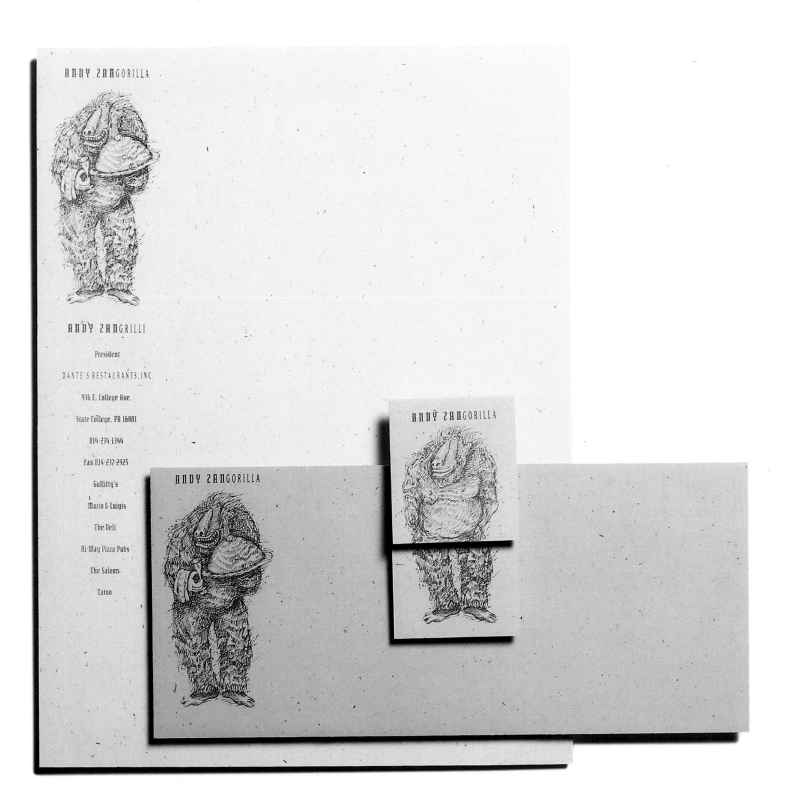

DESIGN FIRM   Sommese Design
ART DIRECTOR   Lanny Sommese, Kristin Sommese
DESIGNER   Kristin Sommese
ILLUSTRATOR   Lanny Sommese
CLIENT   Dante's Restaurants Inc., Andy Zangrilli
PAPER/PRINTING   Cross Pointe Genesis Script

DESIGN FIRM	Choplogic
ART DIRECTOR	Walter McCord
DESIGNER	Walter McCord
ILLUSTRATOR	Bud Hixson
CLIENT	Deitrich's
PAPER/PRINTING	Curtis Flannel, 2 colors

DESIGN FIRM	Raven Madd Design
ART DIRECTOR	Mark Curtis
DESIGNER	Mark Curtis
ILLUSTRATOR	Mark Curtis
CLIENT	Villa Cuppachino Café

DESIGN FIRM	Mac By Night
ART DIRECTOR	Damion Hickman, Hector Garcia
DESIGNER	Damion Hickman
ILLUSTRATOR	Damion Hickman
CLIENT	Napa Valley Gourmet Salsa
PAPER/PRINTING	Deluxe Color

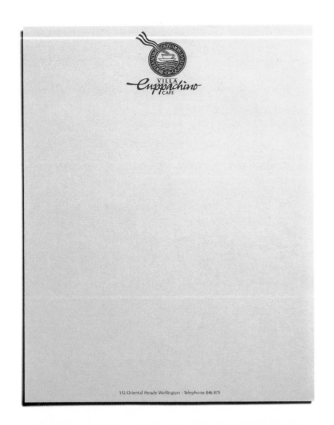

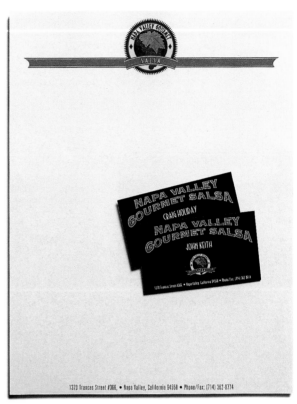

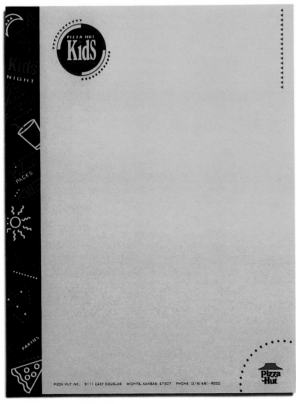

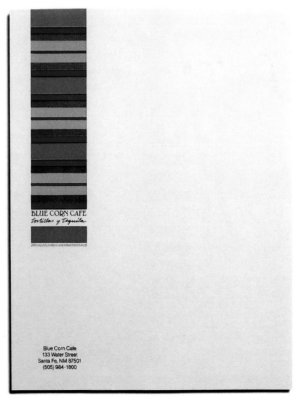

DESIGN FIRM	Creative Services by Pizza Hut
ART DIRECTOR	Lisa Voss, Lori Cox
DESIGNER	Lisa Voss
ILLUSTRATOR	Lisa Voss
CLIENT	Pizza Hut Kids Marketing
PAPER/PRINTING	Champion Carnival, 4 PMS

DESIGN FIRM	William Field Design
ART DIRECTOR	Fred Cisneros
DESIGNER	Fred Cisneros
ILLUSTRATOR	Fred Cisneros
CLIENT	Blue Corn Cafe
PAPER/PRINTING	Classic Crest

DESIGN FIRM David Carter Design
ART DIRECTOR Gary Fobue
DESIGNER Gary Fobue
ILLUSTRATOR Linda Bleck
CLIENT Disney Land Hotel,
Euro Disney, Paris

DESIGN FIRM Hornall Anderson
Design Works
ART DIRECTOR Jack Anderson
DESIGNER Jack Anderson,
David Bates
ILLUSTRATOR David Bates,
George Tanagi
CLIENT Capons Rotisserie
Chicken

DESIGN FIRM Segura Inc.
ART DIRECTOR Carlos Segura
DESIGNER Carlos Segura
ILLUSTRATOR Carlos Segura
CLIENT FreeStyle (drink)

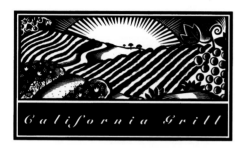

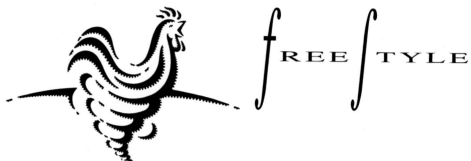

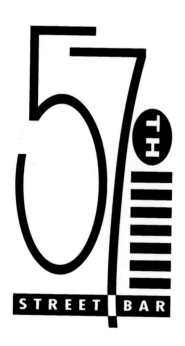

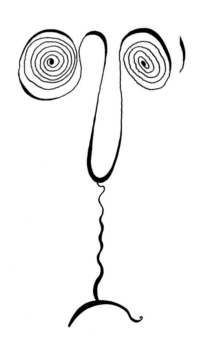

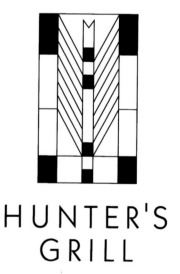

DESIGN FIRM David Carter Design
ART DIRECTOR Sharon Lejune
DESIGNER Sharon Lejune
ILLUSTRATOR Sharon Lejune
CLIENT Euro Disney,
New York,
Euro Disney, Paris

DESIGN FIRM Segura Inc.
ART DIRECTOR Carlos Segura
DESIGNER Carlos Segura
ILLUSTRATOR Carlos Segura
CLIENT Bud Dry

DESIGN FIRM David Carter Design
ART DIRECTOR David Brashier
DESIGNER David Brashier
ILLUSTRATOR David Brashier
CLIENT Sequoia Lodge,
Euro Disney, Paris

DESIGN FIRM   David Carter Design
ART DIRECTOR   Gary Fobue,
                  Lori Wilson
DESIGNER   Gary Fobue,
              Lori Wilson
ILLUSTRATOR   Gary Fobue,
                  Lori Wilson
CLIENT   Amapola Resturant,
            Hotel Principe Felipe

DESIGN FIRM   THARP DID IT
DESIGNER   Rick Tharp
ILLUSTRATOR   Jana Heer,
                  Rick Tharp
CLIENT   The Occidental Grille
PAPER/PRINTING   Simpson Paper,
                    Stormm
                    Graphicworks

DESIGN FIRM   Palmquist & Palmquist
                  Design
ART DIRECTOR   Kurt & Denise Palmquist
DESIGNER   Kurt & Denise Palmquist
CLIENT   The Bistro

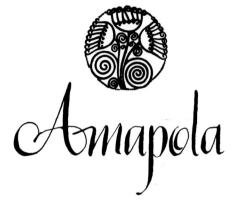

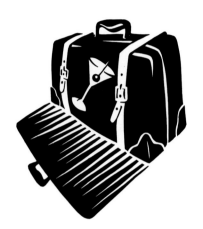

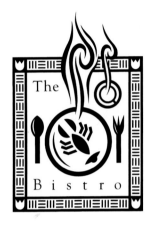

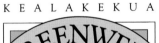

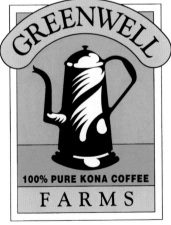

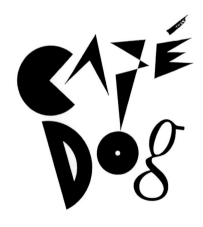

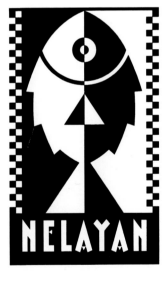

DESIGN FIRM   The Weller Institute
                  for the Cure of
                  Design, Inc.
ART DIRECTOR   Don Weller
DESIGNER   Don Weller
ILLUSTRATOR   Don Weller
CLIENT   Greenwell Farms

DESIGN FIRM   Choplogic
ART DIRECTOR   Walter McCord,
                  Mary Cawein
DESIGNER   Walter McCord,
              Mary Cawein
ILUSTRATOR   Walter McCord,
                Mary Cawein
CLIENT   Café Dog

DESIGN FIRM   David Carter Design
ART DIRECTOR   Kevin Prejean
DESIGNER   Kevin Prejean
ILLUSTRATOR   Kevin Prejean
CLIENT   Grand Hyatt, Bali

DESIGN FIRM	Eilts Anderson Tracy
ART DIRECTOR	Patrice Eilts
DESIGNER	Patrice Eilts,
	Rich Kobs
ILLUSTRATOR	Rich Kobs
CLIENT	PBU Restaurants/
	Grand St. Cafe

DESIGN FIRM	W Designs
ART DIRECTOR	Corinne West
DESIGNER	Corinne West
CLIENT	Carretto Cafes Inc.

DESIGN FIRM	Sommese Design
ART DIRECTOR	Lanny Sommese
DESIGNER	Lanny Sommese
CLIENT	Aquapenn Spring
	Water Co.

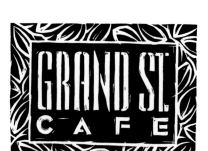

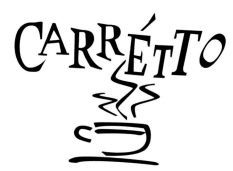

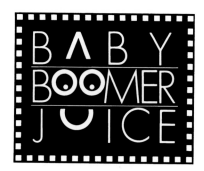

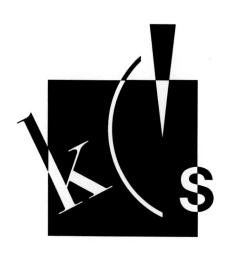

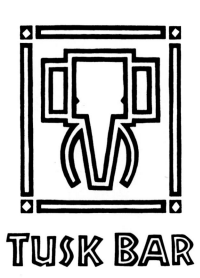

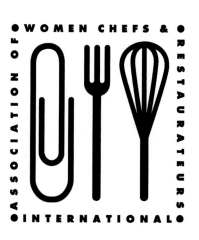

DESIGN FIRM	David Carter Design
ART DIRECTOR	Randall Hill
DESIGNER	Randall Hill
ILLUSTRATOR	Randall Hill
CLIENT	Grand Hyatt, Taipei

DESIGN FIRM	David Carter Design
ART DIRECTOR	Randall Hill,
	Brian Moss
DESIGNER	Randall Hill,
	Brian Moss
ILLUSTRATOR	Randall Hill,
	Brian Moss
CLIENT	Sun International

DESIGN FIRM	Schowalter² Design
ART DIRECTOR	Toni Schowalter
DESIGNER	Ilene Price,
	Toni Schowalter
ILLUSTRATOR	Ilene Price,
	Toni Schowalter
CLIENT	WCRIA

DESIGN FIRM   David Carter Design
ART DIRECTOR David Brashier
DESIGNER   David Brashier
CLIENT   Disney Orlando,
                  Florida

DESIGN FIRM   Luis Fitch Diseño
ART DIRECTOR Luis Fitch
DESIGNER   Luis Fitch
CLIENT   Picante Restaurant

DESIGN FIRM   David Carter Design
ART DIRECTOR Sharon Lejeune
DESIGNER   Sharon Lejeune
ILLUSTRATOR   Pat Foss
CLIENT   Hyatt Regency, Osaka

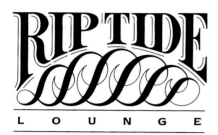

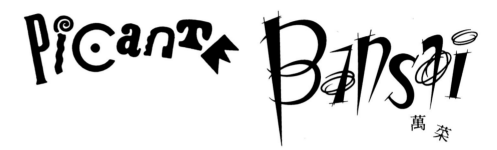

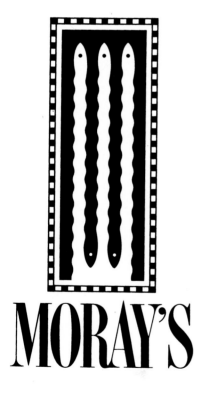

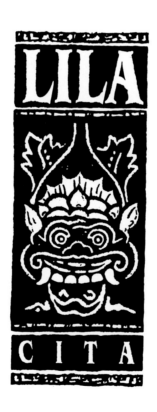

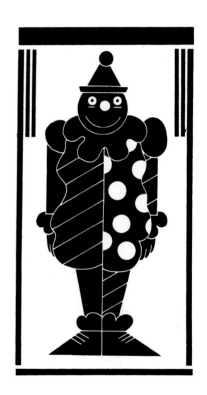

DESIGN FIRM   David Carter Design
ART DIRECTOR Gary Lobue
DESIGNER   Gary Lobue
ILLUSTRATOR   Gary Lobue
CLIENT   Moray's Restaurant

DESIGN FIRM   David Carter Design
ART DIRECTOR Randall Hill
DESIGNER   Randall Hill
ILLUSTRATOR   Randall Hill
CLIENT   Grand Hyatt, Bali

DESIGN FIRM   Sommese Design
ART DIRECTOR Lanny Sommese
DESIGNER   Lanny Sommese
ILLUSTRATOR   Lanny Sommese
CLIENT   Dante's Restaurants Inc.
                  This is the logo for the
                  children's menu.

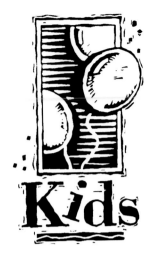

Kids

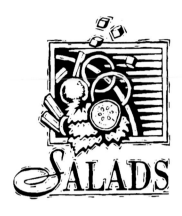

Salads

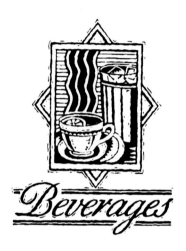

Beverages

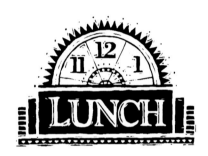

Lunch

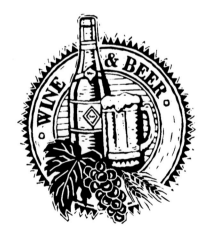

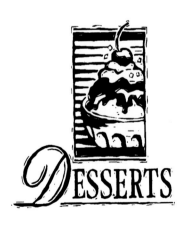

Desserts

DESIGN FIRM   Creative Services by Pizza Hut
ART DIRECTOR   Lisa Voss, Lori Cox
DESIGNER   Lisa Voss
ILLUSTRATOR   Lisa Voss
CLIENT   Pizza Hut Café

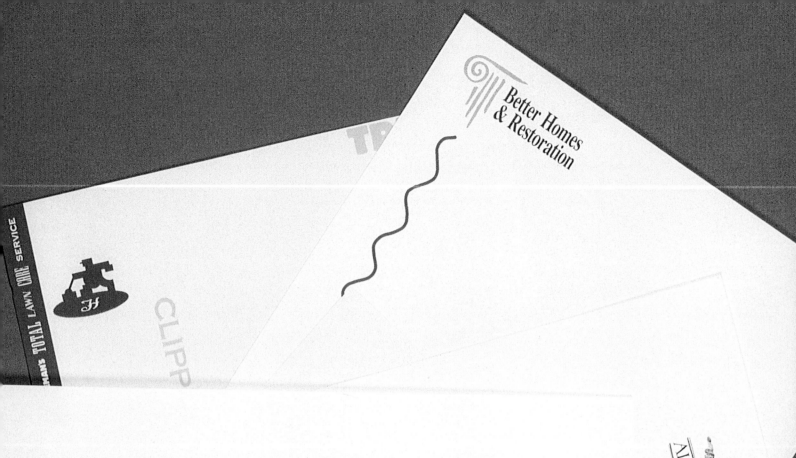

REAL ESTATE/
PROPERTIES

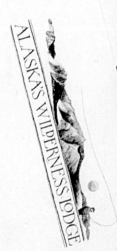

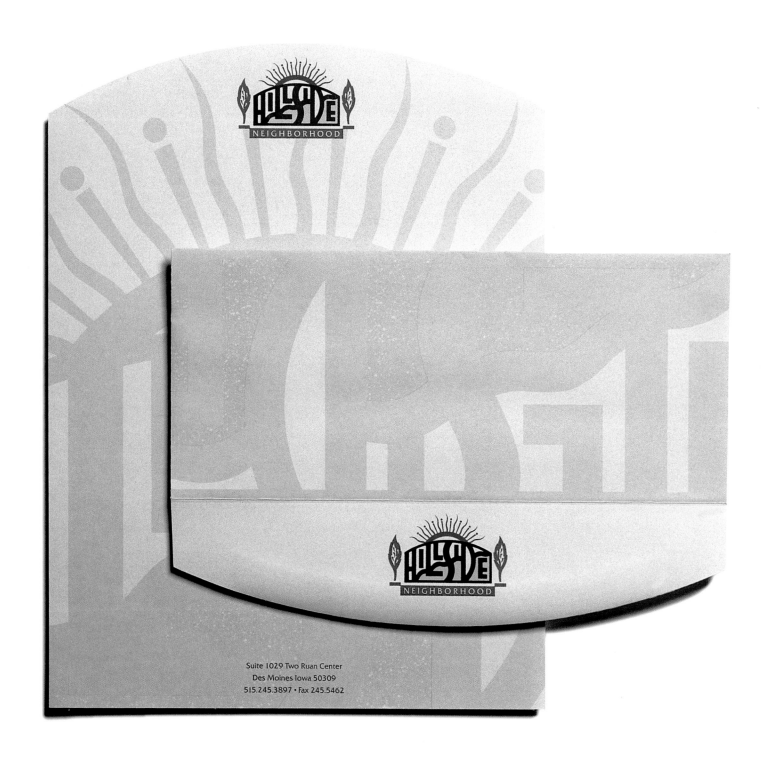

Suite 1029 Two Ruan Center
Des Moines Iowa 50309
515.245.3897 • Fax 245.5462

DESIGN FIRM   Sayles Graphic Design
ART DIRECTOR   John Sayles
DESIGNER   John Sayles
ILLUSTRATOR   John Sayles
CLIENT   Hillside Neighborhood
PAPER/PRINTING   James River, Vellum Gray, 2 colors

DESIGN FIRM   Romeo Empire Design
ART DIRECTOR   Vincent Romeo
DESIGNER   Vincent Romeo
ILLUSTRATOR   Vincent Romeo
CLIENT   Adobe Ranch, New Mexico
PAPER/PRINTING   Curtis Flannel

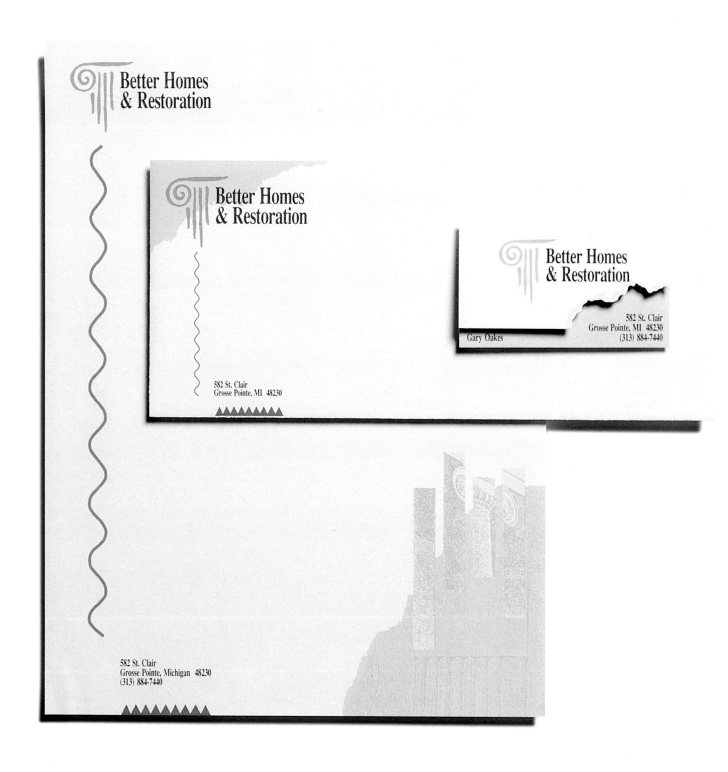

DESIGN FIRM   Ridenour Advertising
ART DIRECTOR   Kerry B. Ridenour
DESIGNER   Kerry B. Ridenour
ILLUSTRATOR   Kerry B. Ridenour
CLIENT   Better Homes & Restoration
PAPER/PRINTING   Passport, 4 colors

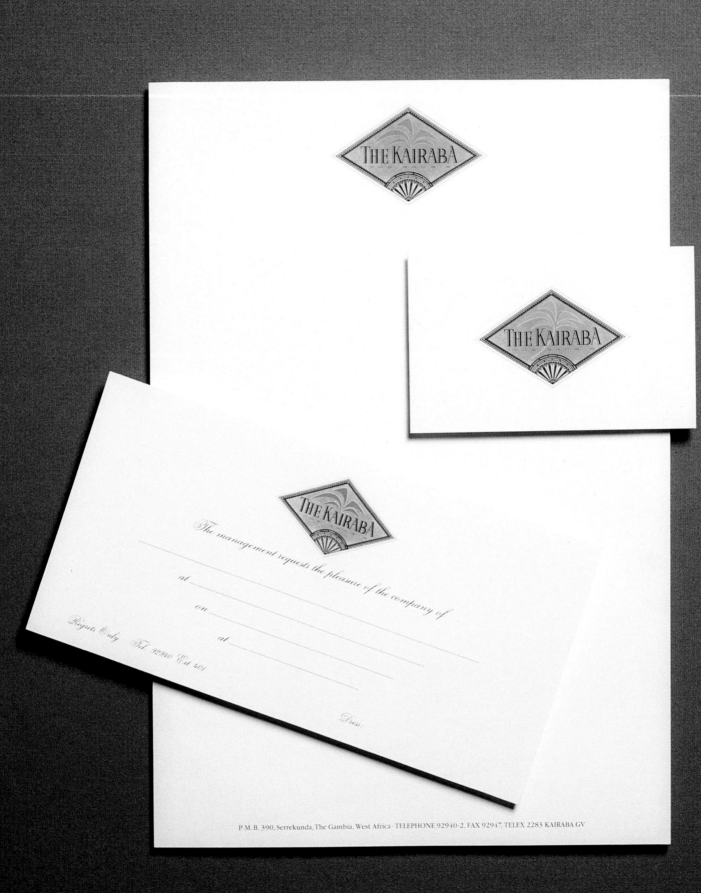

DESIGN FIRM	Hartmann & Mehler Designers GmbH
ART DIRECTOR	Roland Mehler
DESIGNER	Roland Mehler
ILLUSTRATOR	Roland Mehler
CLIENT	Steigenberger Consulting
PAPER/PRINTING	Enhance

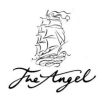
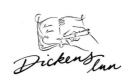
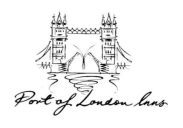
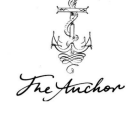

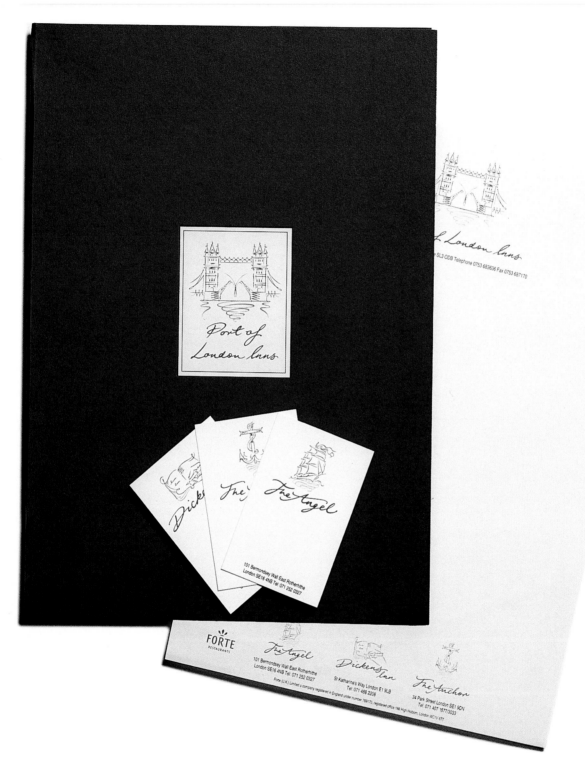

DESIGN FIRM   Hartmann & Mehler Designers GmbH
ART DIRECTOR   Roland Mehler
DESIGNER   Roland Mehler
ILLUSTRATOR   Roland Mehler
CLIENT   Steigenberger Consulting
PAPER/PRINTING   Enhance

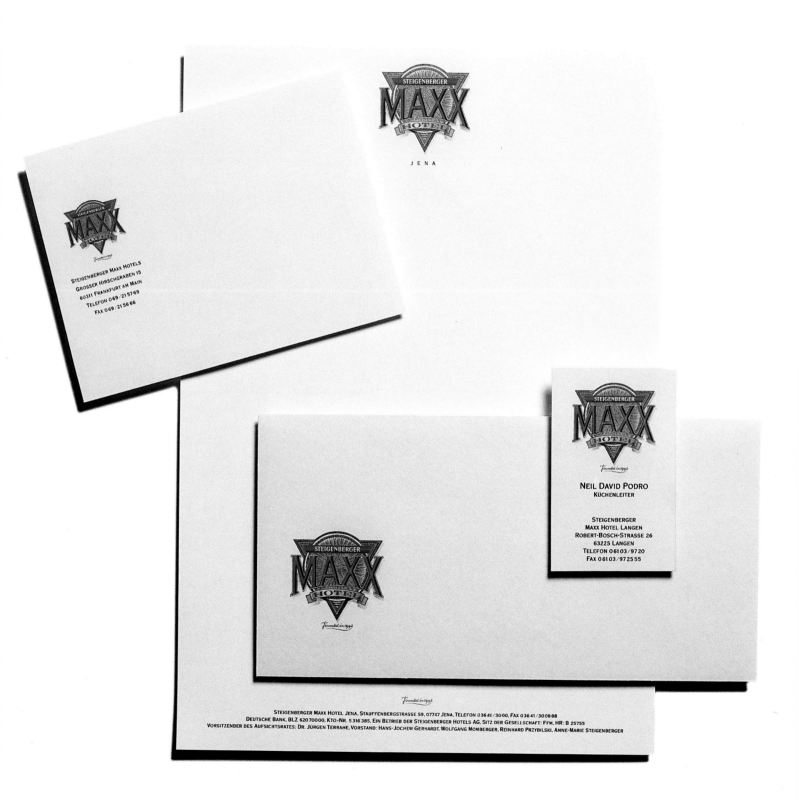

JENA

Neil David Podro
Küchenleiter

Steigenberger
Maxx Hotel Langen
Robert-Bosch-Strasse 26
63225 Langen
Telefon 06103/9720
Fax 06103/972555

Steigenberger Maxx Hotels
Grosser Hirschgraben 15
60311 Frankfurt am Main
Telefon 069/215769
Fax 069/215666

Steigenberger Maxx Hotel Jena, Stauffenbergstrasse 59, 07747 Jena, Telefon 03641/3000, Fax 03641/300888
Deutsche Bank, BLZ 62070000, Kto-Nr. 5316385, Ein Betrieb der Steigenberger Hotels AG. Sitz der Gesellschaft: Ffm, HR: B 25755
Vorsitzender des Aufsichtsrates: Dr. Jürgen Terrahe. Vorstand: Hans-Jochem Gerhardt, Wolfgang Momberger, Reinhard Przybilski, Anne-Marie Steigenberger

DESIGN FIRM   Hartmann & Mehler Designers GmbH
ART DIRECTOR   Roland Mehler
DESIGNER   Roland Mehler
ILLUSTRATOR   Roland Mehler
CLIENT   Steigenberger Maxx Hotels
PAPER/PRINTING   Croxley Heritage

DESIGN FIRM   Signum
ART DIRECTOR   Gregg Snyder
CLIENT   Snyder Appraisals & Analysis
PAPER/PRINTING Gilbert Environment

DESIGN FIRM   William Field Design
ART DIRECTOR   William Field
DESIGNER   William Field
CLIENT   Melanie Peters Real Estate

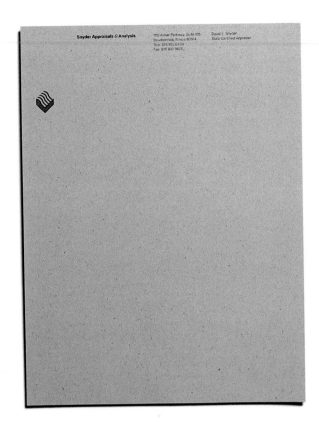

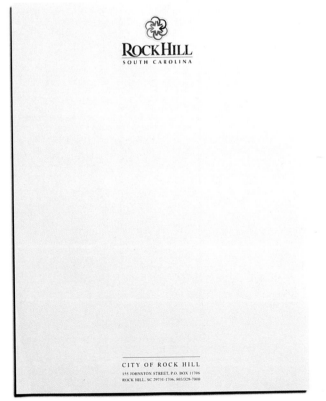

DESIGN FIRM   Debra Nichols Design
ART DIRECTOR   Debra Nichols
DESIGNER   Debra Nichols, Kelan Smith
CLIENT   Stein Kingsley Stein

DESIGN FIRM   Design/Joe Sonderman, Inc.
ART DIRECTOR   Tim Gilland
DESIGNER   Tim Gilland
CLIENT   City of Rock Hill, South Carolina
PAPER/PRINTING Strathmore Writing, 7 colors

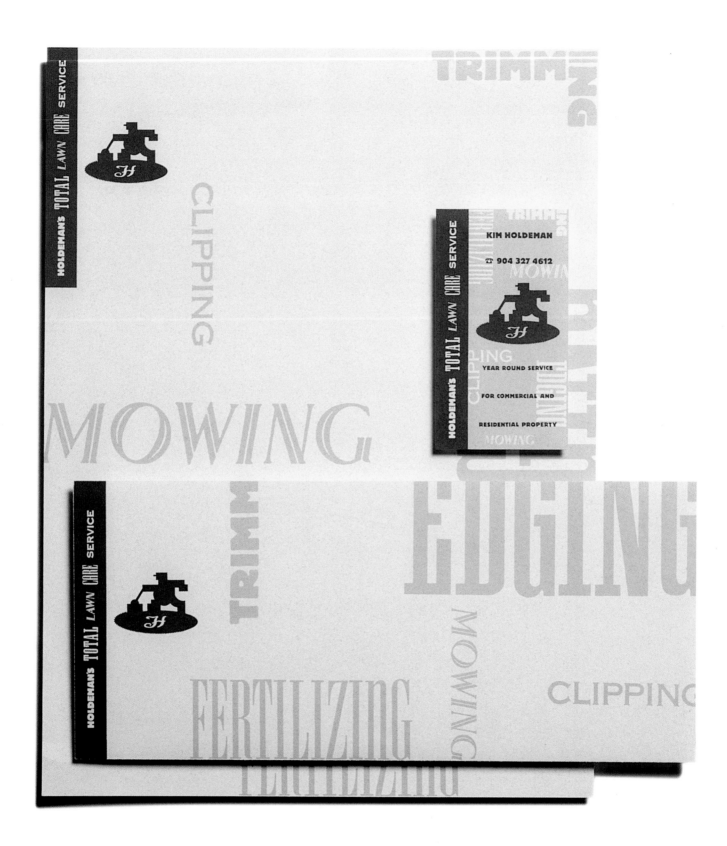

DESIGN FIRM   Love Packaging Group
ART DIRECTOR   Tracy Holdeman
DESIGNER   Tracy Holdeman
ILLUSTRATOR   Tracy Holdeman
CLIENT   Holdeman's Total Lawn Care Service

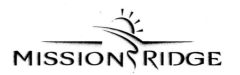

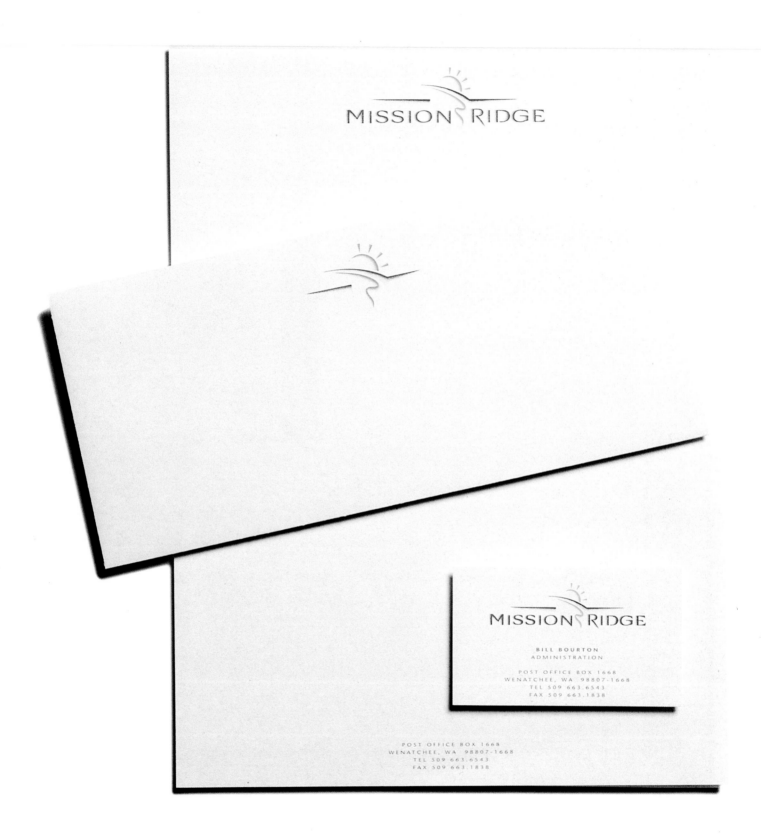

DESIGN FIRM   Hornall Anderson Design Works
ART DIRECTOR   Jack Anderson
DESIGNER   Jack Anderson, Cliff Chung, David Bates, Leo Raymundo, Denise Weir
CLIENT   Mission Ridge
PAPER/PRINTING   Simpson Environment

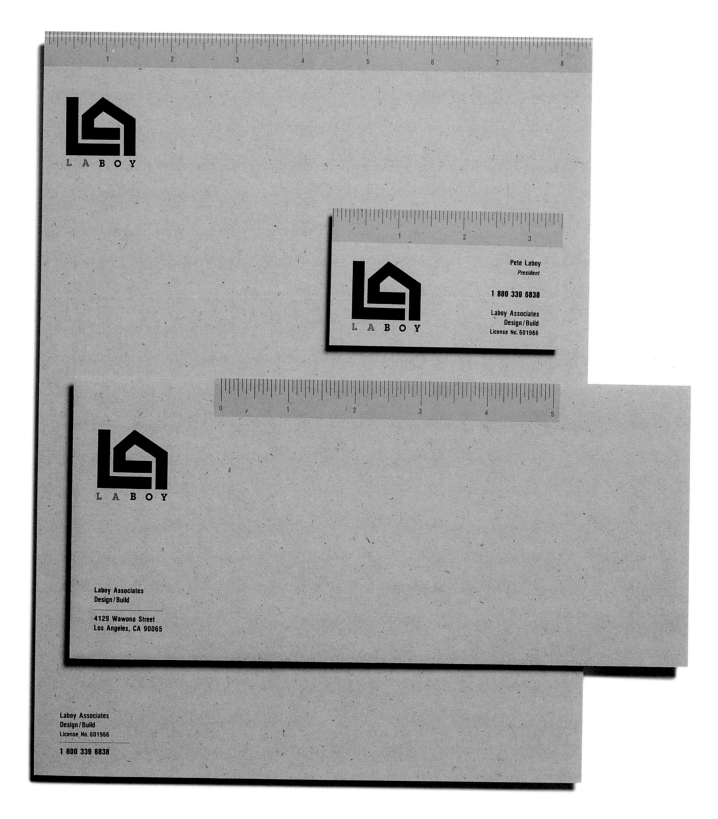

DESIGN FIRM	Adele Bass & Co. Design
ART DIRECTOR	Adele Bass
DESIGNER	Adele Bass
ILLUSTRATOR	Adele Bass
CLIENT	Laboy & Associates
PAPER/PRINTING	Kraft Speckletone, 3 colors

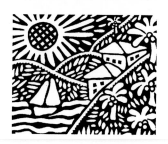

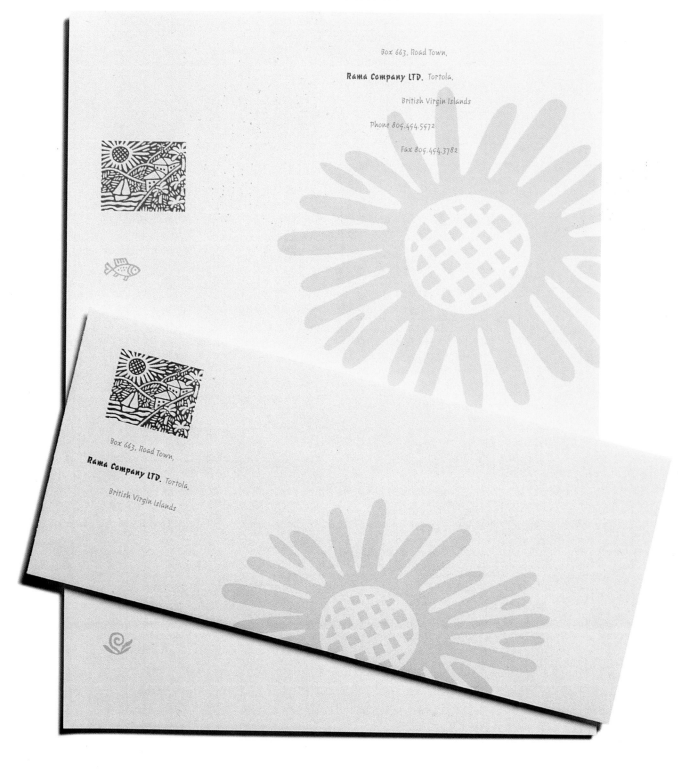

Box 663, Road Town,

Rama Company LTD. Tortola,

British Virgin Islands

Phone 809.494.5572

Fax 809.494.3782

Box 663, Road Town,

Rama Company LTD. Tortola,

British Virgin Islands

DESIGN FIRM	Schowalter² Design
ART DIRECTOR	Toni Schowalter
DESIGNER	Toni Schowalter
ILLUSTRATOR	Toni Schowalter
CLIENT	Rama Villas, Ltd.

DESIGN FIRM	Jenssen Design Pty. Limited
ART DIRECTOR	David Jenssen
DESIGNER	David Jenssen, Karen Lloyd-Jones
ILLUSTRATOR	Karen Lloyd-Jones
CLIENT	Homebush Bay Corporation
PAPER/PRINTING	Mohawk Poseidon High Finish

DESIGN FIRM	Michael Stanard, Inc.
ART DIRECTOR	Michael Stanard, Lisa Fingerhut
DESIGNER	Lisa Fingerhut, Julie Gleason
CLIENT	Hal Stanard Realtor

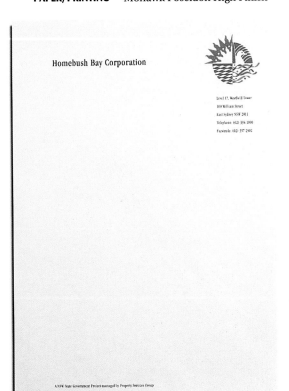

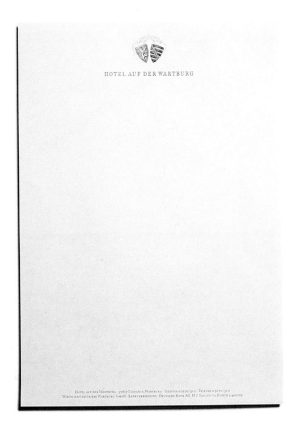

DESIGN FIRM	Hartmann & Mehler Designers GmbH
ART DIRECTOR	Roland Mehler
DESIGNER	Roland Mehler, Hans Bell
ILLUSTRATOR	Hans Bell
CLIENT	Hotel auf der Wartburg
PAPER/PRINTING	Croxley Heritage

DESIGN FIRM	William Field Design
ART DIRECTOR	Fred Cisneros
DESIGNER	Fred Cisneros
ILLUSTRATOR	Fred Cisneros
CLIENT	Custom Properties of Sante Fe
PAPER/PRINTING	Genesis

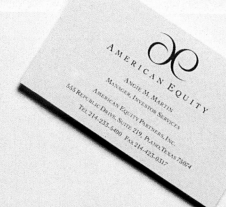

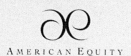

DESIGN FIRM Focus 2
ART DIRECTOR Todd Hart, Shawn Freeman
DESIGNER Todd Hart
ILLUSTRATOR Todd Hart
CLIENT American Equity
PAPER/PRINTING Protocol Writing

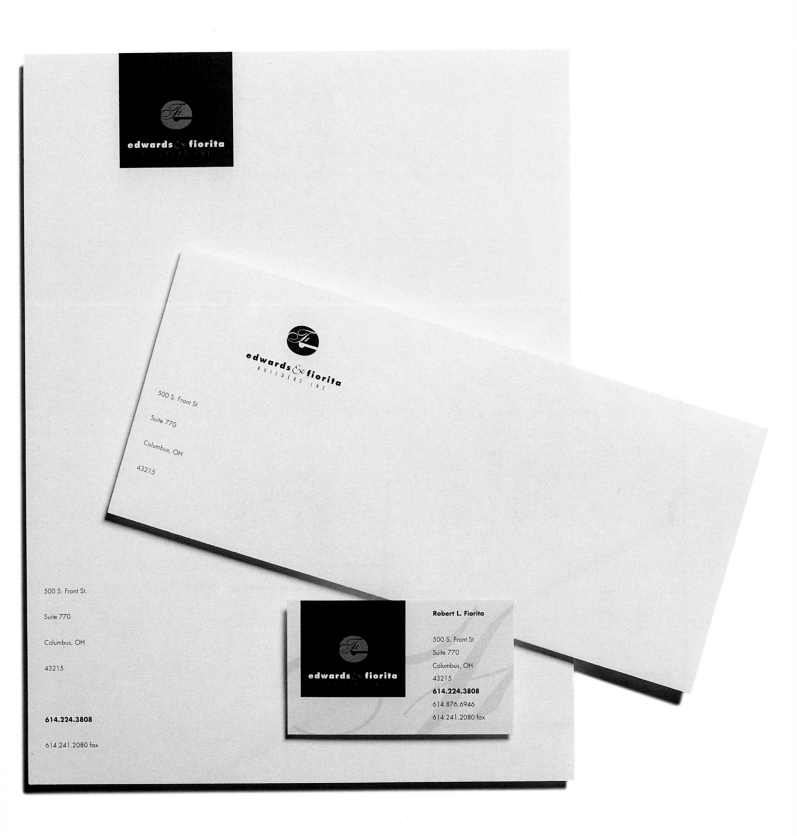

edwards & fiorita
BUILDERS INC.

edwards & fiorita
BUILDERS INC.

500 S. Front St.

Suite 770

Columbus, OH

43215

500 S. Front St.

Suite 770

Columbus, OH

43215

614.224.3808

614.241.2080 fax

Robert L. Fiorita

500 S. Front St.
Suite 770
Columbus, OH
43215
614.224.3808
614.876.6946
614.241.2080 fax

edwards & fiorita

DESIGN FIRM   Integrate Inc.
ART DIRECTOR   Stephen E. Quinn
DESIGNER   Darryl Levering
CLIENT   Edwards & Fiorita Builders

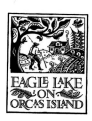

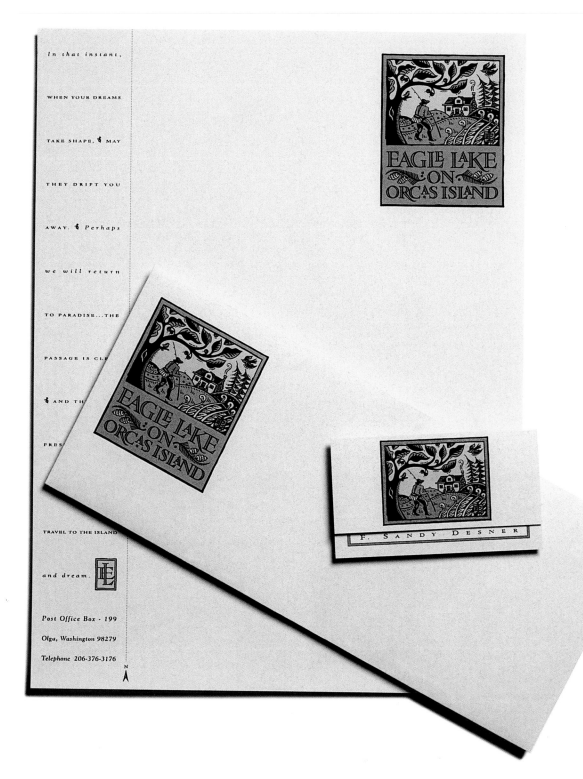

DESIGN FIRM	Hornall Anderson Design Works
ART DIRECTOR	Julia LaPine
DESIGNER	Julia LaPine, Denise Weir
ILLUSTRATOR	Julia LaPine
CLIENT	Eagle Lake on Orcas Island
PAPER/PRINTING	Simpson Environment Recycled

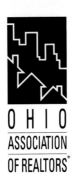

OHIO
ASSOCIATION
OF REALTORS®

DESIGN FIRM   Rickabaugh Graphics
ART DIRECTOR   Eric Rickabaugh
DESIGNER   Mark Krumel
CLIENT   Ohio Association of Realtors

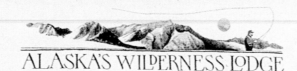

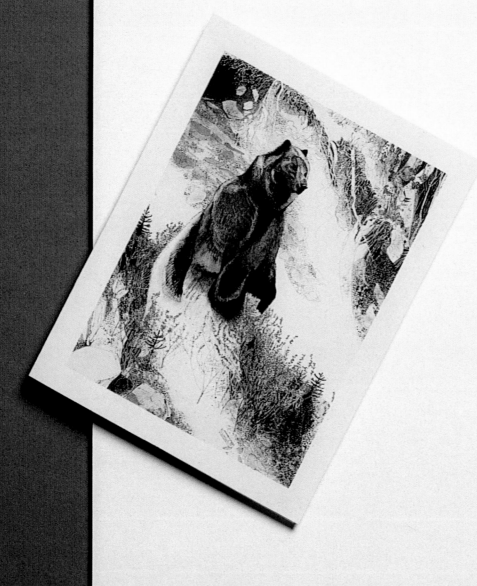

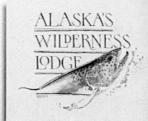

ALASKA'S
WILDERNESS
LODGE

LARRY GEPFERT

Wilderness Point
Port Alsworth, Alaska 99653

FOR RESERVATIONS &
INFORMATION
P.O. Box 700
Sumner, Washington 98390
206 863 6795
Toll-free 800 835 8032

Wilderness Point, Port Alsworth, Alaska 99653
FOR RESERVATIONS & INFORMATION – *P.O. Box 700, Sumner, Washington 98390, 206 863 6795, Toll-free 800 835 8032*

DESIGN FIRM	SHR Perceptual Management
ART DIRECTOR	Barry Shepard
DESIGNER	Douglas Reeder
ILLUSTRATOR	Jack Unruh
CLIENT	Alaska Wilderness Lodge
PAPER/PRINTING	Evergreen Birch

DESIGN FIRM David Carter Design
ART DIRECTOR Randall Hill,
Lori Wilson
DESIGNER Randall Hill,
ILLUSTRATOR Lori Wilson
Randall Hill,
Lori Wilson
CLIENT Hotel Principe Felipe

DESIGN FIRM The Weller Institute
for the Cure of
Design, Inc.
ART DIRECTOR Don Weller
DESIGNER Don Weller
ILLUSTRATOR Don Weller
CLIENT Lewis & Wolcott

DESIGN FIRM David Carter Design
ART DIRECTOR Sharon Lejune
DESIGNER Sharon Lejune
CLIENT Hotel New York, Euro
Disney, Paris

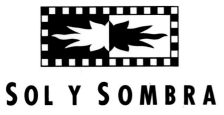

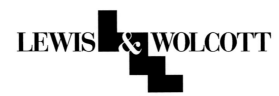

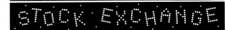

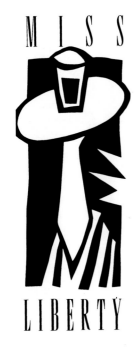

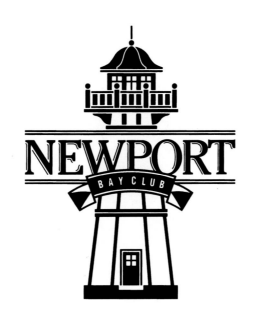

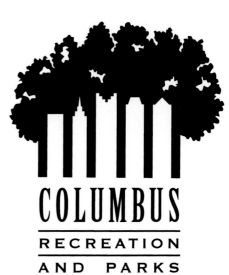

DESIGN FIRM David Carter Design
ART DIRECTOR Kevin Prejean,
Sharon Lejune
DESIGNER Kevin Prejean,
Sharon Lejune
ILLUSTRATOR Kevin Prejean,
Sharon Lejune
CLIENT Hotel New York,
Euro Disney, Paris

DESIGN FIRM David Carter Design
ART DIRECTOR Lori Wilson,
Randall Hill
DESIGNER Lori Wilson,
Randall Hill
ILLUSTRATOR Lori Wilson,
Randall Hill
CLIENT Disney's Newport Bay
Club Hotel

DESIGN FIRM Rickabaugh Graphics
ART DIRECTOR Eric Rickabaugh
DESIGNER Tina Zientarski
ILLUSTRATOR Tina Zientarski
CLIENT City of Columbus/
Recreation & Parks Dept.

DESIGN FIRM	David Carter Design	**DESIGN FIRM**	David Carter Design	**DESIGN FIRM**	Gary Greene Artworks
ART DIRECTOR	David Brashier	**ART DIRECTOR**	Lori Wilson	**ART DIRECTOR**	Gary Greene
DESIGNER	David Brashier	**DESIGNER**	Lori Wilson	**DESIGNER**	Gary Greene
ILLUSTRATOR	David Brashier	**ILLUSTRATOR**	Lori Wilson	**ILLUSTRATOR**	Gary Greene
CLIENT	Sequoia Lodge, Euro Disney, Paris	**CLIENT**	Inn of the Anasazi	**CLIENT**	Robin Eggeman/ Real Estate Broker

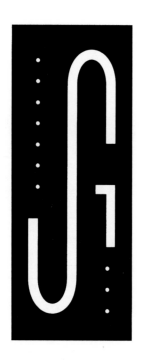

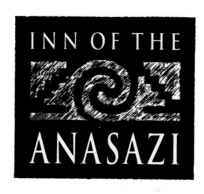

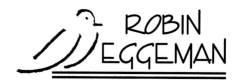

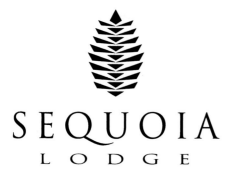

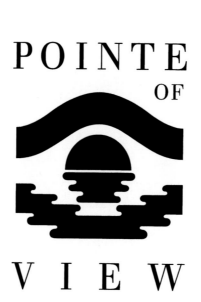

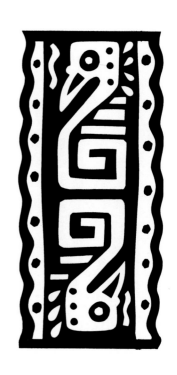

DESIGN FIRM	Lambert Design Studio	**DESIGN FIRM**	The Weller Institue for the Cure of Design, Inc.	**DESIGN FIRM**	David Carter Design
ART DIRECTOR	Christie Lambert			**ART DIRECTOR**	Lori Wilson
DESIGNER	Christie Lambert, Joy Cathey	**ART DIRECTOR**	Don Weller	**DESIGNER**	Lori Wilson
		DESIGNER	Don Weller	**ILLUSTRATOR**	Lori Wilson
CLIENT	The Jorgen Group	**CLIENT**	Pointe of View	**CLIENT**	Grand Hyatt, Bali

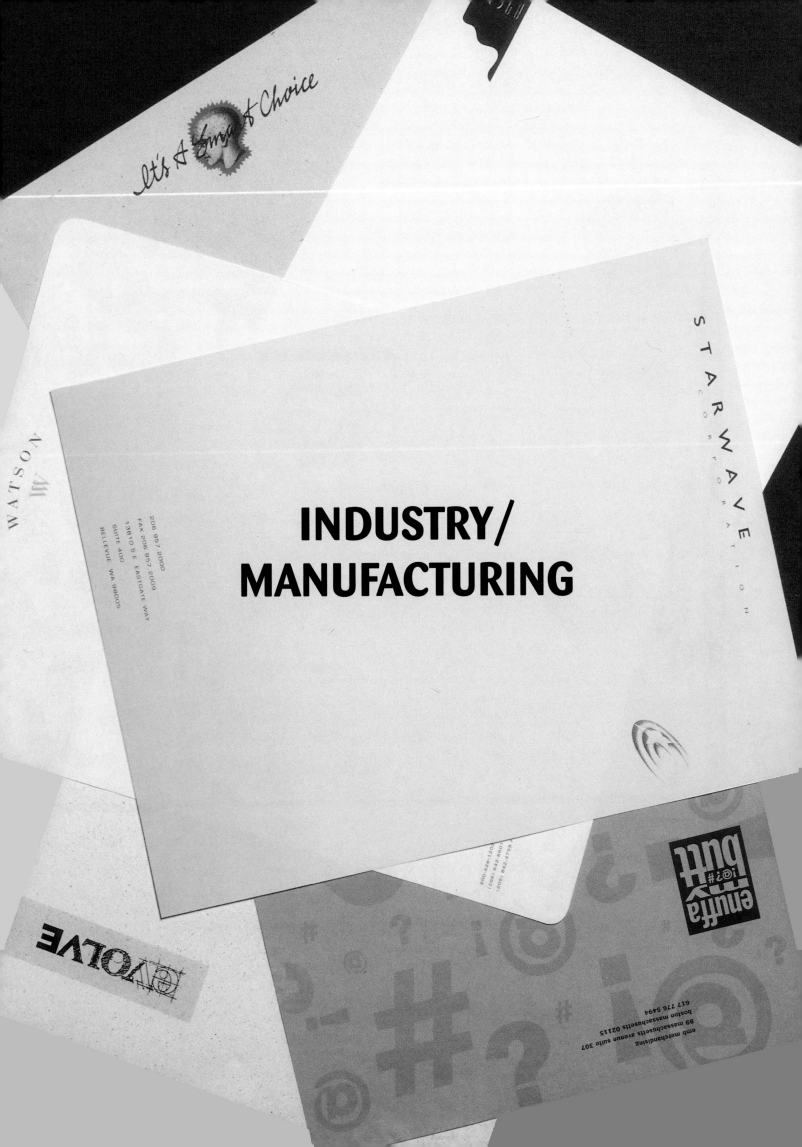

INDUSTRY/
MANUFACTURING

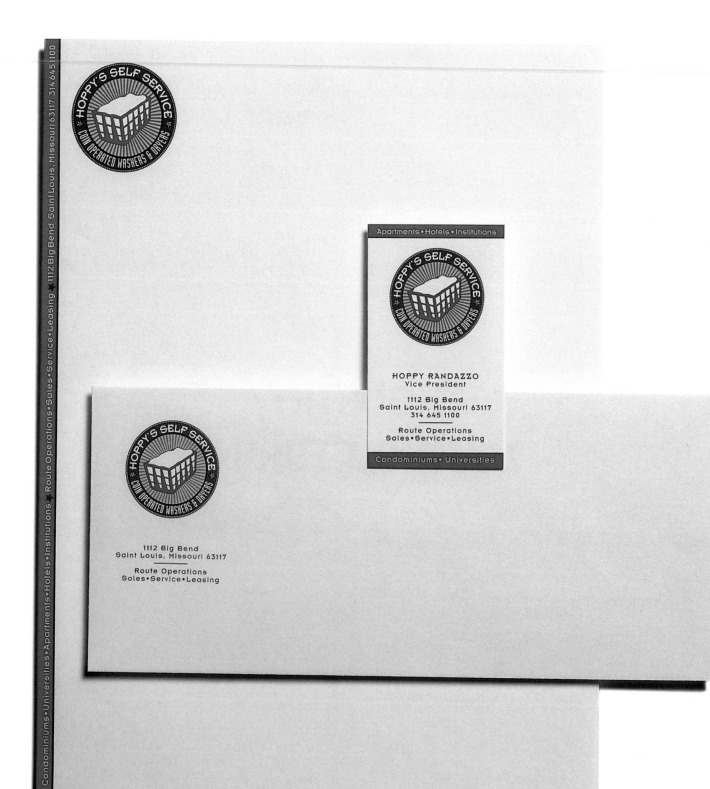

DESIGN FIRM   38 North

ART DIRECTOR   Nida Zada

CLIENT   Hoppy's Self Service

PAPER/PRINTING   3 colors

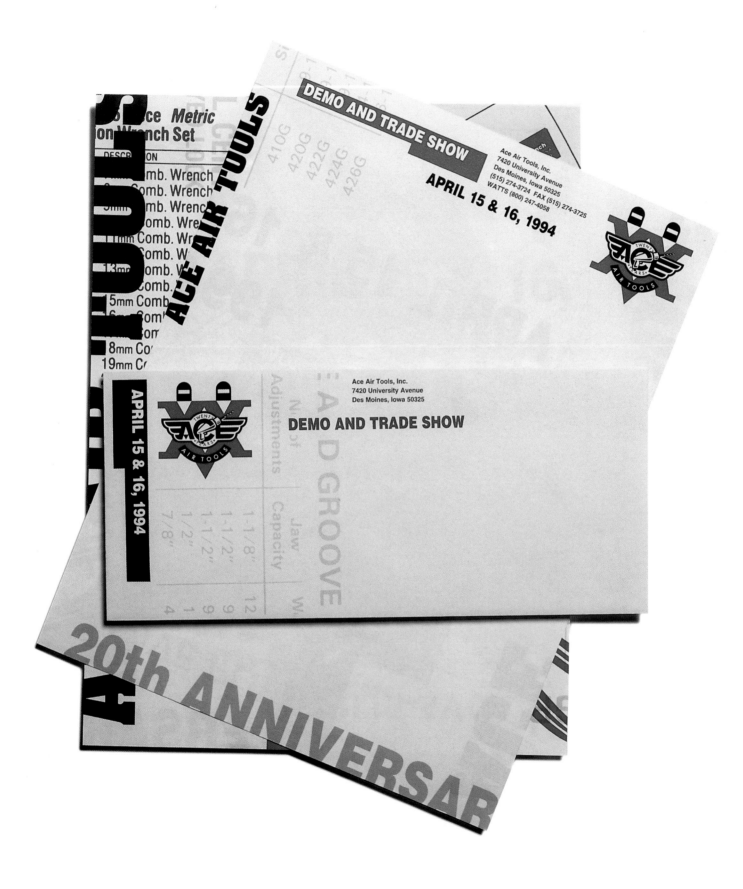

DESIGN FIRM	Sayles Graphic Design
ART DIRECTOR	John Sayles
DESIGNER	John Sayles
ILLUSTRATOR	John Sayles
CLIENT	Ace Air Tools
PAPER/PRINTING	James River, Graphika Vellum White, 2 colors

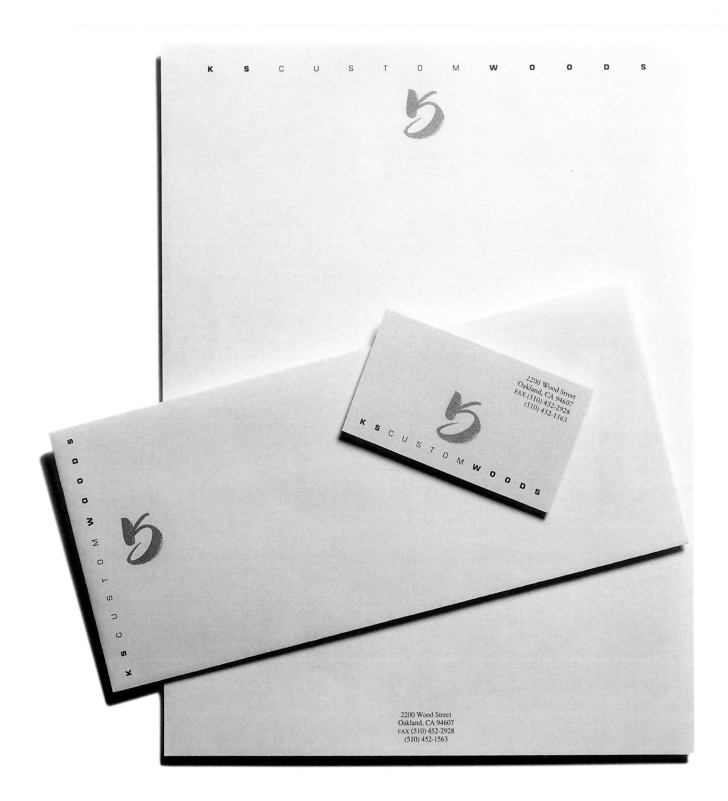

DESIGN FIRM	Dan Frazier Design
ART DIRECTOR	Dan Frazier
DESIGNER	Dan Frazier
ILLUSTRATOR	Sandra Bruce
CLIENT	KS Custom Woods
PAPER/PRINTING	Strathmore Writing

DESIGN FIRM	Carl Seltzer Design Office
ART DIRECTOR	Carl Seltzer
DESIGNER	Carl Seltzer, Luis Alvarado
CLIENT	Grace Cocoa

DESIGN FIRM	Riley Design Associates
ART DIRECTOR	Daniel Riley
DESIGNER	Daniel Riley
ILLUSTRATOR	Daniel Riley
CLIENT	The Bear Group, Inc.
PAPER/PRINTING	1 color, deboss, foil

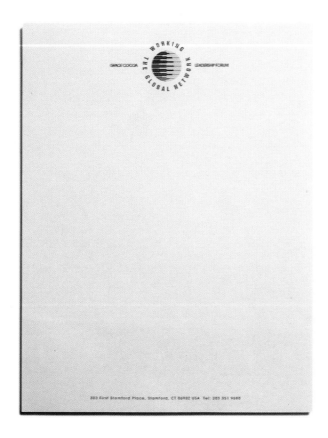

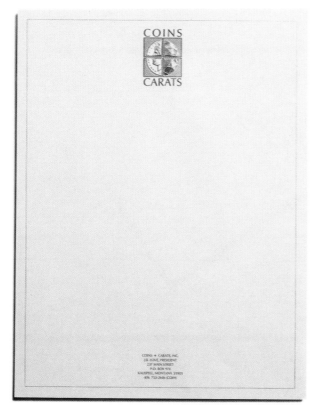

DESIGN FIRM	Ellen Kendrick Creative, Inc.
ART DIRECTOR /DESIGNER	Ellen K. Spalding
ILLUSTRATOR	Ellen K. Spalding
CLIENT	Coins & Carats, Inc.
PAPER/PRINTING	Neenah Classic Crest, black and metallic blue, silver and holographic foils, sculptured brass die

DESIGN FIRM	Elizabeth Resnick Design
ART DIRECTOR	Elizabeth Resnick
DESIGNER	Elizabeth Resnick
CLIENT	CIBA Corning Diagnostics Corporation
PAPER/PRINTING	Curtis Brightwater, 2 colors

ēShop

ēShop

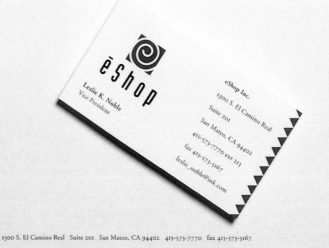

eShop

Leslie K. Noble
Vice President

eShop Inc.
1300 S. El Camino Real
Suite 201
San Mateo, CA 94402
415-573-7770 ext 213
fax 415-573-5167
leslie_noble@ink.com

1300 S. El Camino Real   Suite 201   San Mateo, CA 94402   415-573-7770   fax 415-573-5167

DESIGN FIRM	Mortensen Design
ART DIRECTOR	Gordon Mortensen
DESIGNER	Gordon Mortensen
CLIENT	eShop Inc.
PAPER/PRINTING	Classic Crest/Foreman

S T A R W A V E
C O R P O R A T I O N

S T A R W A V E
C O R P O R A T I O N

13810 S.E. EASTGATE WAY

SUITE 400

BELLEVUE, WA 98005

206.957.2000

FAX 206.957.2009

13810 S.E. EASTGATE WAY

SUITE 400

BELLEVUE, WA 98005

S T A R W A V E
C O R P O R A T I O N

RICHARD O'KEEFE
SENIOR SYSTEMS ENGINEER
206.957.2704
13810 S.E. EASTGATE WAY
SUITE 400
BELLEVUE, WA 98005
FAX 206.957.2009
RICHARD0@STARWAVE.COM

DESIGN FIRM   Hornall Anderson Design Works
ART DIRECTOR   Jack Anderson
DESIGNER   Jack Anderson, David Bates, Lian Ng, Denise Weir
ILLUSTRATOR   John Fretz
CLIENT   Starwave Corporation
PAPER/PRINTING   Neenah Classic Crest, embossed

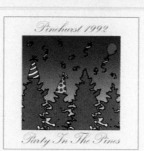

DESIGN FIRM	Beauchamp Design
ART DIRECTOR	Michele Beauchamp
DESIGNER	Michele Beauchamp
CLIENT	Hunter
PAPER/PRINTING	Classic Crest

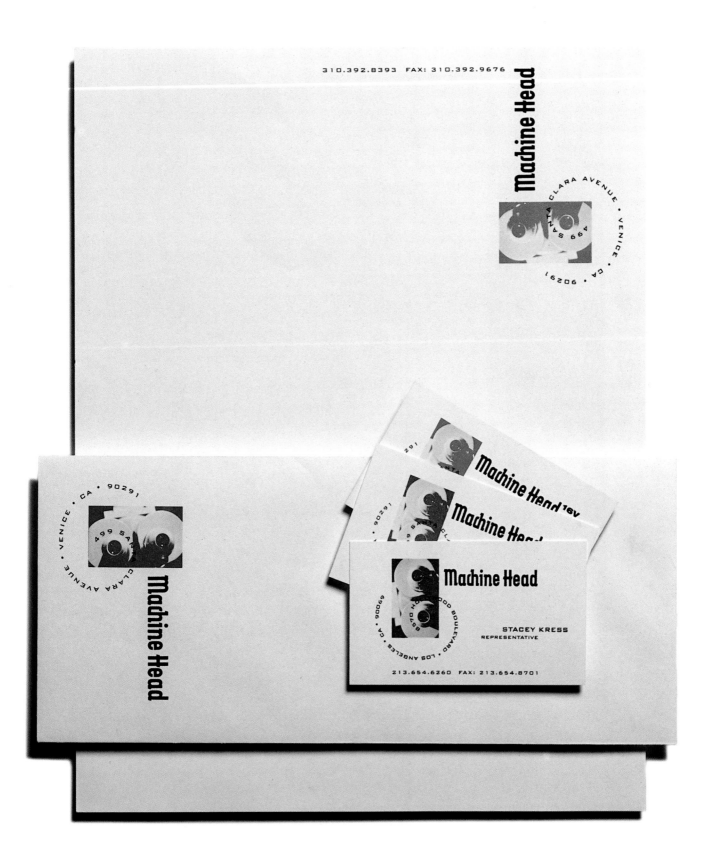

DESIGN FIRM   Lorna Stovall Design
ART DIRECTOR   Lorna Stovall
DESIGNER   Lorna Stovall
CLIENT   Machine Head
PAPER/PRINTING   Starwhite Vicksberg

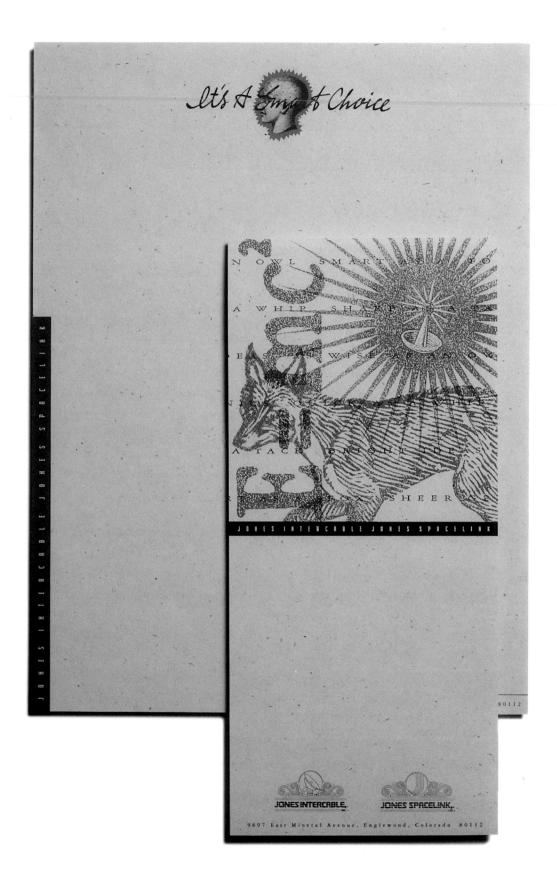

DESIGN FIRM	Vaughn Wedeen Creative
ART DIRECTOR	Steve Wedeen, Daniel Michael Flynn
DESIGNER	Daniel Michael Flynn
ILLUSTRATOR	Bill Gerhold
CLIENT	Jones Intercable
PAPER/PRINTING	French Speckletone Old Green text.

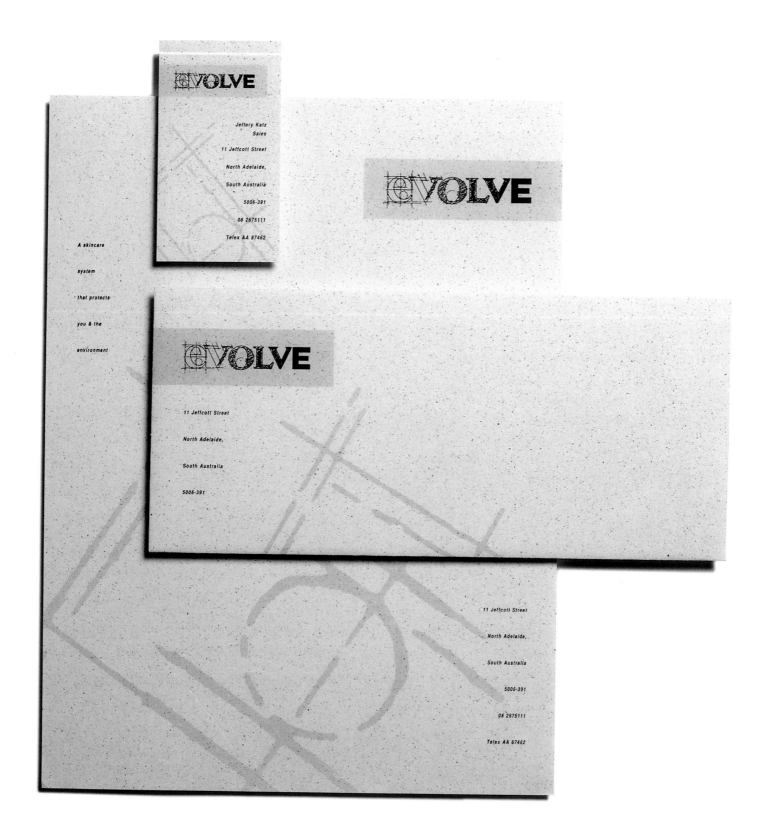

DESIGN FIRM E.M. Design
DESIGNER Elise Moyer
ILLUSTRATOR Elise Moyer
CLIENT Evolve

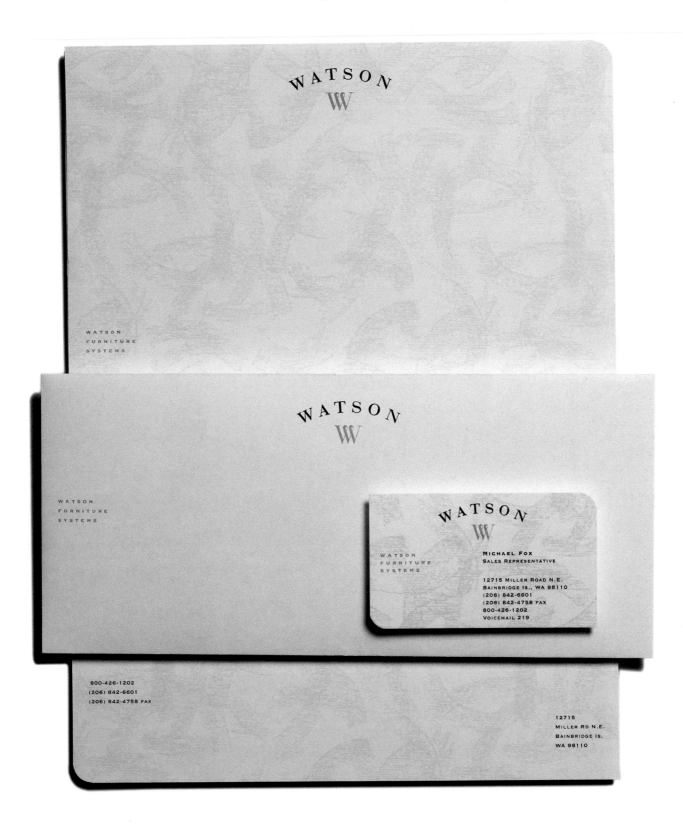

DESIGN FIRM	Hornall Anderson Design Works
ART DIRECTOR	Jack Anderson
DESIGNER	Jack Anderson, Mary Hermes, Leo Raymundo
ILLUSTRATOR	Yutaka Sasaki
CLIENT	Watson Furniture

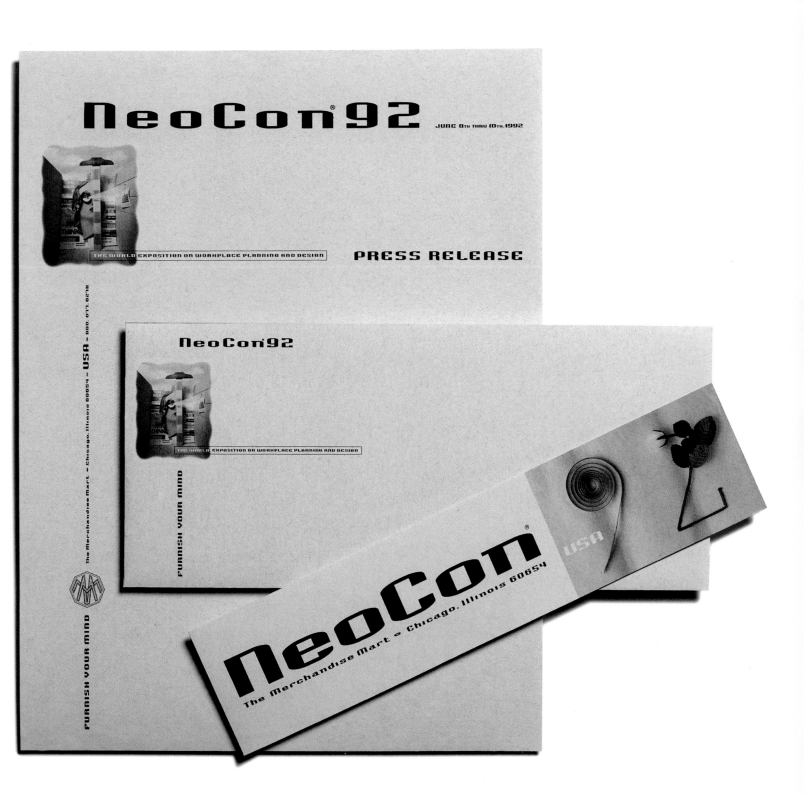

DESIGN FIRM   Segura Inc.
ART DIRECTOR   Carlos Segura
DESIGNER   Carlos Segura
PHOTOGRAPHY   Geof Kern
CLIENT   Merchandise Mart
PAPER/PRINTING   Argus

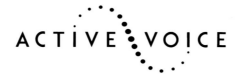

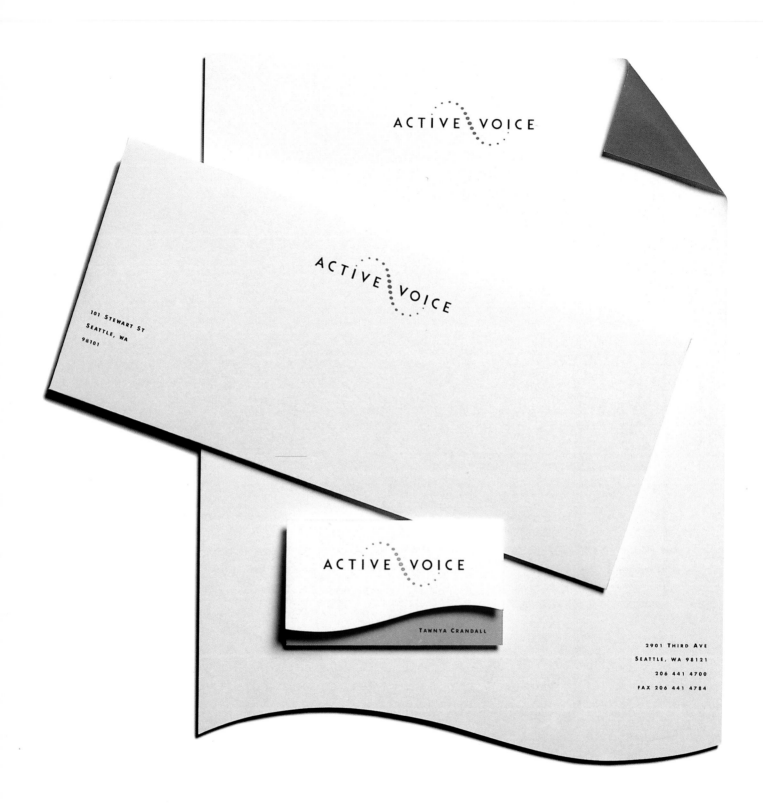

DESIGN FIRM	Hornall Anderson Design Works
ART DIRECTOR	Jack Anderson
DESIGNER	Jack Anderson, Julia LaPine, David Bates, Mary Hermes, Lian Ng
CLIENT	Active Voice
PAPER/PRINTING	Starwhite Vicksburg Tiara Smoothtext

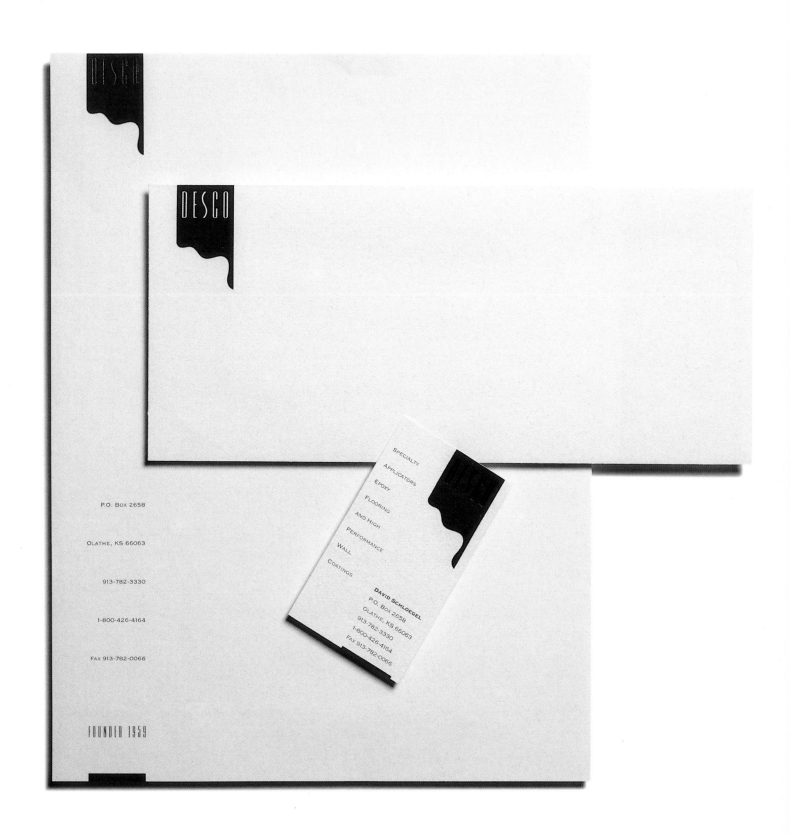

DESIGN FIRM	Muller & Company
ART DIRECTOR	David Shultz
DESIGNER	David Shultz
CLIENT	Desco Coatings, Inc.
PAPER/PRINTING	Cross Pointe, Passport/LaGue

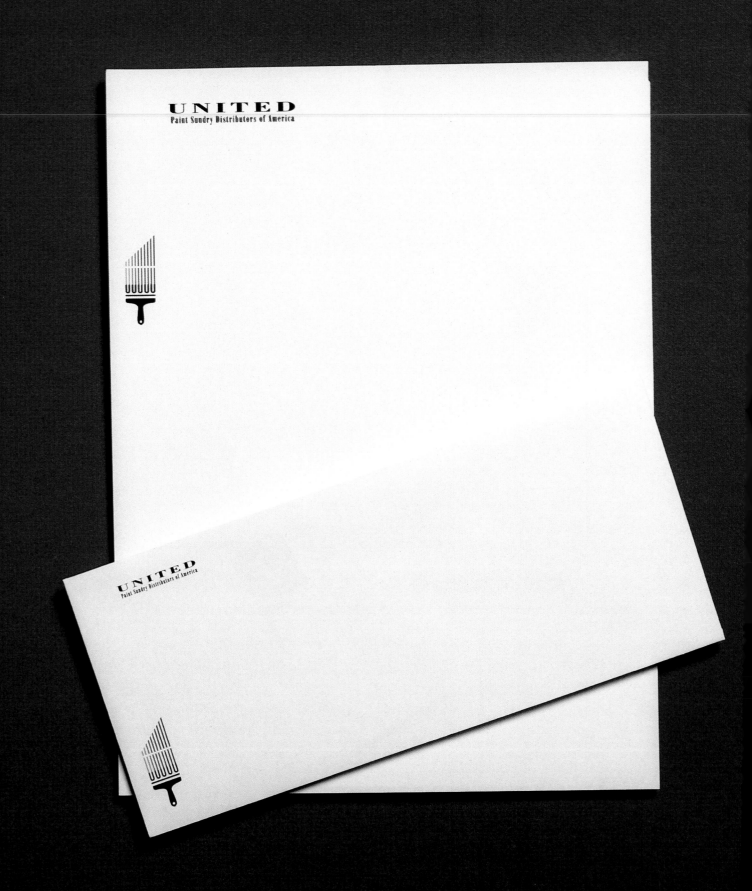

DESIGN FIRM	James Clark Design Images
ART DIRECTOR	James Clark
DESIGNER	James Clark, Linda Sewell
ILLUSTRATOR	Linda Sewell
CLIENT	United Paint Sundry Distributor of America

DESIGN FIRM   Visual Dialogue
ART DIRECTOR   Fritz Klaetke
DESIGNER   Fritz Klaetke, Karen Striebeck
CLIENT   EMB Merchandising
PAPER/PRINTING   French Durotone, construction gold

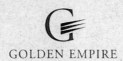

GOLDEN EMPIRE

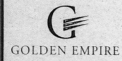

GOLDEN EMPIRE

Jim Ruiter
Buyer

Wholesalers & Distributors
810 Oak Street
Chico, CA 95928
916.342.1857
· 916.342.8097
800.342.2639

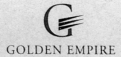

GOLDEN EMPIRE

Wholesalers & Distributors
810 Oak Street
Chico, CA 95928
916.342.1857
916.342.8097

DESIGN FIRM   Image Group
ART DIRECTOR   David Zavala, Eric Sanchez
DESIGNER   David Zavala, Eric Sanchez
CLIENT   Golden Empire Distributing
PAPER/PRINTING   Classic Crest Recycled

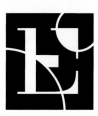

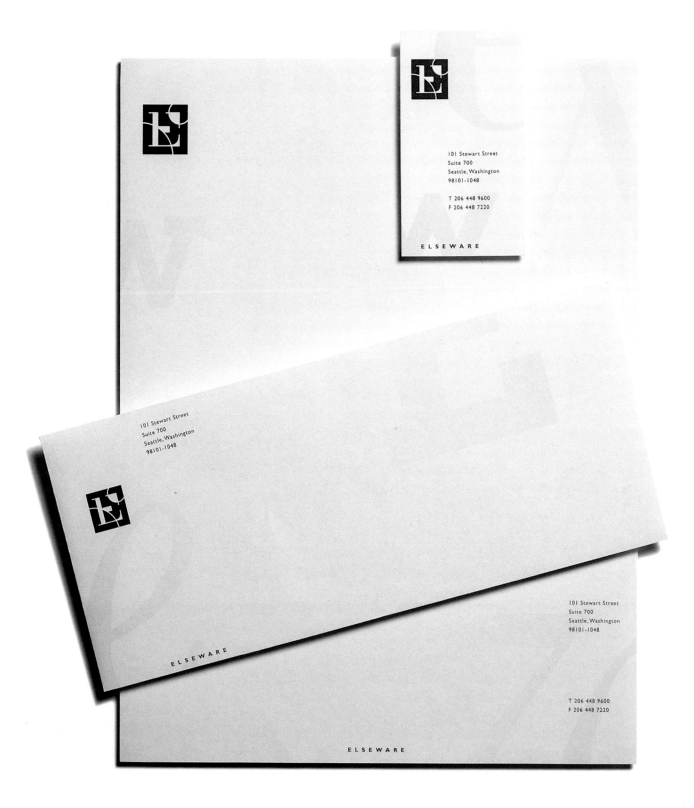

101 Stewart Street
Suite 700
Seattle, Washington
98101-1048

T 206 448 9600
F 206 448 7220

ELSEWARE

101 Stewart Street
Suite 700
Seattle, Washington
98101-1048

ELSEWARE

101 Stewart Street
Suite 700
Seattle, Washington
98101-1048

T 206 448 9600
F 206 448 7220

ELSEWARE

DESIGN FIRM	Hornall Anderson Design Works
ART DIRECTOR	Jack Anderson
DESIGNER	Jack Anderson, Debra Hampton, Leo Raymundo
CLIENT	Elseware Corporation
PAPER/PRINTING	Neenah Classic Crest

GRANITE SOFTWARE

GRANITE SOFTWARE

300 EAST MAIN STREET MILFORD, MA 01757

300 EAST MAIN STREET MILFORD, MA 01757 TEL 508 634.3200 FAX 508 634.8381

DESIGN FIRM	Steven Gulla Graphic Design
ART DIRECTOR	Steven Gulla
DESIGNER	Steven Gulla
CLIENT	Granite Software
PAPER/PRINTING	Passport Pumice

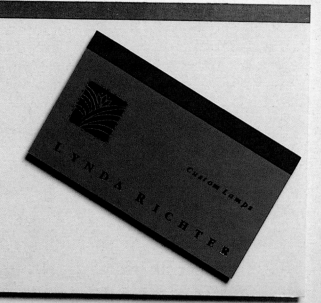

LYNDA RICHTER

Custom Lamps

16904 McCourtney Rd.
Grass Valley,
California 95949

16904 McCourtney Rd.
Grass Valley,
California 95949
(916) 477-1858

DESIGN FIRM   LeeAnn Brook Design
ART DIRECTOR   LeeAnn Brook
DESIGNER   LeeAnn Brook
ILLUSTRATOR   LeeAnn Brook
CLIENT   Lynda Richter
PAPER/PRINTING   Classic Laid Millstone, foil emboss

DESIGN FIRM	Aslan Grafix	DESIGN FIRM	Armin Vogt	DESIGN FIRM	Hornall Anderson
ART DIRECTOR	Tracy Grubbs		Partner/Corporate &		Design Works
DESIGNER	Tracy Grubbs		Packaging Design	ART DIRECTOR	Jack Anderson
CLIENT	Aus-tech Mold &	ART DIRECTOR	Armin Vogt	DESIGNER	Jack Anderson,
	Design	DESIGNER	Armin Vogt		Cliff Chung,
		CLIENT	Electro Bauer AG		David Bates
				CLIENT	Nordstrom

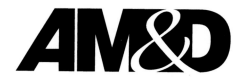

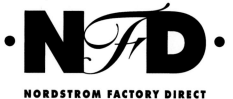

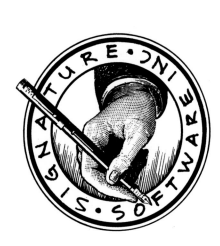

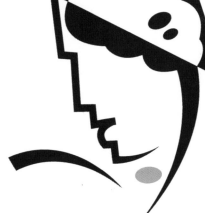

DESIGN FIRM	Strategic	DESIGN FIRM	Porter, Matjasich &	DESIGN FIRM	Earl Gee Design
	Communications		Associates	ART DIRECTOR	Earl Gee
ART DIRECTOR	Charles Drummond,	ART DIRECTOR	Carol Matjasich	DESIGNER	Earl Gee
	Rick Tharp	DESIGNER	Robert Rausch	ILLUSTRATOR	Earl Gee
DESIGNER	Designer Jana Heer,	ILLUSTRATOR	Maria Stroster	CLIENT	Sun Microsystems –
	Rick Tharp	CLIENT	Abbott Laboratories		FIT @ SUN (employee
CLIENT	Signature		Diagnostics Division		fitness center)
	Software, Inc.				

DESIGN FIRM	Earl Gee Design
ART DIRECTOR	Earl Gee
DESIGNER	Earl Gee, Fani Chung
ILLUSTRATOR	Earl Gee
CLIENT	Sun Microsystems "SMART" Program

DESIGN FIRM	Turner Design
ART DIRECTOR	Bert Turner
DESIGNER	Bert Turner
ILLUSTRATOR	Bert Turner
CLIENT	I-Ware

DESIGN FIRM	Armin Vogt Partner/Corporate & Packaging Design
ART DIRECTOR	Armin Vogt
DESIGNER	Armin Vogt
CLIENT	Grafothek Basel

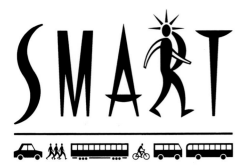

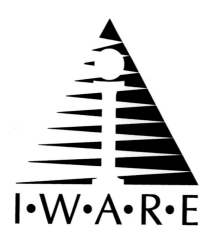

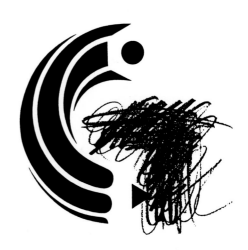

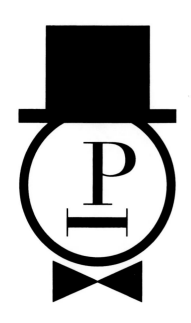

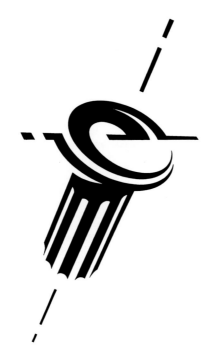

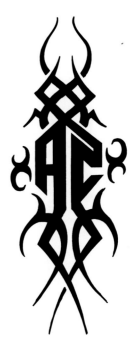

DESIGN FIRM	Ron Kellum Inc.
ART DIRECTOR	Ron Kellum
DESIGNER	Ron Kellum
CLIENT	Topix

DESIGN FIRM	Hornall Anderson Design Works
ART DIRECTOR	Jack Anderson
DESIGNER	Jack Anderson, David Bates, Cliff Chung
CLIENT	Microsoft Corporation

DESIGN FIRM	Modern Dog
ART DIRECTOR	Brent Turner, Luke Edgar
DESIGNER	Michael Strassburger
ILLUSTRATOR	Michael Strassburger
CLIENT	K2 Snowboards

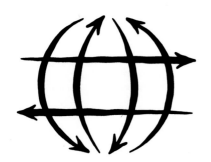

$$\left[\begin{array}{c} \text{WORLDWIDE} \\ \text{OPERATIONS} \end{array} \right]$$

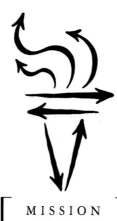

$$\left[\begin{array}{c} \text{MISSION} \\ \text{STATEMENT} \end{array} \right]$$

$$\left[\begin{array}{c} \text{STRATEGIC} \\ \text{INITIATIVES} \end{array} \right]$$

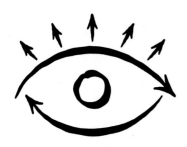

$$\left[\text{VALUES} \right]$$

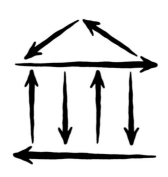

$$\left[\begin{array}{c} \text{ARCHITECTURAL} \\ \text{DIRECTION} \end{array} \right]$$

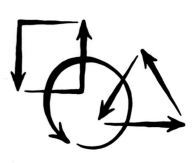

$$\left[\text{COMPONENTS} \right]$$

DESIGN FIRM	Earl Gee Design
ART DIRECTOR	Earl Gee
DESIGNER	Earl Gee, Fani Chung
ILLUSTRATOR	Earl Gee
CLIENT	Sun Microsystems Worldwide Operations

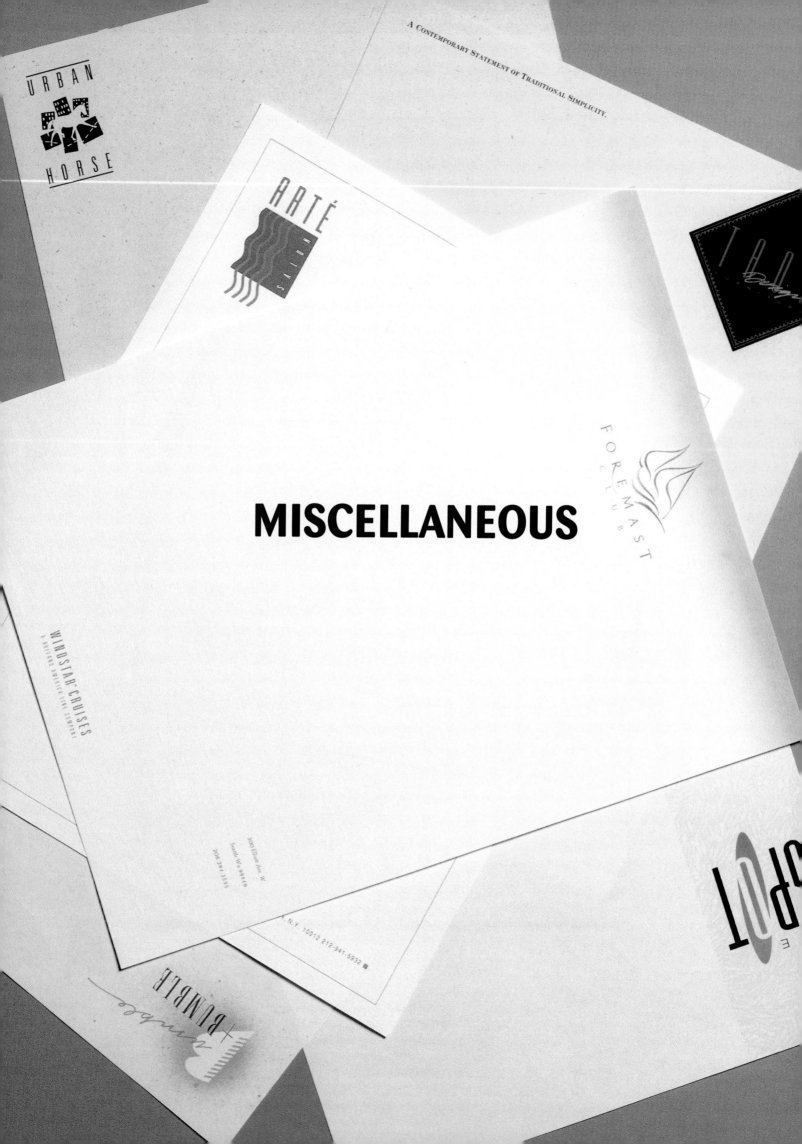

MISCELLANEOUS

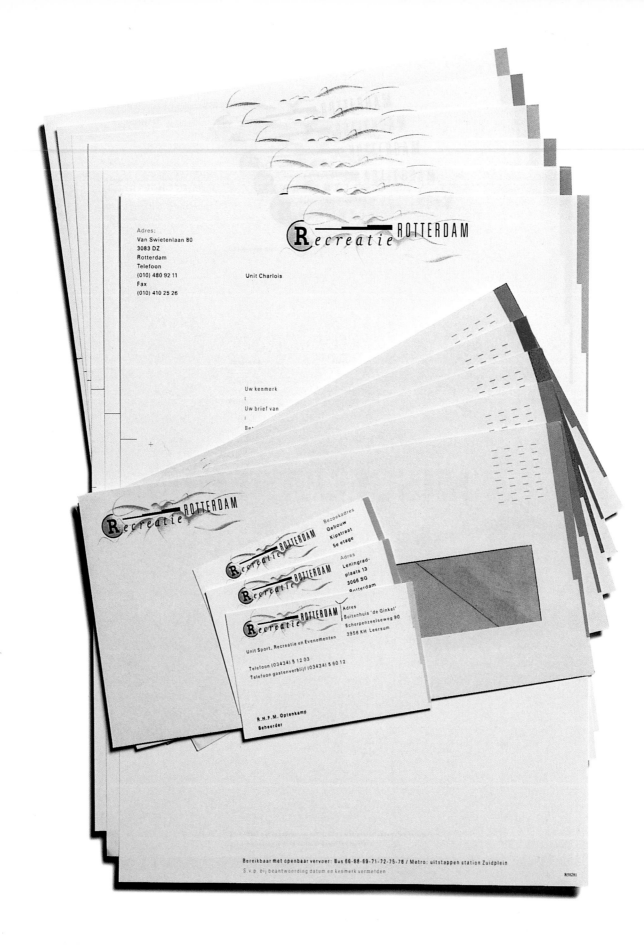

DESIGN FIRM	Proforma Rotterdam
ART DIRECTOR	Aadvan Pommelen
DESIGNER	Gert Jan Rooijakkers
CLIENT	Recreative Rotterdam
PAPER/PRINTING	Bankpost

DESIGN FIRM	Sayles Graphic Design
ART DIRECTOR	John Sayles
DESIGNER	John Sayles
ILLUSTRATOR	John Sayles
CLIENT	Adam Katzman
PAPER/PRINTING	James River, Gray Parchment

DESIGN FIRM	Mike Salisbury Communications
ART DIRECTOR	Mike Salisbury
DESIGNER	Mike Salisbury
ILUSTRATOR	Mike Salisbury
CLIENT	Mike Salisbury
PAPER/PRINTING	Recycled

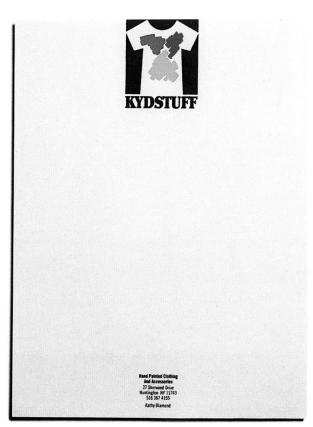

DESIGN FIRM	The Green House
ART DIRECTOR	Brian Green
DESIGNER	Brian Green
ILLUSTRATOR	Brian Green
CLIENT	Crucial Films
PAPER/PRINTING	Connoseur, 1 color, foil thermography

DESIGN FIRM	Handler Design Ltd.
ART DIRECTOR	Bruce Handler
DESIGNER	Bruce Handler
ILLUSTRATOR	Bruce Handler
CLIENT	Kidstuff
PAPER/PRINTING	Curtis Flannel

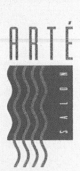

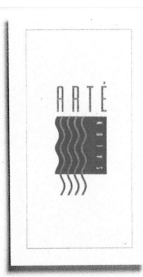

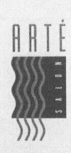

Arté Salon, 284 Lafayette Street, New York, N.Y. 10012

Arté Salon, 284 Lafayette Street New York, N.Y. 10012 212-941-5932

DESIGN FIRM   Platinum Design
ART DIRECTOR   Sandy Quinn
DESIGNER   Kathleen Phelps, Sandy Quinn
ILLUSTRATOR   Kathleen Phelps
CLIENT   Arté Salon
PAPER/PRINTING   Strathmore Writing Laid

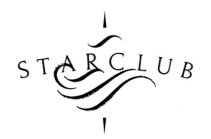

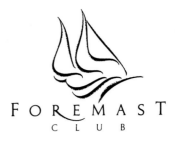

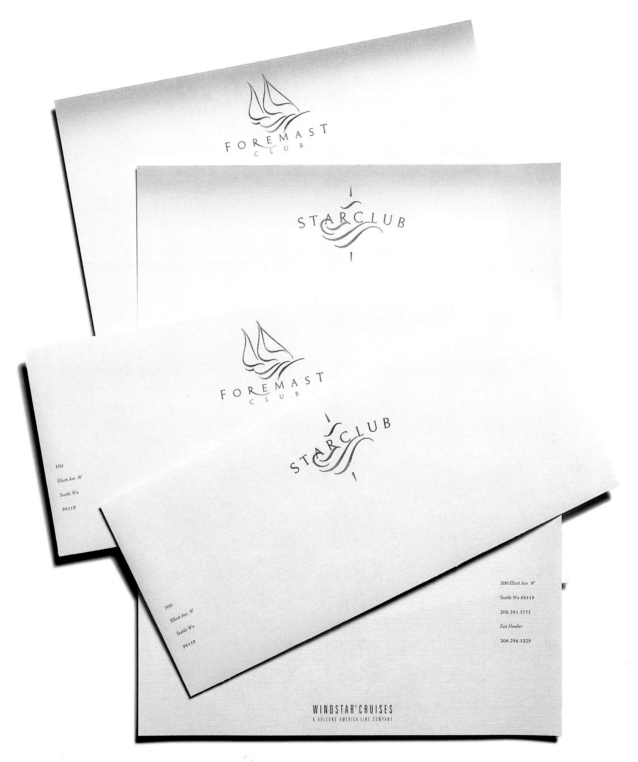

DESIGN FIRM	Hornall Anderson Design Works
ART DIRECTOR	Jack Anderson
DESIGNER	Jack Anderson, Denise Weir, Lian Ng, David Bates
ILLUSTRATOR	Glenn Yoshiyama
CLIENT	Windstar Cruises
PAPER/PRINTING	Neenah Classic Laid

DESIGN FIRM   Proforma Rotterdam
ART DIRECTOR   Mirjam v.d. Haspel
DESIGNER   Michael Snitker
CLIENT   Kop van Zuid
PAPER/PRINTING   Bankpost

Frankenallee 24, Postfach 1148, D-6233 Kelkheim
Telefon 06195/73067, Telefax 06195/73060

AMPRO

Elektro
Akustik
GmbH

AMPRO

Elektro
Akustik
GmbH

HANS-PETER EHL

Geschäftsführer

AMPRO
Elektroakustik GmbH
Frankenallee 24
D-6233 Kelkheim
Telefon 06195/73067
Telefax 06195/73060

Geschäftsführer Hans-Peter Ehl
AG Königstein/Ts. HRB Nr. 2660

Postgiroamt Frankfurt/M. (BLZ 50010060) Kto. 419611-603
Volksbank Kelkheim e.G. (BLZ 50092200) Kto. 50011305

DESIGN FIRM	Hartmann & Mehler Designers GmbH
ART DIRECTOR	Roland Mehler
DESIGNER	Roland Mehler
ILLUSTRATOR	Roland Mehler
CLIENT	Ampro
PAPER/PRINTING	Croxley Heritage

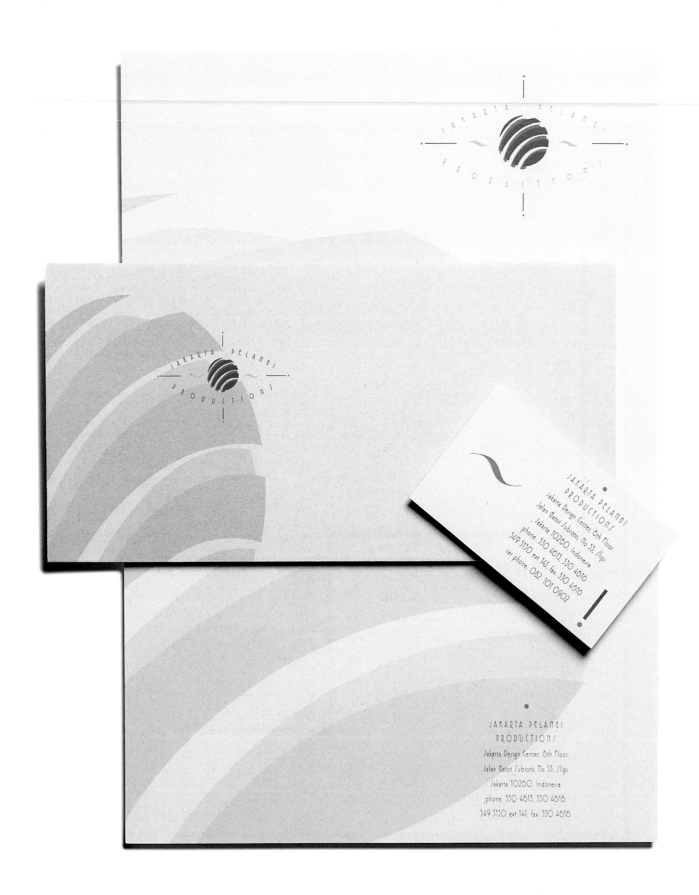

DESIGN FIRM   Wigwam Designs Pte. Ltd.
ART DIRECTOR   Rustam Moh'd
DESIGNER   Rustam Moh'd
CLIENT   Jakarta Pelangi Productions

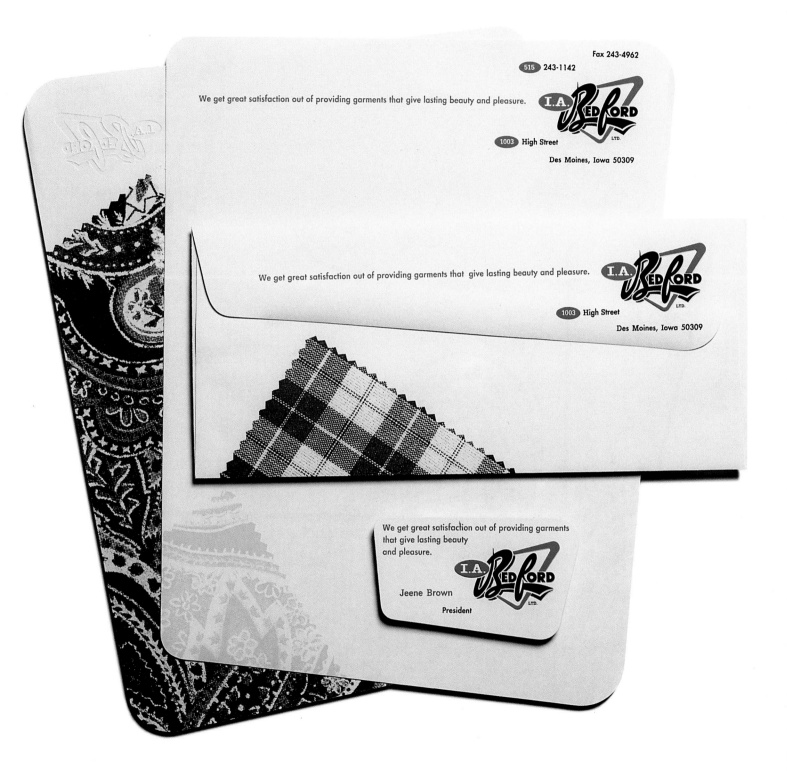

We get great satisfaction out of providing garments that give lasting beauty and pleasure.

I.A. Bedford LTD.

Fax 243-4962

515 243-1142

1003 High Street

Des Moines, Iowa 50309

We get great satisfaction out of providing garments that give lasting beauty and pleasure.

I.A. Bedford LTD.

1003 High Street

Des Moines, Iowa 50309

We get great satisfaction out of providing garments that give lasting beauty and pleasure.

Jeene Brown

President

I.A. Bedford LTD.

DESIGN FIRM Sayles Graphic Design
ART DIRECTOR John Sayles
DESIGNER John Sayles
ILLUSTRATOR John Sayles
CLIENT I.A. Bedford
PAPER/PRINTING James River, Graphika Vellum Natural, 3 colors

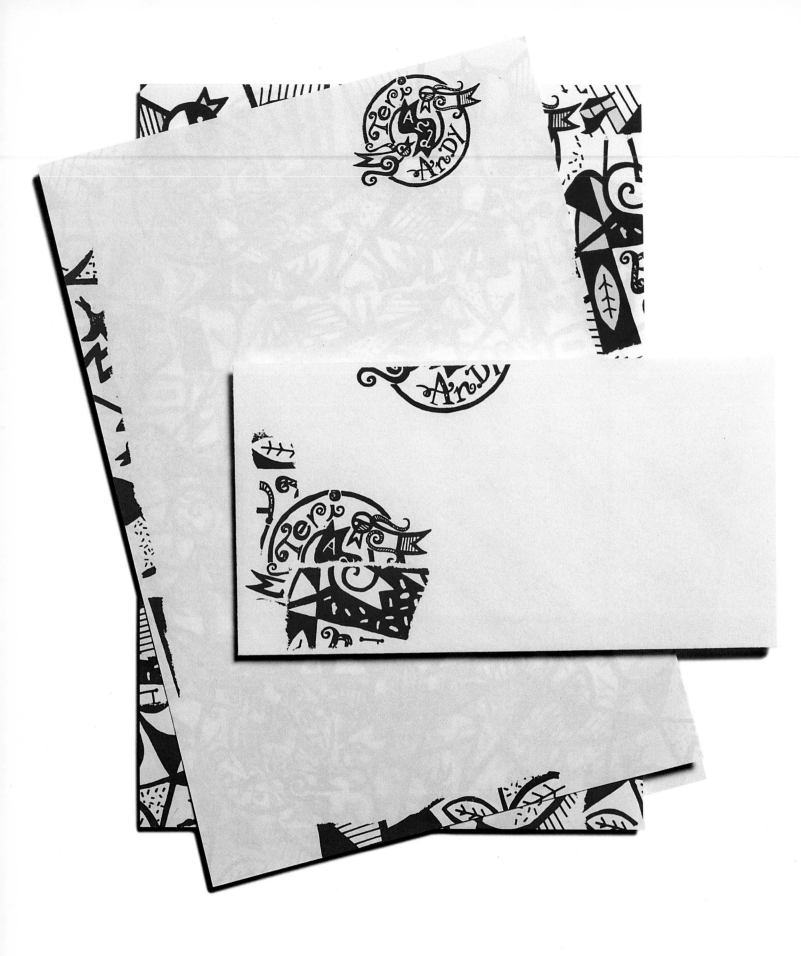

DESIGN FIRM	Sayles Graphic Design
ART DIRECTOR	John Sayles
DESIGNER	John Sayles
ILLUSTRATOR	John Sayles
CLIENT	Teri & Andy TeBockhorst
PAPER/PRINTING	Hammermill, White

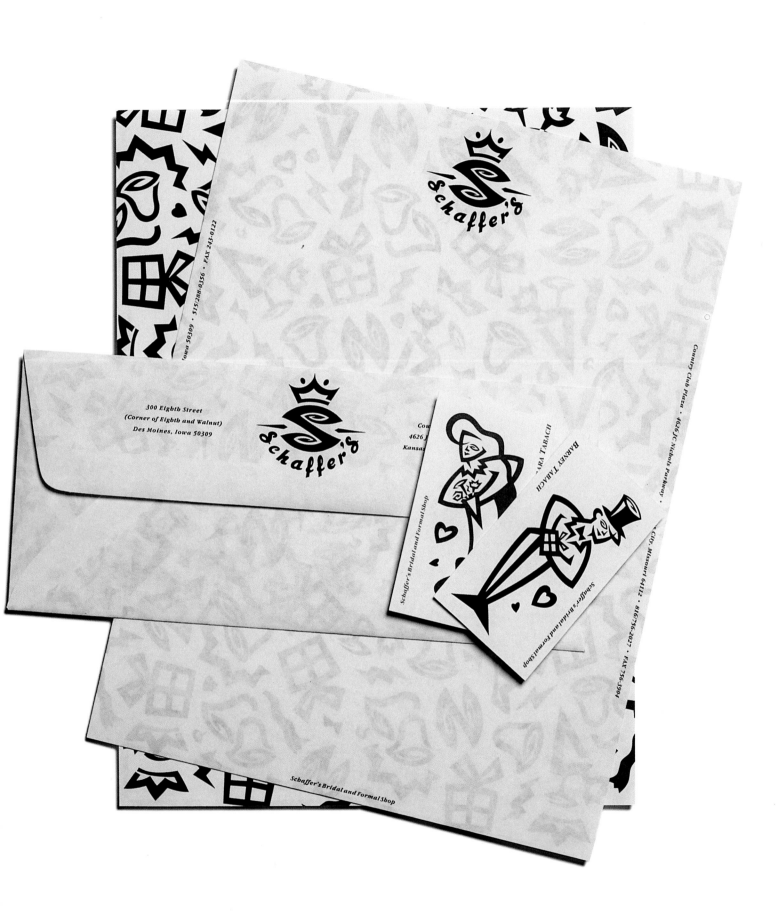

DESIGN FIRM Sayles Graphic Design
ART DIRECTOR John Sayles
DESIGNER John Sayles
ILLUSTRATOR John Sayles
CLIENT Schaffer's Bridal Shop
PAPER/PRINTING James River, Parchment White

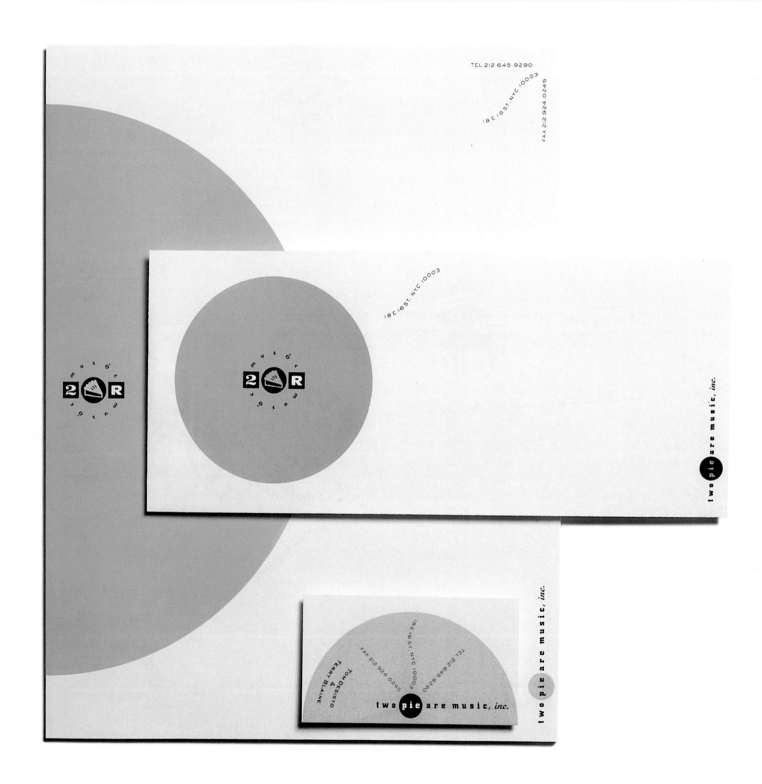

DESIGN FIRM   Pig Studios
ART DIRECTOR   Brandon Griffin
DESIGNER   Sandra Smarp, Brandon Griffin
ILLUSTRATOR   Sandra Smarp
CLIENT   Two Pie Are Music, Inc.
PAPER/PRINTING   Strathmore Writing, Bright White, 2 PMS

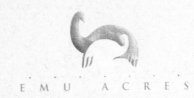

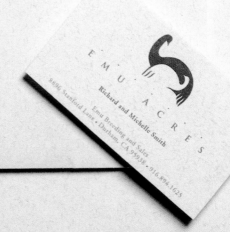

DESIGN FIRM   Image Group
ART DIRECTOR   Dan Frazier
DESIGNER   David Zavala
ILLUSTRATOR   David Zavala
CLIENT   EMU Acres
PAPER/PRINTING Evergreen

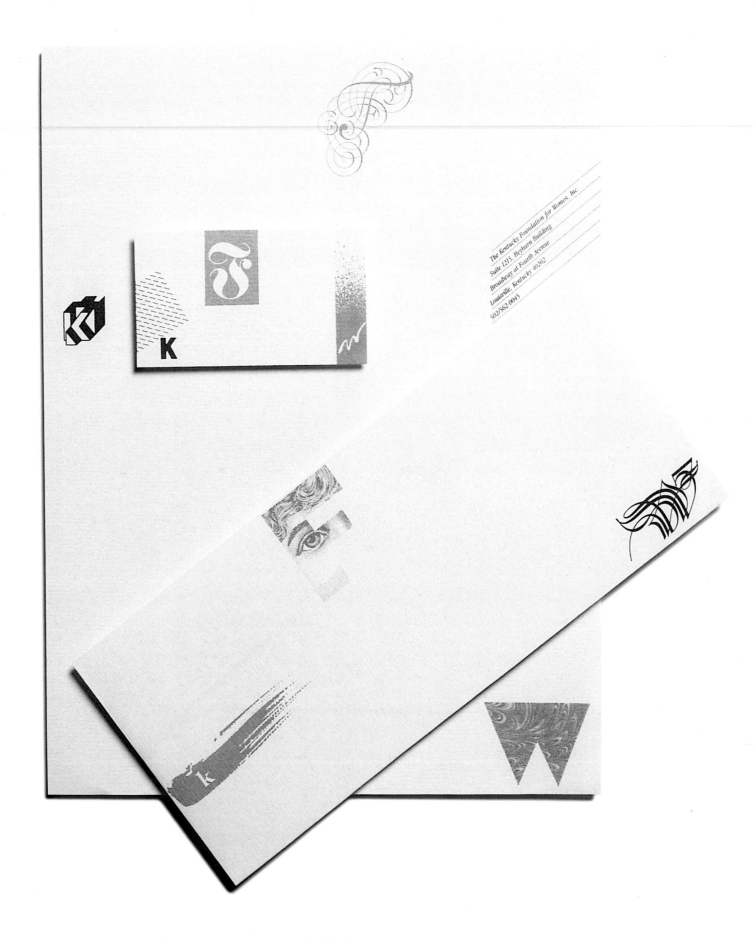

DESIGN FIRM	Choplogic
DESIGNER	Walter McCord, Julius Friedman
ILLUSTRATOR	Walter McCord, Julius Friedman
CLIENT	Kentucky Foundation for Women
PAPER/PRINTING	Simpson Gainsborough, 3 colors

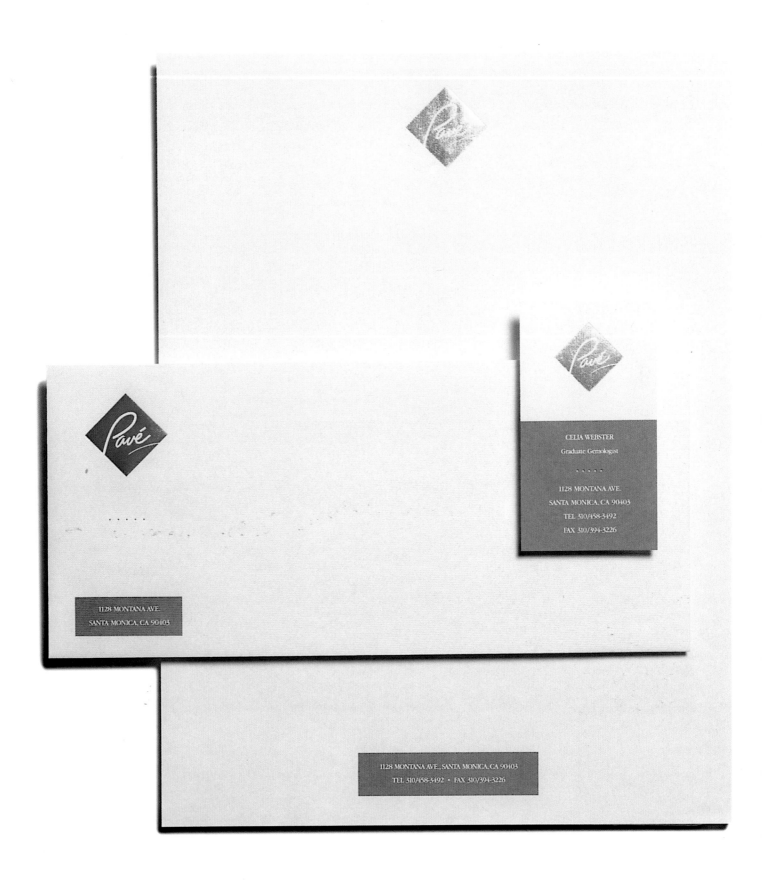

DESIGN FIRM   Shimokochi/Reeves
ART DIRECTOR   Mamoru Shimokochi, Anne Reeves
DESIGNER   Mamoru Shimokochi, Anne Reeves
CLIENT   Pavé
PAPER/PRINTING   Graphika

ADVERTISING
PROFESSIONALS
OF DES MOINES

ADDYS
1993

POST OFFICE
BOX 133
DES MOINES
IOWA 50301

ADDYS
1993

ADVERTISING
PROFESSIONALS
OF DES MOINES

REACH
FOR THE
STARS

REACH
FOR THE
STARS

DESIGN FIRM	Sayles Graphic Design
ART DIRECTOR	John Sayles
DESIGNER	John Sayles
ILLUSTRATOR	John Sayles
CLIENT	Advertising Professionals of Des Moines
PAPER/PRINTING	James River, Graphika Natural, 2 colors

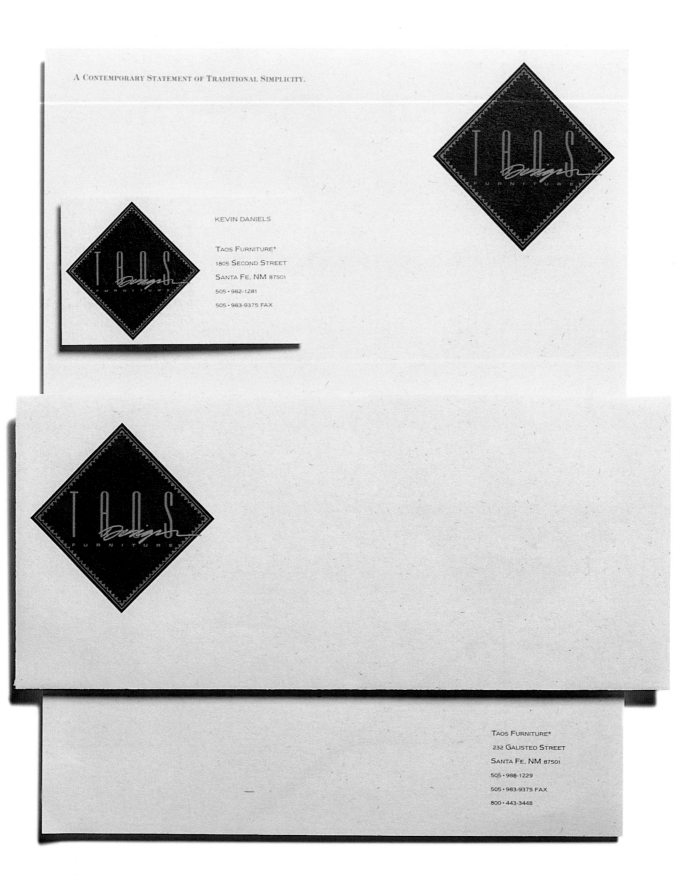

DESIGN FIRM	Vaughn Wedeen Creative
ART DIRECTOR	Rick Vaughn
DESIGNER	Rick Vaughn
CLIENT	Taos Furniture
PAPER/PRINTING	French Speckletone Creme Text

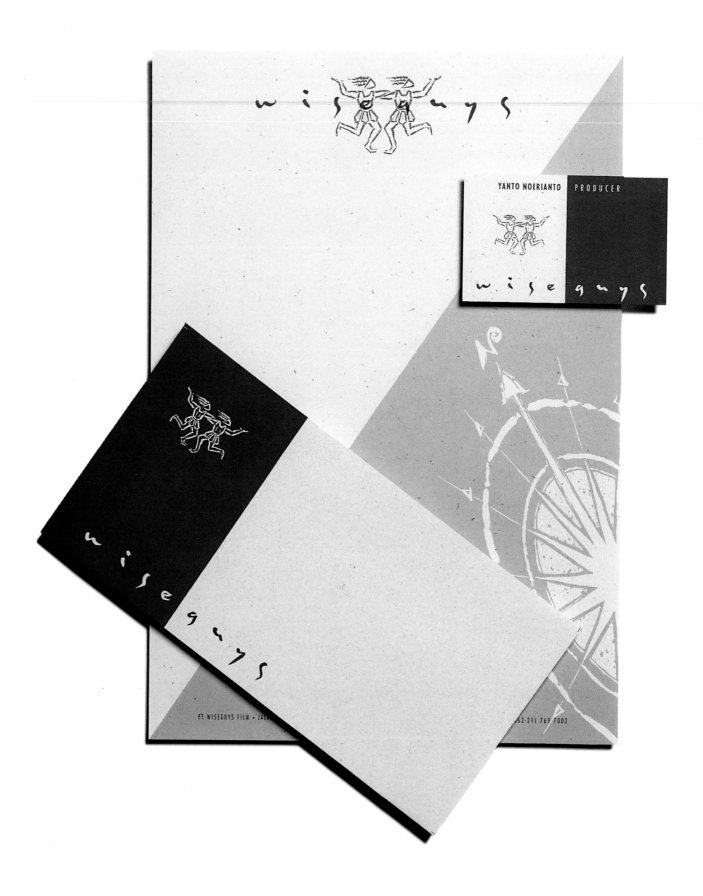

DESIGN FIRM   Wigwam Designs Pte. Ltd.
ART DIRECTOR   Rustam Moh'd
DESIGNER   Rustam Moh'd
ILLUSTRATOR   Rustam Moh'd
CLIENT   Wiseguys Pte. Ltd.
PAPER/PRINTING Recycled

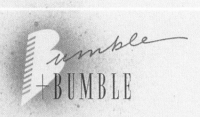

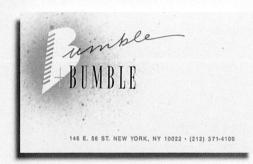

146 E. 56 ST. NEW YORK, NY 10022 • (212) 371-4100

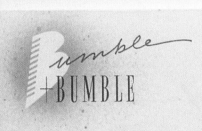

146 EAST 56 STREET, NEW YORK, NY 10022

146 EAST 56 STREET, NEW YORK, NY 10022 TEL. (212) 371-4100

DESIGN FIRM   Mike Quon Design Office
ART DIRECTOR   M. Gordon, Mike Quon
DESIGNER   Mike Quon
ILLUSTRATOR   Mike Quon
CLIENT   Bumble & Bumble/Hair Salon

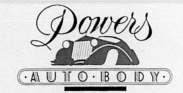

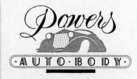

custom paint, detailing, fiberglass repairs
complete restoration, reproduction parts
all makes
specializing in classic/antique autos
Harley-Davidson motorcyles
free estimates, free pick up & delivery

Frederick Powers, Jr.
Manager

39 Old Salt Road
Old Orchard Beach, ME 04064
207-934-1314
home 207-967-3997

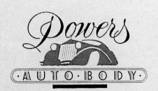

39 Old Salt Road
Old Orchard Beach, ME 04064

39 Old Salt Road ■ Old Orchard Beach, Maine 04064 ■ Telephone 207-934-1314 ■ home 207-967-3997

DESIGN FIRM	Bayon Marketing Design
ART DIRECTOR	Cecile Bayon
DESIGNER	Cecile Bayon
ILLUSTRATOR	Cecile Bayon
CLIENT	Powers Auto Body
PAPER/PRINTING	Classic Crest

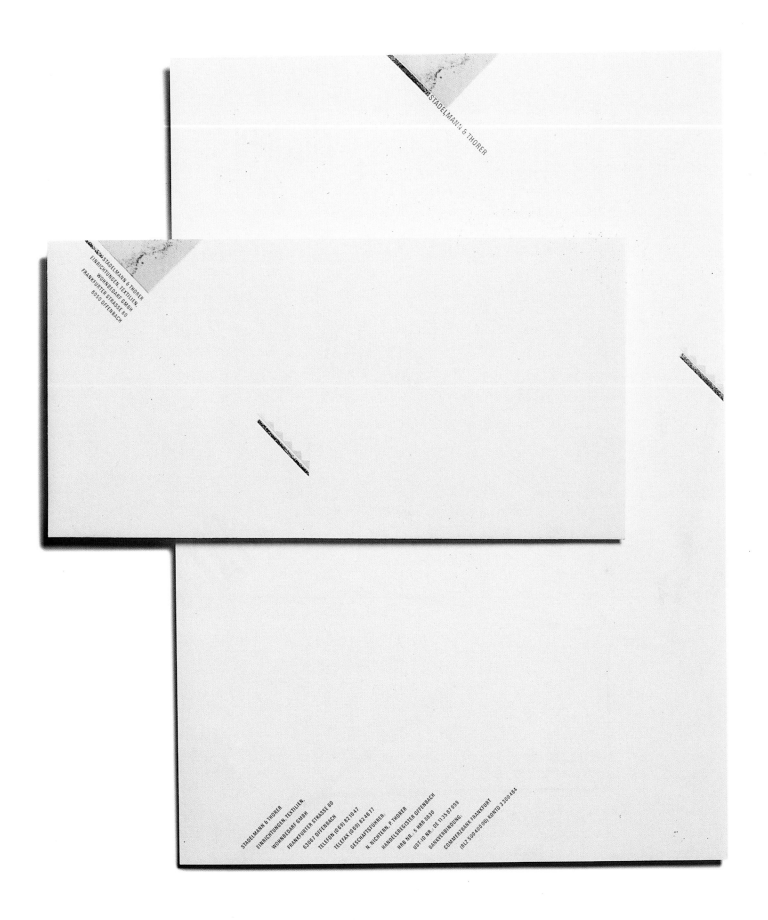

DESIGN FIRM   Hartmann & Mehler Designers GmbH
ART DIRECTOR   Roland Mehler
DESIGNER   Roland Mehler
ILLUSTRATOR   Roland Mehler
CLIENT   Stadelmann & Thorer

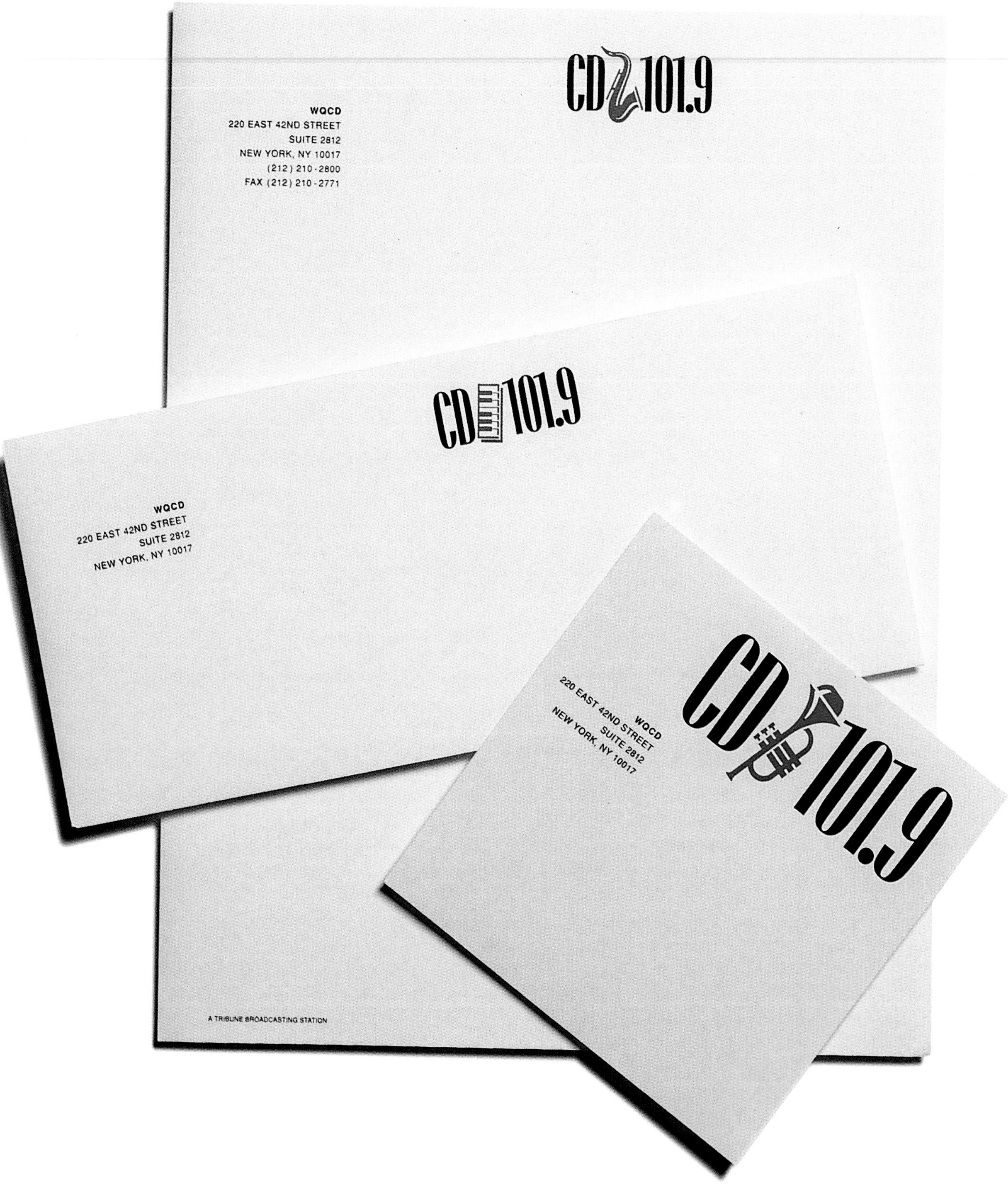

CD 101.9

CD 101.9

WQCD
220 EAST 42ND STREET
SUITE 2812
NEW YORK, NY 10017
(212) 210-2800
FAX (212) 210-2771

WQCD
220 EAST 42ND STREET
SUITE 2812
NEW YORK, NY 10017

WQCD
220 EAST 42ND STREET
SUITE 2812
NEW YORK, NY 10017

CD 101.9

A TRIBUNE BROADCASTING STATION

DESIGN FIRM	Mike Quon Design Office
ART DIRECTOR	Dale Pon, Mike Quon
DESIGNER	Mike Quon
ILLUSTRATOR	Mike Quon
CLIENT	CD 101.9

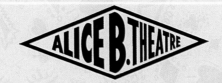

A Gay And Lesbian Theatre For All People

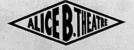

The Third Floor • 1100 East Pike
Seattle, WA 98122

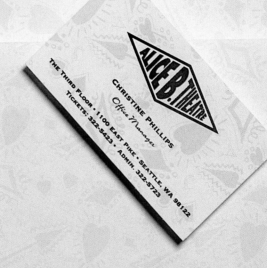

The Third Floor • 1100 East Pike • Seattle, WA 98122 • Tickets 322-5423 • Admin. 322-5723

DESIGN FIRM	Modern Dog
ART DIRECTOR	Rick Rankin
DESIGNER	Michael Strassburger, Robynne Raye
CLIENT	Alice B. Theatre
PAPER/PRINTING	Simpson Evergreen

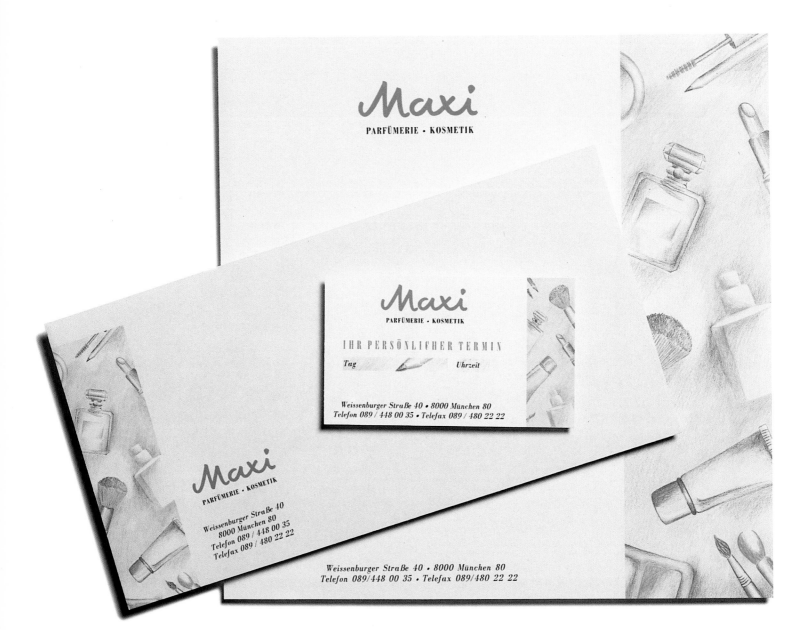

DESIGN FIRM   Kom Design Munich
ART DIRECTOR   Caren Schindelwick
ILLUSTRATOR   Caren Schindelwick
CLIENT   Maxi (a perfume shop)
PAPER/PRINTING   4 colors

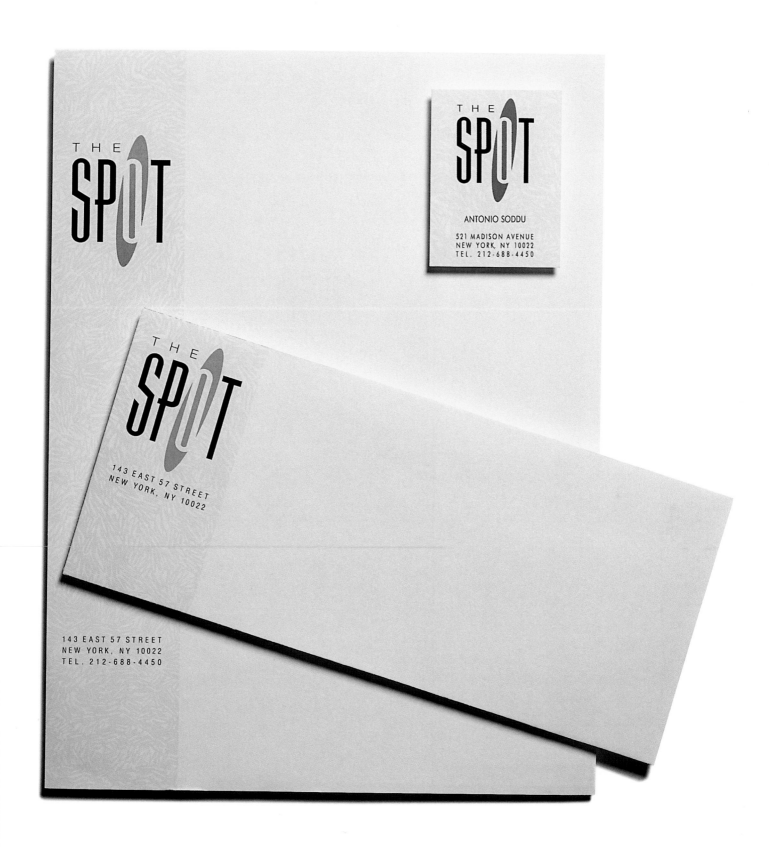

DESIGN FIRM   Mike Quon Design Office
ART DIRECTOR   Mike Quon
DESIGNER   Mike Quon
ILLUSTRATOR   Mike Quon
CLIENT   The Spot/Hair Salon

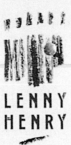

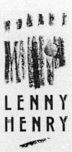

WITH COMPLIMENTS

DESIGN FIRM   The Green House
ART DIRECTOR   Judi Green
DESIGNER   Brian Green
ILLUSTRATOR   Brian Green
CLIENT   Lenny Henry
PAPER/PRINTING   Evergreen, 1 color with 2 foils.

DESIGN FIRM	L. F. Banks, Associates
ART DIRECTOR	Lori Banks
DESIGNER	Dorie Phillips
ILLUSTRATOR	Dorie Phillips
CLIENT	American Karate Studio

DESIGN FIRM	Modern Dog
ART DIRECTOR	Robynne Raye, Sheila Hughes
DESIGNER	Robynne Raye, Michael Strassburger
CLIENT	One Reel
PAPER/PRINTING	Simpson Vicksburg

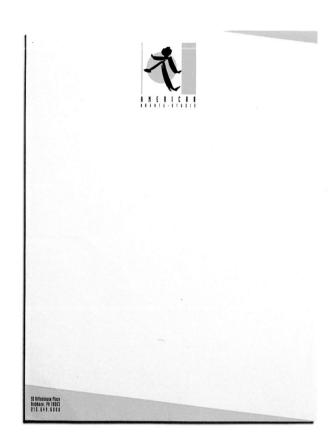

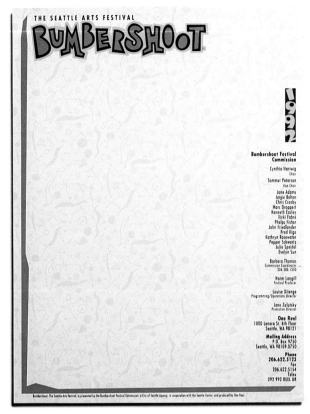

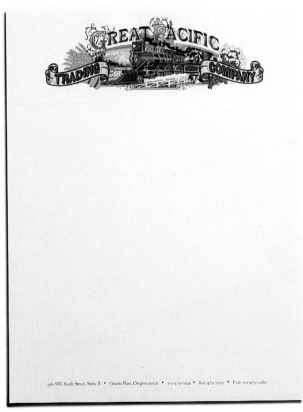

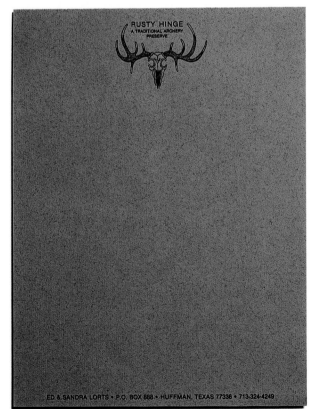

DESIGN FIRM	Shields Design
ART DIRECTOR	Charles Shields
DESIGNER	Charles Shields
ILLUSTRATOR	Doug Hansen
CLIENT	Great Pacific Trading Company
PAPER/PRINTING	Classic Crest

DESIGN FIRM	Total Designers
ART DIRECTOR	Ed Lorts
DESIGNER	Ed Lorts
ILLUSTRATOR	Ed Lorts
CLIENT	The Rusty Hinge Lodge
PAPER/PRINTING	100% Recycled Rag

CRITTERS AND

CHRYSANTHEMUMS

GOES COUNTRY

The Dallas Arboretum

and Botanical Garden

8617 Garland Road

Dallas, Texas 75218

CRITTERS AND
CHRYSANTHEMUMS
GOES COUNTRY

The Dallas Arboretum

and Botanical Garden

8617 Garland Road

Dallas, Texas 75218

Society for Prevention

of Cruelty to Animals

349 South Industrial

Dallas, Texas 75207

DESIGN FIRM	Focus 2
ART DIRECTOR	Todd Hart, Shawn Freeman
DESIGNER	Todd Hart
ILLUSTRATOR	Todd Hart
CLIENT	SPCA of Texas
PAPER/PRINTING	Evergreen

BRETTELL ENTERPRISES

4c Island View, Discovery Bay, Lantau, Hong Kong.

tel: (852) 987 6260 *fax:* (852) 987 0740

Brettell
ENTERPRISES

LINDA LITTELL

4c Island View, Discovery Bay
Lantau, Hong Kong
tel: (852) 987 6260
fax: (852) 987 0740

Brettell
ENTERPRISES

Brettell
ENTERPRISES

Brettell
ENTERPRISES

4c Island View, Discovery Bay, Lantau, Hong Kong.

DESIGN FIRM	The Design Associates
ART DIRECTOR	Victor Cheong
DESIGNER	Victor Cheong, Philip Sven
CLIENT	Brettell Enterprises
PAPER/PRINTING	Gilbert

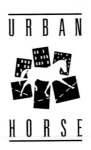

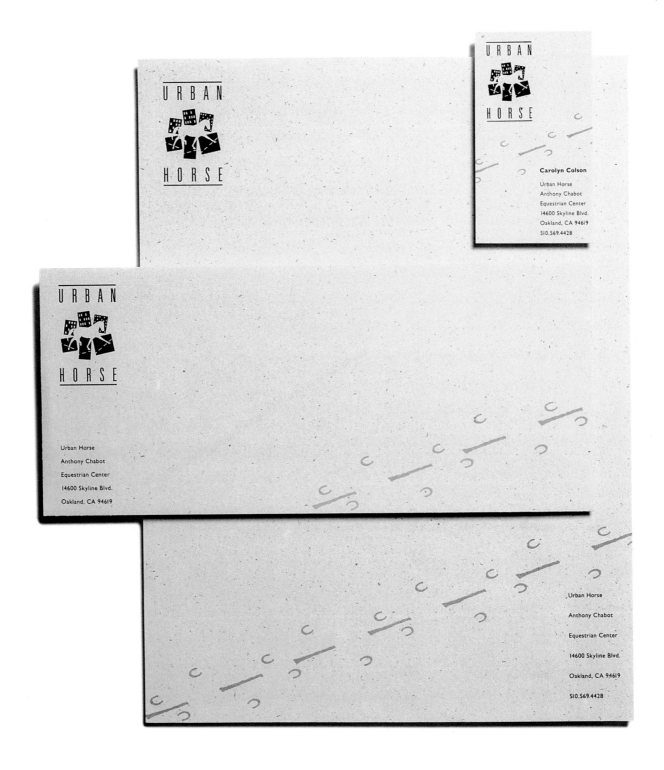

DESIGN FIRM   Bruce Yelaska Design

ART DIRECTOR   Bruce Yelaska

DESIGNER   Bruce Yelaska

ILLUSTRATOR   Bruce Yelaska

CLIENT   Urban Horse

PAPER/PRINTING   Champion Benefit

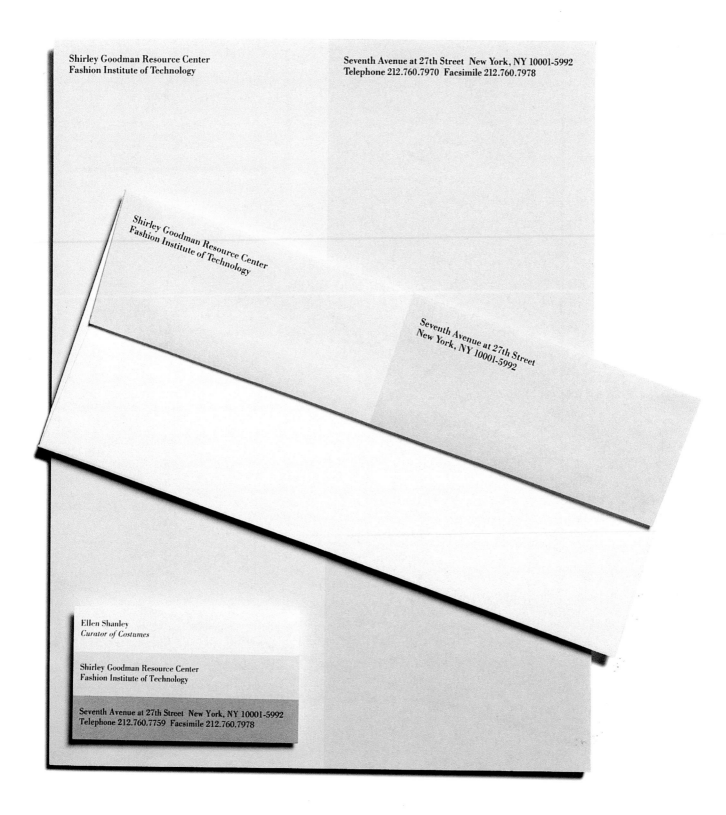

Shirley Goodman Resource Center
Fashion Institute of Technology

Seventh Avenue at 27th Street New York, NY 10001-5992
Telephone 212.760.7970 Facsimile 212.760.7978

Shirley Goodman Resource Center
Fashion Institute of Technology

Seventh Avenue at 27th Street
New York, NY 10001-5992

Ellen Shanley
Curator of Costumes

Shirley Goodman Resource Center
Fashion Institute of Technology

Seventh Avenue at 27th Street New York, NY 10001-5992
Telephone 212.760.7759 Facsimile 212.760.7978

DESIGN FIRM   M Plus M Incorporated
ART DIRECTOR   Takaaki Matsumoto, Michael McGinn
DESIGNER   Takaaki Matsumoto
CLIENT   Fashion Institute of Technology

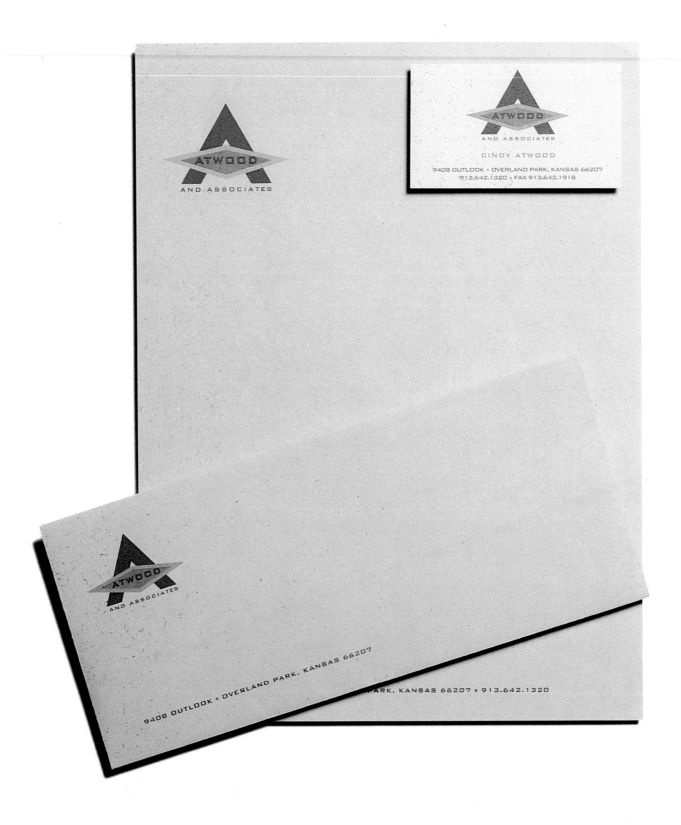

DESIGN FIRM	WRK
ART DIRECTOR	Deb Robinson
DESIGNER	Deb Robinson
CLIENT	Atwood and Associates
PAPER/PRINTING	Speckletone/Colormark

DESIGN FIRM	Design Art, Inc.	**DESIGN FIRM**	Design Art, Inc.	**DESIGN FIRM**	Design Art, Inc.
ART DIRECTOR	Norman Moore	**ART DIRECTOR**	Norman Moore	**ART DIRECTOR**	Norman Moore
DESIGNER	Norman Moore	**DESIGNER**	Norman Moore	**DESIGNER**	Norman Moore
CLIENT	Roger Davies Records	**CLIENT**	Patty Smyth	**CLIENT**	Riverhorse Music

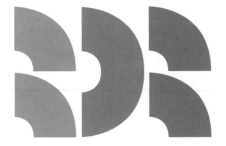

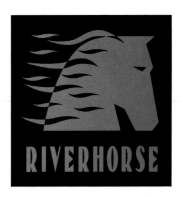

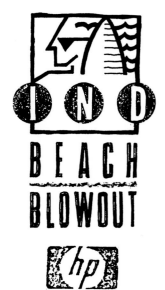
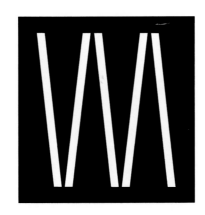
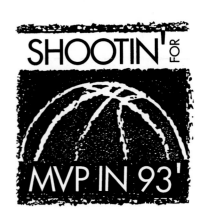

DESIGN FIRM	Riley Design Associates	**DESIGN FIRM**	Muller + Company	**DESIGN FIRM**	Riley Design Associates
ART DIRECTOR	Daniel Riley	**ART DIRECTOR**	John Muller	**ART DIRECTOR**	Daniel Riley
DESIGNER	Daniel Riley	**DESIGNER**	David Shultz	**DESIGNER**	Daniel Riley
ILLUSTRATOR	Daniel Riley	**CLIENT**	Weideman	**ILLUSTRATOR**	Daniel Riley
CLIENT	Hewlett Packard			**CLIENT**	Ernst & Young

DESIGN FIRM	Schowalter² Design	**DESIGN FIRM**	Segura Inc.	**DESIGN FIRM**	M Plus M Incorporated
ART DIRECTOR	Toni Schowalter	**ART DIRECTOR**	Carlos Segura	**ART DIRECTOR**	Takaaki Matsumoto,
DESIGNER	Ilene Price,	**DESIGNER**	Carlos Segura		Michael McGinn
	Toni Schowalter	**ILLUSTRATOR**	Carlos Segura	**DESIGNER**	Takaaki Matsumoto
CLIENT	Towers Perrin	**CLIENT**	Elements	**ILLUSTRATOR**	Takaaki Matsumoto
				CLIENT	Congregation Rodeph
					Sholom

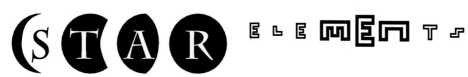

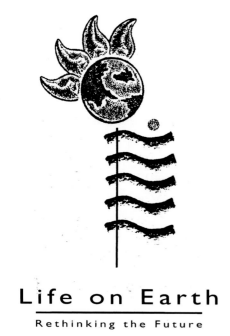

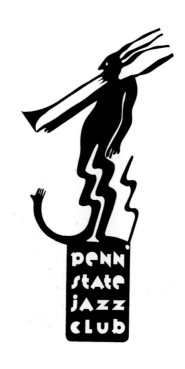

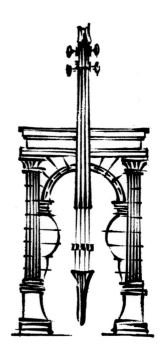

DESIGN FIRM	Bruce Yelaska Design	**DESIGN FIRM**	Sommese Design	**DESIGN FIRM**	Hornall Anderson
ART DIRECTOR	Bruce Yelaska	**ART DIRECTOR**	Lanny Sommese		Design Works
DESIGNER	Bruce Yelaska	**DESIGNER**	Kristin Sommese	**ART DIRECTOR**	Jack Anderson
ILLUSTRATOR	Bruce Yelaska	**ILLUSTRATOR**	Lanny Sommese	**DESIGNER**	Jack Anderson,
CLIENT	Bank of America	**CLIENT**	Penn State Jazz Club		David Bates
	This logo is for a traveling			**ILLUSTRATOR**	David Bates
	exhibit on the rain forest			**CLIENT**	Seattle Camerata
	and the environment.				

DESIGN FIRM	Lambert Design Studio	**DESIGN FIRM**	Segura Inc.	**DESIGN FIRM**	David Carter Design
ART DIRECTOR	Christie Lambert	**ART DIRECTOR**	Carlos Segura	**ART DIRECTOR**	Sharon Lejune
DESIGNER	Joy Cathey	**DESIGNER**	Carlos Segura	**DESIGNER**	Sharon Lejune
CLIENT	The Family Place	**ILLUSTRATOR**	Carlos Segura	**ILLUSTRATOR**	Sharon Lejune
		CLIENT	Glade	**CLIENT**	Anzu

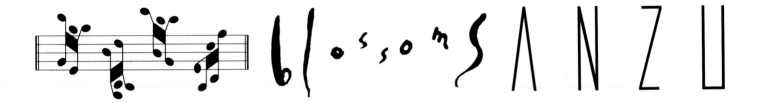

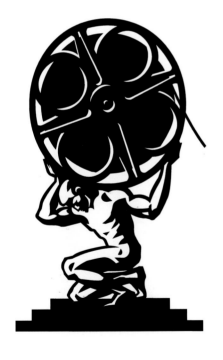

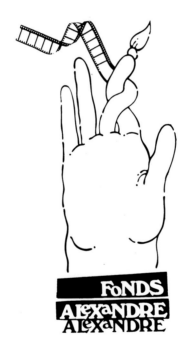

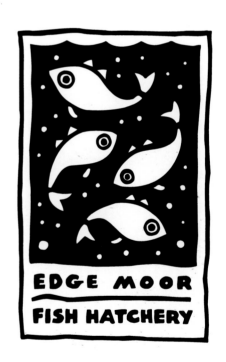

DESIGN FIRM	Tracy Sabin, Illustration & Design	**DESIGN FIRM**	Sommese Design	**DESIGN FIRM**	Delmarva Power Visual Communications Design Firm
ART DIRECTOR	Alison Hill	**ART DIRECTOR**	Lanny Sommese		Christy MacIntyre
DESIGNER	Tracy Sabin	**DESIGNER**	Lanny Sommese	**ART DIRECTOR**	John Alfred
ILLUSTRATOR	Tracy Sabin	**ILLUSTRATOR**	Lanny Sommese	**DESIGNER**	John Alfred
CLIENT	Turner Entertainment Co.	**CLIENT**	Fonds Alexandre Alexandre.	**ILLUSTRATOR**	John Alfred
				CLIENT	Edge Moor Fish Hatchery

DESIGN FIRM Smith Group
Communications
ART DIRECTOR Gregg Frederickson
DESIGNER Gregg Frederickson
CLIENT Waterhouse Place

DESIGN FIRM Segura Inc.
ART DIRECTOR Carlos Segura
DESIGNER Carlos Segura
ILLUSTRATOR Carlos Srgura
CLIENT Arete Furniture

DESIGN FIRM Design Art, Inc.
ART DIRECTOR Norman Moore
DESIGNER Norman Moore
CLIENT Digital Design Centre

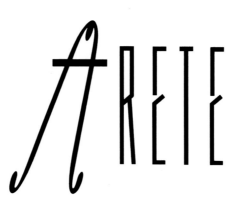

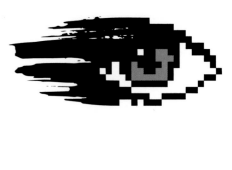

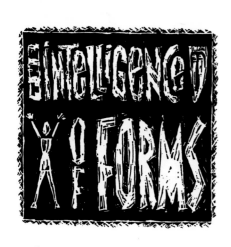

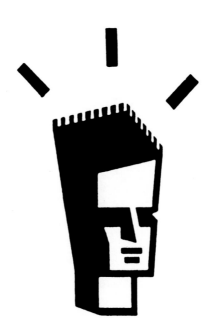

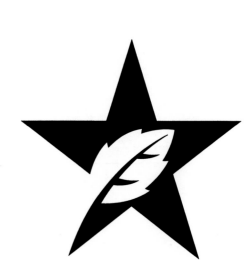

DESIGN FIRM Eilts Anderson Tracy
ART DIRECTOR Patrice Eilts
DESIGNER Patrice Eilts
ILLUSTRATOR Patrice Eilts
CLIENT Nelson Adluns
Museum of Art for
"Intelligence of Forms,
an African Exhibit."

DESIGN FIRM Luis Fitch Diseño
ART DIRECTOR Luis Fitch
DESIGNER Luis Fitch
CLIENT Fletop (hair salon)

DESIGN FIRM Smith Group
Communications
ART DIRECTOR Gregg Frederickson
DESIGNER Gregg Frederickson
CLIENT United States
Botanic Garden

DESIGN FIRM Segura Inc.
ART DIRECTOR Carlos Segura
DESIGNER Carlos Segura
ILLUSTRATOR Carlos Segura
CLIENT Deni Furniture

DESIGN FIRM Lambert Design Studio
ART DIRECTOR Christie Lambert
DESIGNER Joy Cathey
CLIENT The Family Place
(children's art and
music festival)

DESIGN FIRM Regal Airport/Art Dept.
DESIGNER Timmy Kan
CLIENT Regal Airport Hotel

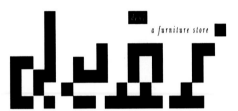

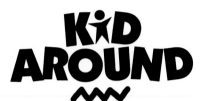

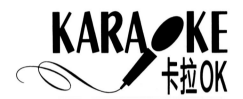

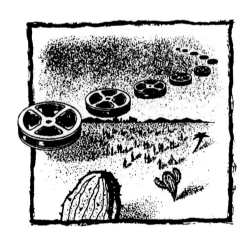

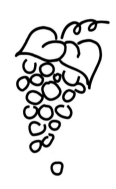

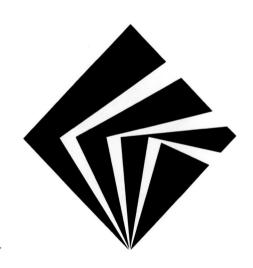

DESIGN FIRM Tieken Design &
Creative Services
ART DIRECTOR Fred E. Tieken
DESIGNER Fred E. Tieken
ILLUSTRATOR Fred E. Tieken
CLIENT Arizona International
Film Festival

DESIGN FIRM Lambert Design Studio
ART DIRECTOR Christie Lambert
DESIGNER Christie Lambert,
Joy Cathey
ILLUSTRATOR Joy Cathey
CLIENT Anita Misra. The client
used this logo for her
bridal shower — a bar
and lingerie shower.

DESIGN FIRM MacVicar Design &
Communications
ART DIRECTOR John Vance
DESIGNER William A. Gordon
CLIENT Marketing International
Corporation

DESIGN FIRM	Luis Fitch Diseño
ART DIRECTOR	Luis Fitch
DESIGNER	Luis Fitch
CLIENT	Freak's
	This client is a "young" clothing company for skateboarders.

DESIGN FIRM	Luis Fitch Diseño
ART DIRECTOR	Luis Fitch
DESIGNER	Luis Fitch
CLIENT	Scott Foresman Publishers

DESIGN FIRM	Segura Inc.
ART DIRECTOR	Carlos Segura
DESIGNER	Carlos Segura
ILLUSTRATOR	Carlos Segura
CLIENT	Source Lotion/ Helene Curtis

celebrate

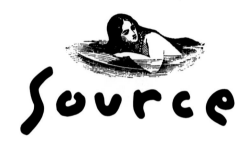

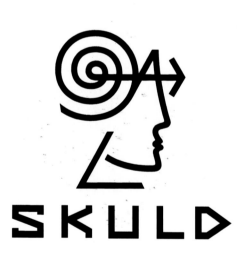

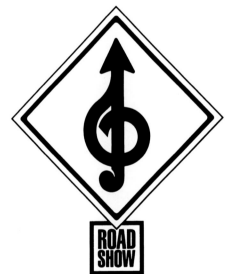

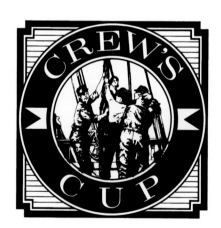

DESIGN FIRM	Studio Seireeni
ART DIRECTOR	Richard Seireeni
DESIGNER	Jim Pezzullo
ILLUSTRATOR	Bob Maile
CLIENT	Skuld

DESIGN FIRM	Eilts Anderson Tracy
ART DIRECTOR	Patrice Eilts
DESIGNER	Patrice Eilts
ILLUSTRATOR	Patrice Eilts
CLIENT	Total Entertainment

DESIGN FIRM	David Carter Design
ART DIRECTOR	Lori Wilson
DESIGNER	Lori Wilson
ILLUSTRATOR	Faith Delong
CLIENT	Disney Orlando, Florida

DESIGN FIRM	Design Art, Inc.	**DESIGN FIRM**	Studio Seireeni	**DESIGN FIRM**	Riley Design Associates
ART DIRECTOR	Norman Moore	**ART DIRECTOR**	Romane Cameron	**ART DIRECTOR**	Daniel Riley
DESIGNER	Norman Moore	**DESIGNER**	Romane Cameron	**DESIGNER**	Daniel Riley
CLIENT	Digital Art 3D	**ILLUSTRATOR**	Romane Cameron	**ILLUSTRATOR**	Daniel Riley
	Graphics	**CLIENT**	Wilshire Designs	**CLIENT**	Randy Licht Inc.

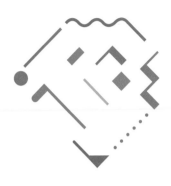

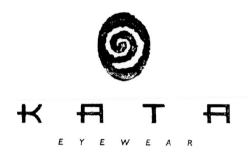

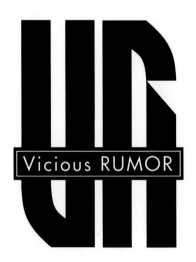

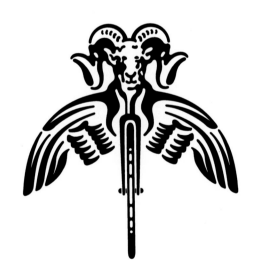

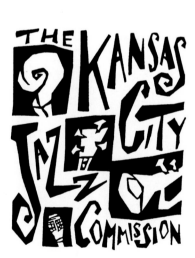

DESIGN FIRM	Segura Inc.	**DESIGN FIRM**	Hornall Anderson	**DESIGN FIRM**	Muller + Compnay
ART DIRECTOR	Carlos Segura		Design Works	**ART DIRECTOR**	John Muller
DESIGNER	Carlos Segura	**ART DIRECTOR**	Jack Anderson	**DESIGNER**	Mike Muller
ILLUSTRATOR	Carlos Segura	**DESIGNER**	Jack Anderson,	**CLIENT**	Kansas City Jazz
CLIENT	Vicous Rumor/band		Brian O'Neill		Commission
		CLIENT	Gang of Seven		

INDEX/DIRECTORY

Ace Architects
330 2nd Street
Oakland, CA 94607

Adam, Filippo & Associates
1206 Fifth Avenue
Pittsburgh, PA 15219

Adele Bass & Co. Design
758 E. Colorado Boulevard #209
Pasadena, CA 91101

Albert Juarez Design &
Illustration
2900 McKinley
El Paso, TX 79930

Animus Communicacao
LaDeira Do Ascurra 115-A
22241-320/RIO/RJ/Brazil

Armin Vogt Partner
Corporate & Packaging Design
Munsterplatz 8
CH-4001 Basel

Aslan Grafix
6507 Rain Creek Parkway
Austin, TX 78759

Barbara Raab Design
3105 Valley Drive
Alexandria, VA 22302

Bartels & Company, Inc.
3284 Ivanhoe Avenue
St. Louis, MO 63139

Bayon Marketing Design
P.O. Box 214
Kennebunk, ME 04043

Beauchamp Design
9848 Mercy Road No. 8
San Diego, CA 92129

Bi-design
502 Alabama Drive
Herndon, VA 22070

Blue Sky Design
6401 SW 132 Ct. Circle
Miami, FL 33183

Bruce Yelaska Design
1546 Grant Avenue
San Francisco, CA 94133

Cactus Design
312 Montgomery Street
Alexandria, VA 22314

Carl Seltzer Design Office
120 Newport Center Drive
Suite 206
Newport Beach, CA 92660

Cheryl Waligory Design
145 W. 12th St. #25
New York, NY 10011

Choplogic
2014 Cherokee Parkway
Louisville, KY 40204

Cisneros Design
3168 Plaza Blanca
Santa Fe, NM 87505

Clifford Selbert Design
2067 Massachusetts Avenue
Cambridge, MA 02140

Coker Golley Ltd.
101 Marietta Street
Suite 3310
Atlanta, GA 30303

Communication Design, Inc.
One North Fifth Street
Suite 500
Richmond, VA 23219

Creative EDGE
2 Church Street
Burlington, VT 05401

Creative Services by Pizza Hut
9111 E. Douglas
Wichita, KS 67207

Dan Frazier/Image Group
25 Main Street
Suite 203
Chico, CA 95928

David Carter Design
4112 Swiss Avenue
Dallas, TX 75204

Debra Nichols Design
468 Jackson Street
San Francisco, CA 94111

Delmarva Power Corp. Comm.
P.O. Box 231
Wilmington, DE 19899

Design Art, Inc.
6311 Romaine Street #7311
Los Angeles, CA 90038

The Design Associates
89 Wellington St. 5A1
Central, Hong Kong

Design/Joe Sonderman, Inc.
P.O. Box 35146
Charlotte, NC 28235

Designs N Logos
24 Wilson Avenue NE
P.O. Box 6159
St. Cloud, MN 56302

Dewitt Kendall-Chicago
5000 Marine Drive 4D
Chicago, IL 60640

Stephen Divoky
1048 N.E. 95th Street
Seattle, WA 98115

E.M. Design
9526 S. 207th Place
Kent, WA 98031

Earl Gee Design
501 Second Street, Suite 700
San Francisco, CA 94107

Eilts Anderson Tracy
4111 Baltimore
Kansas City, MO 64111

Elizabeth Resnick Design
126 Payson Road
Chestnut Hill, MA 02167

Ellen Kendrick Creative, Inc.
1707 Nicholasville Road
Lexington, KY 40503

Ema Design
1228 Fifteenth Street
Suite 301
Denver, CO 80202

Envision Communications, Inc.
120 South Brook Street
Louisville, KY 40202

Eskind Waddell
260 Richmond Street West
Suite 201
Toronto M5V 1W5 Ontario
Canada

Focus 2
3333 Elm Suite 203
Dallas, TX 75226

Fountainhead Graphics
6740 Clough Pike
Suite 202-206
Cincinnati, OH 45244

Frank D'Astonfo Design
80 Warren Street #32
New York, NY 10007

Gary Greene Artworks
21820 NE 156th Street
Woodinville, WA 98072

GrandPre and Whaley, Ltd.
475 Cleveland Avenue North
Suite 222
St. Paul, MN 55104

The Great American Logo
Company
14800 N.W. Cornell Road #4C
Portland, OR 97229

The Green House
64 High St.
Harrow-on-the-Hill
London HA1 3LL UK

Handler Design Ltd.
17 Ralph Avenue
White Plains, NY 10606

Hartmann & Mehler Designers
GmbH
CorneliusstraBe 8
60325 Frankfurt am Main
Germany

Hawley & Armian
Marketing/Design
305 Newbury #22
Boston, MA 02115

Heart Graphic Design
501 George Street
Midland, MI 48640

Peter Hermesmann
306 Bainbridge Street
Philadelphia, PA 19147

Allan Hill
2535 Tulip Lane
Langhorne, PA 19053

Hoffmann & Angelic Design
317-1675 Martin Drive
White Rock, B.C.
Canada V4A 6E2

Hornall Anderson Design Works
1008 Western, Suite 600
Seattle, WA 98104

i4 Design
55C Gate 5 Road
SaulSalito, CA 94965

Ilan Geva & Friends
1340 N. Astor #1608
Chicago, IL 60610

Image Group
25 Main Street
Suite 203
Chico, CA 95928

Images
1835 Hampden Court
Louisville, KY 40205

Inkwell Publishing Co., Inc.
10 San Pablo Street
Bo. KapitolYo Pasig
Metro Manila, Philippines 1603

Integrate Inc.
503 S. High Street
Columbus, OH 43215

James Clark Design Images
200 West Mercer #102
Seattle, WA 98119

Jenssen Design Pty. Limited
2A Glen Street
Milsons Point NSW 2061
Australia

Jim Ales Design
123 Townsend Street #480
San Francisco, CA 94107

Jon Wells Associates
407 Jackson Street
Suite 206
San Francisco, CA 94111

Kom Design Munich
Georg-Brauchle-Ring 68
80992 Munich

L. F. Banks Associates
8th & Chestnut Street
Philadelphia, PA

Lambert Design Studio
7007 Twin Hills Avenue
Suite 213
Dallas, TX 75231

Laura Herrmann Design
69 Atlantic Road
Gloucester, MA 01930

Leann Brook Design
P.O. Box 1788
Nevada City, CA 95959

Let Her Press
1544 Westerly Terrace
Los Angeles, CA 90026

Linnea Gruber Design
1775 Hancock Street #190
San Diego, CA 92110

Lipson Alport Glass
666 Dundee Road #103
Northbrook, IL 60062

Lorna Stovall Design
1088 Queen Anne Place
Los Angeles, CA 90019

Love Packaging Group
700 E. 37th Street North
Wichita, KS 67201

Luis Fitch Diseno
1116 Harrison Avenue
Columbus, OH 43201

M. Renner Design
Weiherway 3
CH-4123 Australia

M Plus M Incorporated
17 Cornelia Street
New York, NY 10014

Mac By Night
22975 Caminito Olivia
Laguna Hills, CA 92653

MacVicar Design &
Communications
2615-A Fhirlington Road
Arlington, VA 22206

Mark Oldach Design
3525 N. Oakly
Chicago, IL 60614

The Marketing & Design Group
297 Garfield Avenue
Oakhurst, NJ 07755

Randall McCafferty
305 Edgewood Road
Pittsburgh, PA 15221

Metalli Lindberg Adv.
Via Garibaldi, 5/D
31015 Conegliano (Treviso) Italy

Michael Stanard, Inc.
One Thousand Main Street
Evanston, IL 60202

Mike Salisbury Communications
2200 Amapola Ct.
Torrance, CA 90504

Mike Quon Design Office
568 Broadway #703
New York, NY 10012

Modern Dog
601 Valley Street No. 309
Seattle, WA 98109

Mortensen Design
416 Bush Street
Mountain View, CA 94041

Muller & Company
4739 Belleview
Kentuck City, MO 64112

Musikar Design
7524 Indian Hills Drive
Rockville, MD 20855

Nesnadny & Schwartz
10803 Magnolia Drive
Cleveland, OH 44106

New Idea Design Inc.
3702 S. 16th Street
Omaha, NE 68107

O & J Design, Inc.
9 West 29th Street
New York, NY 10001

Ortega Design Studio
1735 Spring Street
St. Helena, CA 94574

Palmquist & Palmquist Design
P.O. Box 325
Bozeman, MT 59771

Pandamonium
14 Mt. Hood Road
Suite 3
Boston, MA 02135

Patri-Keker Design
1859 Mason St. #1
San Francisco, CA 94133

Pig Studios
41 Wooster Street
New York, NY 10013

Platinum Design
14 W. 23rd Street
New York, NY 10010

Porter/Matjasich & Associates
154 West Hubbard
Chicago, IL 60610

Proforma Rotterdam
Slepersvest 5-7
3011 MK Rotterdam

Puccinelli Design
114 E. De La Guerra #5
Santa Barbara, CA 93101

Punctuation
3-14, 3rd Floor, Berjaya
Plaza, 55100 KL, West Malaysia

Ramona Hutko Design
9607 Bulls Run Parkway
Bethesda, MD 20817

Raven Madd Design
P.O. Box 11331
Wellington, New Zealand

Regal Airport Hotel
SA PO Road
Kowloon City
Kowloon Hong Kong

Reliv, Inc.
1809 Clarkson Road
Chesterfield, MO 63017

Richard Danne & Associates Inc.
126 Fifth Avenue
New York, NY 10011

Rickabaugh Graphics
384 W. Johnstown Road
Gahanna, OH 43230

Ridenour Advertising
33975 Dequindre
Suite 106
Troy, MI 48083

Riley Design Associates
214 Main Street Suite A
San Mateo, CA 94401

Nora Robbins
19 Holden Road
Belmont, MA 02178

Romeo Empire Design
154 Spring Street
New York, NY 10012

Ron Kellum Inc.
151 First Avenue PH-1
New York, NY 10003

Sayles Graphic Design
308 Eighth Street
Des Moines, Iowa 50309

Caren Schindelwick
Longwiedo Str. 26a
85221 Dachen, Germany

Schmeltz & Warren
74 Sheffield Road
Columbus, OH 43214

Schowalter[2] Design
21 The Crescen
Short Hills, NJ 07078

Segura, Inc.
361 W. Chestnut
Chicago, IL 60610

Sharpe Grafikworks
815 Main Street
Cincinnati, OH 45202

Jeff Shelly
300 Mercer Street
Apt. 28I
New York, NY 10003

Shields Design
415 E. Olive Avenue
Fresno, CA 93728

Shimokochi/Reeves
4465 Wilshire Blvd. #100
Los Angeles, CA 90010

SHR Perceptual Management
8700 E. Via De Ventura
Suite 100
Scottsdale, AZ 85258

Signum
1904 Nancy Court Number 7
Champaign, IL 61821

Smith Group Communications
614 SW 11th
Portland, OR 97205

Sommese Design
481 Glenn Road
State College, PA 16803

Source/Inc.
116 S. Michigan Avenue
Chicago, IL 60451

Steven Gulla Graphic Design
65 Sullivan Street
Suite 8A
New York, NY 10012

Strategic Communications
308 Southwest 1st Avenue
Suite 181
Portland, OR 97204

Studio Michael
1775 Hancock #190
San Diego, CA 92110

Studio Seireeni
708 S. Orange Grove
Los Angeles, CA 90036

Teknøs Design Group
111 Cooper Street
Santa Cruz, CA 95060

THARP DID IT
21 University Avenue
Suite 21
Los Gatos, CA 95030

38 North
2001 S. Hanley
Suite 200
St. Louis, MO 63144

Thomas Hillman Design
193 Middle Street
Portland, ME 04101

Tieken Design & Creative Services
2800 N. Central Avenue
Suite 150
Phoenix, AZ 85004

TMCA, Inc.
2231 Devine Street
Suite 304
Columbia, SC 29205

Total Designers
P.O. Box 888
Huffman, TX 77336

Tracy Sabin, Illustration & Design
13476 Ridley Road
San Diego, CA 92129

Trickett & Webb Limited
The Factory, 84 Marchmont Street
London WC1N 1AG

Turner Design
1210 Barkley Rd.
Charlotte, NC 20209

TW Design
3490 Piedmont Road
Suite 1200
Atlanta, GA 30305

Ultimo Inc.
41 Union Sq. West
Suite 209
New York, NY 10003

Vaughn Wedeen Creative
407 Rio Grande NW
Albuquerque, NM 87104

Visual Dialogue
429 Columbus Avenue #1
Boston, MA 02116

Vrontikis Design Office
2021 Pontius Avenue
Los Angeles, CA 90025

W Designs
14 Hollywood Place
Hohokus, NJ 07423

Walsh and Associates, Inc.
4464 Fremont North #310
Seattle, WA 98103

The Weller Institute for the Cure
of Design, Inc.
P.O. Box 726
Park City, UT 84060

Wigwam Designs Pte. Ltd.
32A Sago Street
Singapore 0105

William Field Design
355 E. Palace Avenue
Santa Fe, NM 87501

WRK
602 Westport Road
Kentuck City, MO 64111